Public Sector Organizations

Editors: **B. Guy Peters**, Maurice Falk Professor of Government, Pittsburgh University, USA, and **Geert Bouckaert**, Professor at the Public Management Institute, Katholieke Universiteit Leuven, Belgium.

Organizations are the building blocks of governments. The role of organizations, formal and informal, is most readily apparent in public bureaucracy, but all the institutions of the public sector are composed of organizations, or have some organizational characteristics that affect their performance. Therefore, if scholars want to understand how governments work, a very good place to start is at the level of the organizations involved in delivering services. Likewise, if practitioners want to understand how to be effective in the public sector, they would be well-advised to consider examining the role of organizations and how to make the organizations more effective.

This series will publish research-based books concerned with organizations in the public sector and will cover such issues as: the autonomy of public sector organizations, networks and network analysis, bureaucratic politics, organizational change and leadership, and methodology for studying organizations.

Titles include:

Cristopher Ballinas Valdes
POLITICAL STRUGGLES AND THE FORGING OF AUTONOMOUS
GOVERNMENT AGENCIES

Geert Bouckaert, B.Guy Peters and Koen Verhoest
THE COORDINATION OF PUBLIC SECTOR ORGANIZATIONS
Shifting Patterns of Public Management

Tero Erkkilä
GOVERNMENT TRANSPARENCY
Impacts and Unintended Consequences

Leslie A. Pal
FRONTIERS OF GOVERNANCE
The OECD and Global Public Management Reform

Amanda Smullen
TRANSLATING AGENCY REFORM
Rhetoric and Culture in Comparative Perspective

Koen Verhoest, Paul G. Roness, Bram Verschuere, Kristin Rubecksen and
Muiris MacCarthaigh
AUTONOMY AND CONTROL OF STATE AGENCIES
Comparing States and Agencies

Koen Verhoest, Sandra Van Thiel, Per Lægreid and Geert Bouckaert (*editors*)
GOVERNMENT AGENCIES
Practices and Lessons from 30 Countries

Public Sector Organizations Series
Series Standing Order ISBN 978–0–230–22034–8 (Hardback)
                          978–0–230–22035–5 (Paperback)
                          (*outside North America only*)

You can receive future titles in this series as they are published by placing a standing order. Please contact your bookseller or, in case of difficulty, write to us at the address below with your name and address, the title of the series and one of the ISBNs quoted above.

Customer Services Department, Macmillan Distribution Ltd, Houndmills, Basingstoke, Hampshire RG21 6XS, England

Government Transparency

Impacts and Unintended Consequences

Tero Erkkilä
Lecturer, Department of Political and Economic Studies,
University of Helsinki, Finland

First published 2012 by
PALGRAVE MACMILLAN

Palgrave Macmillan in the UK is an imprint of Macmillan Publishers Limited,
registered in England, company number 785998, of Houndmills, Basingstoke,
Hampshire RG21 6XS.

Palgrave Macmillan in the US is a division of St Martin's Press LLC,
175 Fifth Avenue, New York, NY 10010.

Palgrave Macmillan is the global academic imprint of the above companies
and has companies and representatives throughout the world.

Palgrave® and Macmillan® are registered trademarks in the United States,
the United Kingdom, Europe and other countries.

ISBN: 978–0–230–30005–7

This book is printed on paper suitable for recycling and made from fully
managed and sustained forest sources. Logging, pulping and manufacturing
processes are expected to conform to the environmental regulations of the
country of origin.

A catalogue record for this book is available from the British Library.

A catalog record for this book is available from the Library of Congress.

10 9 8 7 6 5 4 3 2 1
21 20 19 18 17 16 15 14 13 12

Printed and bound in Great Britain by
CPI Antony Rowe, Chippenham and Eastbourne

Contents

Illustrations

Tables

Figures

Preface

Transparency has become a concept of global relevance for responsible governance. As I argue in this book, the transnational discourse of transparency promotes various policy ideas that can be contradictory, and can lead to unintended consequences and paradoxes in governance. In analyzing the related institutional developments in the Nordic context, specifically in Finland, I argue that there has been an economic reframing of access to government information as a result of policies related to transparency. Throughout this analysis, I critically examine whether or not increased transparency actually leads to increased democratic accountability. As will be evident from my empirical analysis, the institutional developments related to the pursuit of transparency may be paradoxical and contain potential unintended consequences.

The idea of writing a book on the shifting information strategies of the state took shape between 2001 and 2003, when I was working on information society projects for the Finnish state. The initial idea was to study the commercialization of public sector information, but it soon occurred to me that the changes were of a more comprehensive nature. The privatization of public information eventually took up a full chapter of this study (Chapter 4). Though the book is problem-oriented, focusing on the emerging concerns of modern governance, I was most impressed by the willingness of civil servants in Finland to discuss the issues with me, and to share their insights and point me towards relevant sources. This book would not have been possible without their help.

I wish to thank my interviewees in the following organizations: the Audit Committee of the Finnish Parliament, the Finnish National Bureau of Statistics, the *Hufvudstadsbladet* newspaper, the KEPA Service Centre for Development Cooperation, the Ministry of Agriculture and Forestry, the Ministry of Finance, the Ministry of Justice, the Ministry of the Interior, the Ministry for Foreign Affairs, the Ministry of Trade and Industry, the Office of the Parliamentary Ombudsman, the Population Register Centre, the Prime Minister's Office, SAK – the Central Organisation of Finnish Trade Unions, and University of Helsinki. The Ministry of Finance, the Ministry for Foreign Affairs, and the Prime Minister's Office kindly permitted the use of one table and three figures appearing in the book.

Several people have helped and supported me in my work during this study. I particularly wish to thank Niilo Kauppi, whose comments and encouragement have been invaluable. I am also indebted to Henri Vogt and Jan-Erik Johanson, who read earlier versions of the manuscript. I had the privilege of discussing the work in detail with Guy B. Peters, whose insightful editorial comments helped to shape the book into its current form. I also thank Tom Christensen, Seppo Tiihonen, and my anonymous reviewer for their excellent comments.

I would like to thank my colleagues at the Department of Economic and Political Studies and in the Network for European Studies at the University of Helsinki, with whom I have greatly enjoyed working. In particular, my thanks go to Turo Virtanen, Kyösti Pekonen, Teija Tiilikainen, Satu Sundström, Johanna Rainio-Niemi, Norbert Götz, and Juhana Aunesluoma for their help with the work. My collaboration with Ossi Piironen on governance indices is also reflected in this book. I have greatly enjoyed the academic environment of the Network for Public Sphere Studies at the University of Helsinki. In particular, my discussions with Henrik Stenius and Pia Letto-Vanamo have been stimulating and encouraging.

I wish to thank Klaus Eder for his generous comments when I was conducting my research at the Humboldt Universität zu Berlin in 2005. I spent spring 2009 at the Zeppelin University. I am grateful to Eckhard Schröter and Patrick von Maravic for the invitation and the time I spent in Friedrichshafen. I am also grateful to Patrick for his encouragement throughout the process. I have very much benefited from my affiliation (2008–10) with the University of Strasbourg and the Maison Interuniversitaire des Sciences de l'Homme Alsace (MISHA). Strasbourg has become my home. Different parts of this book have been presented at numerous conferences over the years, and I would like to express my gratitude to all those who commented on the work in its various stages.

I also wish to thank Mark Waller for his work on the language. Max Eklund provided reliable assistance in formatting the manuscript for publication. My research has been mainly funded by the Academy of Finland and the Finnish Cultural Foundation, for which I am most grateful. I have also received funding from the Kone Foundation and the Network for European Studies.

My deepest gratitude goes to Almut Schröder for her love and support. I also want to thank my family for their unconditional support. The book is dedicated to my parents, Helena and Eero.

Abbreviations

EU	European Union
GATT	General Agreement on Tariffs and Trade
NGO	Non-governmental organizations
NPM	New Public Management
OECD	Organisation for Economic Co-operation and Development
PSI	Public Sector Information
PUMA	OECD's Public Management Committee
UN	United Nations

Introduction

Historically, the publicity of government information has been an area of social critique and democratization with differing national traditions and institutional trajectories. In recent years there has been a surge in international policy programs on good governance and the knowledge economy that endorse transparency and access to government information. These contemporary forms of governance tend to blur dichotomies between public and private, market and hierarchy, democracy and efficiency. This blurring of dichotomies allows us to see efficiency where before we saw democracy, and vice versa. It challenges previous perceptions of government, causing shifts in the beliefs, ideas and norms constituting institutional practices. The aspirations towards democracy *and* efficiency come together in the concept of *transparency*.

Social-scientific studies of transparency tend to fall into two categories, looking at the issue either from the perspective of democracy or from that of economic efficiency. Interestingly, 'transparency' works as a mirror for these studies, often reflecting the authors' own aspirations, and simultaneously concealing another perspective: that in a democratic framework, transparency enhances democratization, while from an economic perspective it brings economic gains and better performance. This study assesses the shifts between the categories of democracy and efficiency in which there are re-descriptions of certain public activities as efficient, or of certain efficiency-enhancing activities as open and transparent, and hence democratic.

I will argue that the new economic- and performance-driven understanding of transparency poses often paradoxical and unintended consequences for public administration. Most notably, such increased transparency might not lead to increased democratic accountability. In Part I, I will present a framework for studying these ideational changes and their outcomes. Empirically, this study explores new ideational changes in the information strategy of the Finnish state between 1998 and 2007, following a juncture in Finnish governance in the early 1990s. Part II scrutinizes the economic reframing of institutional openness in Finland that entails significant and often unintended institutional consequences. In this context, the constitutional *principle of publicity* – a Nordic institutional peculiarity allowing public access to state information – is now becoming an instrument of economic performance and result-based accountability. While I consider that, since the mid-1990s, access to public information has become a stronger citizen's right than it was before, I also argue that there are institutional developments that run counter to this trend.

These changes are visible in state agencies and government ministries whose work is information-intensive in domains such as registry-keeping and cartography, but we also find them in the administration of foreign affairs. When exposed to the new ideas of performance management and transparency, these organizations start to perceive their information resources as assets of economic value. This has altered the way such resources have come to be allocated, leading to surprising institutional outcomes. On a larger scale, states are now exposed to external scrutiny by market actors, leading to their perceived need to produce market-relevant information on their institutional activities, often presented in numerical form. This is manifested in the rise of global governance indices and country rankings that render the performance of state institutions visible to external audiences.

International policy discourses such as that of transparency often tend, when they are adopted, to take nationally specific forms. In Finland, 'openness' has become a central concept of governance, and the narrative that the Finns now relate about themselves depicts institutional openness as a central characteristic of Finnish government. Seen as part of a broader Nordic tradition, this is often referred to as *Nordic openness*. However, the discourse of openness also legitimizes various other acts of government. Along with the commercialization of public information, openness is a Finnish national asset in the globalizing economy that now endorses transparency. Access to government information is increasingly interlinked with Finnish national competitiveness and Finland's fate in the global economy. In this study I explore how the above ideational changes in the state information strategy came about between 1998 and 2007 in Finland, and why they took place. This process therefore relates to research on a shift in the ideology of the state – from that of a Welfare State to that of a Competitive State – revealing a new theme in institutional adaptation.

I will focus strongly on the role of ideas in institutional change, and thereby draw on previous studies on new institutionalism and political economy. Methodologically, this study combines interviews with civil servants, textual analysis of general and case-specific government documents, and analyses of statistical time-series data. As I will show, there has been a general shift towards the economic conception of transparency, resulting in tensions with the previous democratic understanding of public access to government information. Formerly, government openness was seen as a component of democratization, potentially even opposed to efficiency. There is now a broadly shared understanding that transparency is beneficial for economic efficiency and national economic competitiveness. In this study I question how the above ideational changes have been possible, and indicate the importance of policy discourses and normative concepts and narratives of governance.

However, the very shift from an old to a new understanding of openness in government has injected a conceptual incoherence into the various policies adopted in the name of transparency. As we will see, when we look at the paradoxical effects of transparency, there is no single rationale behind the current emphasis on transparency; rather, a proliferation of rationales creates the potential for unintended consequences and counter-finalities, such as the privatization of information, effectively reducing public access to government records, or diminishing public debate through the pressures of globalization. In relation to institutional developments, this study observes changes in central steering mechanisms (political, normative, and financial), institutional developments at the central government level (in the judiciary, information services and performance management), and in two specific areas: census data (from the Population Register Centre) and foreign political information (from the Ministry for Foreign Affairs). I also look at the new policy domain of governance indices as means of achieving transparency. A further question raised here is: What are the institutional transformations and unintended consequences that we find in the above cases and in systems of accountability?

In looking at ideational changes, I draw on various studies of policy discourses (Schmidt 2002, 2006a; Marcussen 2000; Bacchi 1999). The process of conceptual change in Finland has proceeded hand-in-hand with the new discourse of 'openness' or 'Nordic openness' that emerged in the mid-1990s. This discourse communicates new policy ideas concerning transparency and the knowledge economy. Policy discourses tend to be shaped into a contextually appealing form, resonating with prevailing norms and values, and with perceived traditions. In Finland the new discourse on openness resonates with a range of current values and narratives that present the Finns as being Nordic, open, progressive and competitive. Nevertheless, the discourse on Nordic openness is a variant of the international policy discourse on transparency.

The transnational discourse of transparency has various modalities. It emphasizes freedom of information as a civil right ('the right to know'), implying a conflict of interest between the government and the general public. Transparency is also evoked in the calls for new forms of collaborative governance, where it is seen to enhance citizen trust, making governance more effective. Finally, transparency is an economic concept, referring to public information on the performance of organizations and countries. These different modalities are also present in the conceptual constituents of the discourse on Nordic openness. While access to government information in the Finnish context was already understood in terms of democratic control and consensual governance, the perceptions of effectiveness and economic competitiveness are altogether new additions to thinking on governance.

I also use conceptual historical analysis to identify and examine conceptual shifts from 'publicity' to 'openness' and 'transparency' (Skinner 2002a; Koselleck 2004). Adding to current theoretical treatments of discursive institutionalism, I wish to stress that political concepts carry policy ideas and prescriptions (Skinner 1969, 1989). Such concepts are exchanged between actors, and they tend to be part of a wider narrative. With the help of such concepts as 'transparency', 'openness', and 'public sector information', the publicity of government information is framed differently from one context to another. Though I see these concepts as reflections of the current drive for economic transparency, they have differing underlying rationales and pursue different ends.

This political adversity (Palonen 2003) – combined with contextual path-dependencies (Thelen 2004; Streeck and Thelen 2005) – causes unexpected and often paradoxical outcomes in governance (Hood and Peters 2004). The perspective of a long institutional history in the Nordic countries renders the general ideational changes visible, as access to government information is actively reframed from a previous democratic understanding of publicity to one of trust-based openness and economic transparency. Though their intensity and frequency might vary from one country to another, the paradoxes and unintended consequences of transparency presented in this book are also potentially more general problems for contemporary governance.

The understanding reached by this study is that transparency is the vector of the recent conceptualization that public acts of governing can be economically efficient. While this is a broad idea, often discussed in Finland in relation to the idea of openness more generally, it is most apparent in new attempts to provide standardized information on government, even to the extent that it can be expressed numerically. The specific observations on economic transparency are mostly made in relation to governance measurements – namely performance-management measurements, or in global governance indices and country rankings.

I will begin with a brief overview of the history of the publicity of government information, with a focus on legal developments in Europe. I will outline various historical trajectories that are now converging, with most countries now having passed legislation on information access. Yet there is a clear shift to be observed from old ideas of publicity to the new performance-driven ideas of transparency. I will then present the theoretical framework for this study, concentrating on ideational changes in accountability and their potential for producing paradoxical outcomes and unintended consequences (Chapter 1).

In Part II, I will explore how the discourse on Nordic openness emerged in Finland in the 1990s, and how it has evolved with respect to economic performance, including conceptual changes (Chapter 2). I will then explore ideational changes in the area of central steering – particularly legal and financial steering – and analyze the communication of the new performance rationales and economic beliefs concerning 'openness' among policy actors. I will also present institutional developments in accessing government information on a national level in Finland (Chapter 3), pointing to the low level of conflict in attaining information but growing concerns about privacy. Although there is currently an increased awareness of citizens' rights to information following public debate on openness and transparency, I intend to show that many of the economic re-descriptions come together in the current performance-management initiatives and governance indices, which strive for calculable results.

I will then examine organizational cases (Part III), analyzing the interplay of contemporary performance management, renewed legal frameworks, and the economic perceptions of 'public sector information' in managing census information (Chapter 4). I will conclude that the drive for budget transparency has led to the marketization of census information in Finland, accommodated by a historical narrative of openness and citizens' trust. I will then move to assess openness and transparency in the context of the Ministry for Foreign Affairs, showing that a rhetorical shift from secrecy to openness was a consequence of budget transparency and demands for measurable results (Chapter 5). In both of the above cases, civil servants are exposed to a new type of transparency through external governance assessments, making them increasingly responsible for performance, including with respect to market actors.

Finally, I will discuss the findings of the previous chapters, critically exploring current governance reforms, especially in relation to unintended consequences, democratic accountability and perceptions of history (Conclusions). I will conclude that, while there is an increasing awareness of the historical trajectories of government openness as a democratic institution, it is paradoxically being reframed as economic transparency, with significant and often unintended institutional consequences and trade-offs.

Part I
Background and Theory

1
Paradoxes and Unintended Consequences of Transparency

1.1 Introduction

Historically, states have differed from one another in terms of the scope of the information they have collected – and, more importantly, its allocation and publicity. There is now pressure for convergence in the standards of public access to government information. There is a new interest in making government information public, often debated under the headings of 'openness', 'transparency' and 'public sector information'. Some of these developments are contextually specific, but many of their aspects are part of a wider international agenda of 'good governance', the 'knowledge economy' and 'better regulation'. In looking at this process of change from an institutional perspective, this study analyzes the ideational changes in institutional practices governing state information. I explore the ideational and ideological aspects of this process, and thus indicate the sorts of shifts in belief systems that are driving these changes, and that stress efficiency and economic competitiveness. At the institutional level, I will consider the changes that are taking place and certain unintended consequences of the above reforms. The second part of the book analyzes developments in Finland, where there is arguably a long-standing tradition of openness in public administration. This Nordic tradition has been rethought since the mid 1990s, when Finnish governance underwent much transformation and adopted an altogether different course.

When it comes to access to government information, there has been a shift from the democratic understanding of *publicity* to one of *transparency*, which entails a more economic understanding of the issue, emphasizing efficiency. This can be seen in the geographical spread of government information access laws – now even reaching autocratic states; in shifts in ideas of accountability that increasingly stress results; and in the emergence of performance management and global governance indices. Moreover, I will argue that this ideational shift is leading to unintended and often paradoxical institutional outcomes. The most pronounced paradoxical outcome is that the drive for transparency might not lead to increased democratic accountability. I will conclude by proposing a framework for studying the above ideational changes and their institutional consequences.

1.2 Institutional openness in historical perspective: from publicity to transparency

The organizational evolution of the modern state and sovereign rule was made possible by its ability to collect and analyze information (Sheehan 2006, p. 9). In looking at the history of institutional openness, we can conclude that the social conflicts between markets, (state) institutions and citizen rights have been at the heart of the developments of the public sphere and the normative boundaries of the 'public' (cf. Schulz-Forberg and Stråth 2010; Habermas 1989; Arendt 1958; Tocqueville 1991; Emirbayer and Sheller 1999).

Technological developments are also noteworthy drivers of change. The development of printing in the eighteenth century arguably increased the pressure to undo the secrecy of absolutist rule (Habermas 1989; Konstari 1977; Gestrich 1994). It also contributed to another trans-historical process – namely, the building of pan-European and wider networks of communication (Schulz-Forberg and Stråth 2010; Würgler 2002).[1] Starting in the mid twentieth century, the general politicization of government, and the computerization of public administration and transnational communication, have driven countries to adopt information access laws, though to varying extents (Bennett 1997).

The public sphere has been a central theme in studies of nation-building, explaining contextual differences in collective identities, nationhood and nationalism (Eisenstadt and Schluchter 2001; Eder 2006). In the world of convergence through grand processes, such as modernization and globalization, there remain a variety of national trajectories in political and economic institutions and citizen freedoms and rights, as well as in the narrative boundaries of nations ('us and them'). The public sphere can be understood as a structure or as a discursive space (Eder 2006; Marx Ferree et al. 2002).[2] The latter position marks an opening for a genealogical conceptual analysis of the 'public', also adopted in this text. It makes concepts such as 'publicity', 'openness' and 'transparency' instrumental in defining the institutional boundaries of the public sphere (see Somers 1995, 2005).[3] Whereas publicity has been primarily understood as a democratic concept, the notion of transparency increasingly carries economic connotations. As we shall see, this shift in conceptualization is also driving contemporary institutional changes. The geographical spread of information access laws is also revealing in terms of the shift that has accompanied it from old ideas of *publicity* to new governance modes that stress *transparency.*

The institutional European history of administrative openness, depicted in Table 1.1, outlines the variations in time and political argument for adopting legislation on the publicity of government information up to late twentieth century.[4] Ideationally, the institutional practice of making government documents public dates as far back as eighteenth-century Sweden. Though the dissemination of state affairs was already occurring in several locations in eighteenth-century Europe, it was in Sweden in 1766 that it first acquired institutional status (Konstari 1977; Knudsen 2003; cf. Gestrich 1994; Würgler 2002; van Dülmen 1986; Martens 1971; van Eijnatten 2004).[5] There are common features of the adoption (and non-adoption) of access laws in the twentieth century (Bennett 1997), but country-specific studies stress local historical explanations (Durham Peters 2005; Rose-Ackerman 2005; Knudsen 2003; Thurlow 1994; Owen

Table 1.1 Adoption of information access laws in Europe (EU-27) [and in selected other countries][6]

Pre-20th century	1950–1969	1970–1989	1990s	2000s
Sweden (1766)	Finland (1951) [United States of America (1966)]	Denmark (1970) [Norway (1970)] [New Zealand (1970)] Austria (1974) France (1978) Netherlands (1978, into force 1980) Luxemburg (1979) [Australia (1982)] [Canada (1982)]	Hungary (1992) Spain (1992) Italy (1992) Portugal (1993) Belgium (1994) [Iceland (1996, into force 1997)] Ireland (1997, into force 1998) Latvia (1998) Greece (1999) Czech Republic (1999, into force 2000)	Bulgaria (2000) Estonia (2000, into force 2001) Lithuania (2000) Slovakia (2000, into force 2001) UK (2000, into force 2005) Poland (2001, into force 2002) Romania (2001) Slovenia (2003) Germany (2005)

2000, p. 69; Kingdom 2000, p. 42; Timmins 2000, p. 93; Wieland 2000, p. 98; Spence 2000, p. 142; Grønlie and Nagel 1998; Tant 1993; Häner 1990, pp. 281–4; Robertson 1982; Høgetveit 1981; Konstari 1977).

There has been a distinctive historical trajectory in the Nordic countries, where access to government documents forms a constitutional principle of governance, namely the 'principle of publicity', meaning that all government documents are public unless otherwise indicated (Swedish: *offentlighetsprincipen*, Finnish: *julkisuusperiaate*).[7] In terms of comparative administrative law, this feature of governance separates the Nordic countries from other administrative traditions (Harlow 2006, p. 193). Initial conditions do not predetermine historical developments, but they are often of great importance (Pierson 2000a). This is apparent in the Swedish case, where the law allowing public access remained an unmatched institutional peculiarity for some 200 years (see Table 1.1). In Sweden, the world's first law allowing citizens access to government documents was issued as early as 1766, along with a statute on the liberalization of printing.

The issue of accessing government information became topical in eighteenth-century Sweden amid a transition from absolutist rule to liberal bourgeois rule (Konstari 1977; Knudsen 2003, p. 63; cf. Habermas 1989; 1997, p. 105). The process leading to a right of access to state documents was related to the degrading of the absolutism (see Anderson 1993, pp. 190–1; Tiihonen 1994, p. 57). The Habermasian narrative on the structural transformations of the 'public sphere' has been seen as explaining the institutional developments that have made government information public in Sweden (Konstari 1977; Knudsen 2003; cf. Habermas 1989).[8] Yet, in this particular context, the narrative is misconceived due to its anti-religious emphasis. In Sweden the clergy were largely responsible for spreading the ideas of the Enlightenment, and for demanding information on state affairs (see Chapter 2).[9]

Despite similar conflicts elsewhere in eighteenth-century Europe, the Swedish law lasted as an institutional peculiarity until the twentieth century. The issue of institutional openness was debated in Denmark on various occasions from the mid 1800s onwards, but it was 1970 before an actual law providing for such openness was passed (Knudsen 2003, pp. 69–82).[10] Norway, which had been within the Danish sphere of influence, also acquired such legislation in 1970, as part of a process of general democratization within the public administration (Høgetveit 1981, p. 70; Grønlie and Nagel 1998, pp. 308, 329). As a former part of Sweden, Finland had a Swedish administrative model that mostly survived Russia's rule between 1809 and 1917 (Knudsen 2003, pp. 43–4;

Tiihonen 1994, p. 6; Konstari 1977). In Finland, the principle of publicity gained legal status through an access law passed in 1951.

According to Konstari (1977), the principle of publicity had been dormant in Finnish administrative culture since 1766, when Sweden adopted the world's first publicity access legislation, when Finland was still part of Sweden. Finland's period of Russian Tsarist rule, beginning in 1809, brought tightened censorship, making the idea of institutional openness obsolete. After gaining independence in 1917, Finland replicated many of Sweden's state institutions. The openness of government records was first formally adopted in 1951, though the relevant legislation had been drafted in 1939.

On the other hand, Finland differs from the other Scandinavian countries in this area. The Cold War era in Finland was marked by limited public debate and widespread self-censorship, particularly in the sphere of foreign politics – a process often characterized as 'Finlandization'. The post–Cold War era has also brought a normalization of public political debate in Finland. Access to government information was a politicized topic in the 1970s, when there was a failed attempt to reform the access legislation (see Chapter 2). The access law and related legislation were revised in the late 1990s, when transparency had become topical internationally. These events should be seen as potential turning points, in which the institution of access to government information has been explicitly (re)negotiated, enabling it to change (cf. Thelen 2004). Moreover, they are also points of reference at which actors discuss the history of the institution.

In the Finnish case, some remarks are in order on the politics of institutional change and consensus-formation (Peters et al. 2005; Schmidt 2000). Legislative development has generally stagnated during periods of social turmoil, and progressed during periods of consensual government (see Chapter 2). Public debate on the legal framework between the 1930s and the late 1990s was limited, and discussion leading to the legislative revisions defining the boundaries of the 'public' were confined to legal experts. The reforms that led to the 1999 Act on the Publicity of Government Affairs and related laws drew media attention, and a broader range of experts was consulted during the drafting of the new law.

The current international liberalist emphases on 'freedom of information' portray it as a citizen's democratic right. In Finland the principle of publicity is said to have served an integrative function for Finnish society – something that could be applied to the Nordic countries as a whole (Konstari 1977; Larsson 1998).[11] We can also link this with another

Nordic tradition – that of consensus-based policy-making (Kettunen and Kiviniemi 2006; Rainio-Niemi 2008; Larsson 1998). Involving various actors in specific deliberative bodies, this type of openness is likely to create extensive networks of collaborative governance.[12] This implies the contextual specificity of institutional openness, understood in Finland as a principle of governance – an institutional practice – rather than as a citizen's right (see Konstari 1977; cf. Mäenpää 2008a, p. 2; Mäenpää 2008b). Another contextual feature of state information in the Nordic countries is the comprehensive registry infrastructure system, which is the backbone of the Nordic welfare state, allowing for social planning and the allocation of various goods and benefits (Kort & Matrikelstyrelsen 2006; Karimaa 2001). Citizens' unparalleled trust in the state's registry-keeping enables the Nordic countries to maintain an unmatched registry system, and to combine the different registries in ways that would be unthinkable in any other context.

But this state tradition is changing once again, as the new economic and performance-driven perception of institutional openness – often called transparency – advances in Finnish and Nordic governance (see Blomgren 2007; Blomgren and Sahlin 2007). Consequently, the peculiarities of Nordic institutional mechanisms governing public access to state information and the allocation of registry data have been reframed in terms of results-based economic performance and accountability. Alongside the previous control and integration functions, there is now a new economic rationale structuring access to state information.

These new 'theories of state' also have an apparent historical analogy (cf. Chapter 2). While liberalist ideas about governance were spreading among the European communication networks of the eighteenth century, the late twentieth century saw a worldwide spread of political and market liberalism (Schulz-Forberg and Stråth 2010; Simmons et al. 2006; Peters et al. 2005). Both aspects of the diffusion of liberalism are visible in Europe. Democratization in Europe has been most visible in the post-communist countries, where access laws on information have contributed to the democratization process and to a coming to terms with the past (Rose-Ackerman 2005). As for market liberalism, the codifications of New Public Management (NPM) and good governance are enhancing performance through transparency, which has also hastened the process as a whole.

In the twentieth century the diffusion of ideas on freedom of information legislation (as well as on privacy and the Ombudsman institution) have for long been held up as examples of political innovation (Bennett 1997; Rowat 1973, 1979). This diffusion of ideas used to be mostly horizontal (between one national context and another), but it is increasingly becoming vertical: from supranational organizations to national polities (see Sanders and West 2003; Knudsen 2003; Harlow 2006). Standards in ethics and concepts of public information are currently undergoing convergence, and are often discussed under the policy programmes of 'good governance', 'better regulation', and 'e-government'.

The international diffusion of ideas concerning the transparency of public institutions now encompasses newly industrialized countries, and even autocracies (see for example Rodan 2004; Samaratunge et al. 2008; Cejudo 2008; Lynden & Wu 2008; Pietrowski et al. 2009). This development demonstrates the shift from the old idea of *publicity* to the new concept of *transparency*. Policy instruments are also relevant. Most notably, the rise of performance management and global governance indices is inherently related to the drive for transparency.

The evolution of administrative thinking on transparency goes hand-in-hand with the theorizing of governance that now emphasizes the rule of law over laissez-faire, and aims to uproot information asymmetry (opacity) and hidden transaction costs, such as corruption. The role of government information is emphasized in the creation of new economic activities, and in the processes of democratization through deliberation. While accountability systems can be seen as institutional frameworks providing continuity for democratic governance, these systems are not themselves static. They hinge on prevailing ideas of democracy and efficiency, and they reflect policy change.

1.3 Governance, accountability, and transparency: democratic and efficient?

Transparency is often seen as a central element of accountability – the latter an ambiguous concept itself, forthrightly described by some as 'the key to the broadest and most widely applicable definition of "modern representative democracy"' (Schmitter 2005, p. 18).[13] Accountability is increasingly becoming a topic of concern in literature on governance. The growing interest in it is largely explained by the rise of new governance models, which are thought to challenge traditional mechanisms of accountability (Pierre and Peters 2000, p. 67; Mulgan 2000; Van Kersbergen and Van Waarden 2004; Dubnick 2005). As the interest in accountability has increased, the definition of the term itself seems to have become more ambiguous (Mulgan 2000; Sinclair 1995, p. 221; Dubnick 2005, pp. 2–3, 6). The shifts in the conceptualization of accountability can be understood against the shift from 'government' to 'governance' (see Erkkilä 2007).[14] Since the late 1980s, openness and transparency have been seen as a counterbalance to performance-seeking governance programmes. On the other hand, transparency is increasingly becoming a core concept for public sector performance.

1.3.1   Defining accountability

The origins of the concept of accountability can be traced to the emergence of royal legal traditions in England (Dubnick 2005, p. 10). But for a long time the term was little used outside the sphere of financial accounting, and it first acquired wider currency with the New Public Management (NPM) reforms of the 1980s (Mulgan 2003, p. 9; see also Bovens 2005). The concept of accountability has since become more accepted than the term 'responsibility' (Mulgan 2000, pp. 557–8; see also Dwivedi and Jabbra 1988, pp. 3–5). Accountability was first conceptually included in the idea of responsibility, but later gained ground as an individual concept, now outstripping responsibility in both its centrality and scope (Mulgan 2000, p. 558; Sinclair 1995, p. 221; see also Dubnick 2005, p. 6).

In Mulgan's 'core sense', accountability is defined as a *process* of 'being called to account to some authority for one's actions', or of 'giving an account' (Mulgan 2000, p. 555; see also Dubnick 2005, p. 6; Bovens 2005). This core definition of accountability is characterized by externality and social interaction and exchange in terms of rectification and sanctions (Mulgan 2000, p. 555; 2003, p. 10). The account-holder, meaning actor or constituency holding someone accountable has rights of authority over the accountor, the actor held accountable, including rights to demand answers and impose sanctions (Mulgan 2000, p. 555). Some scholars have related accountability to answerability (Dubnick 2005, pp. 410–11; Bovens 2005).

Dubnick finds Mulgan's definition of core accountability somewhat limited, since it stresses external authority as a mechanism of accountability, disregarding personal ethics (Dubnick 2005, p. 6; 2003). Bovens notes that the account-holder or 'accountee' can be a person or an agency – but it can also take the form of an accountability forum, such as the general public. The accountability forum may also be of a more 'virtual' nature – something like personal conscience or faith (Bovens 2005).

The various definitions of accountability all entail an element of control. This was the term commonly used in the literature before the term accountability took over (Hood 1986; Beck Jørgensen and Larsen 1987;

Hood and Schuppert 1988; Beck Jørgensen 1993). The notion of control differs slightly from that of accountability, since the process of calling someone to account is retrospective by nature, whereas control can be proactive (Harlow 2002, p. 10). Yet both of these terms refer to authority over those who govern. As a process, accountability can be reduced to three variables: accountability *for what, to whom* and *how*? (Mulgan 2000). Here, the most important is the 'mechanism of accountability', or *how* the actors are made accountable.

Most definitions of accountability do not specify any particular mechanism for calling someone to account, which causes certain problems in conceptualizing the term consistently. There are various definitions, and even misuses, of the term (Mulgan 2000; Sinclair 1995; Dubnick 2005, p. 6). In my view, the different definitions or types of accountability are contingent on the structures or administrative contexts in which they appear. Different types of accountability apply in different administrative contexts, and there are no universal solutions for organizing accountability systems (cf. Romzek and Dubnick 1987, p. 230; Beck Jørgensen and Larsen 1987; Peters 1989, pp. 252–3; Beck Jørgensen 1993; Sinclair 1995; Romzek 2000, pp. 34–5; Mulgan 2003; Goodin 2003, p. 381; Van Kersbergen and Van Waarden 2004, pp. 155–60; Dubnick 2005, p. 37). Table 1.2 summarizes the types of accountability often cited in governance literature according to their mechanisms of accountability: political accountability, bureaucratic accountability, personal accountability, professional accountability, performance, and deliberation (Erkkilä 2007).[15] These various types tend to overlap, and are not always clear-cut.

I regard political accountability, bureaucratic accountability, personal accountability and professional accountability as traditional types of accountability, each having a long history within the context of the democratic state and public administration. Political accountability refers to actors' responsibility for their actions to a wider public either

Table 1.2 Different types of accountability (after Erkkilä 2007)

Type of accountability	Mechanisms of accountability
Political accountability	Democratic elections, chain of accountability
Bureaucratic accountability	Rules, regulations, supervision
Personal accountability	Culture, values, ethics
Professional accountability	Expert scrutiny, peer review, professional role
Performance	Competition, self-regulation, transparency
Deliberation	Public debate, openness, transparency

directly, when politically elected or appointed, or indirectly as subordinates of democratically elected bodies. Bureaucratic accountability has traditionally been based on the hierarchic relationship between superiors and subordinates, with its attendant rules, regulations and supervision. In relation to civil servants, personal accountability refers to the personal values and ethics used as guides to their action. Professional accountability refers to deference to expertise and peer review.

Governance literature often sees performance and deliberation as new or alternative types of accountability; since the early 1990s, performance in particular has been identified in this way. Consequently, public sector institutions and civil servants alike have been exposed to new efficiency-seeking programmes and means of control. This has diminished public political debate, increased the prestige of expert authority, and privatized bureaucratic processes (Erkkilä 2007). New deliberative models of governance have arisen as a counterbalance to this trend. In the debates over accountability, performance and deliberation are often seen as being opposed to one another.

But credible arguments have been made that neither 'performance' nor 'deliberation' should be regarded as types of accountability in any strict sense, since they do not necessarily provide a mechanism of accountability (Mulgan 2003; Dubnick 2005). Mere deliberation does not imply that its conclusions must be taken into account, or that the public may hold the civil service accountable through deliberation after some wrongdoing. Deliberation is therefore meaningful only as a component of political or bureaucratic accountability, or as an input channel to the experts, where an informed public can provide peer review. Similarly, the notion of performance does not provide a mechanism for calling someone to account when things go wrong (Dubnick 2005).

Nevertheless, the discussion about performance and deliberation has undeniably influenced the understanding of available means for controlling government. We should perhaps perceive them as two governance ideologies that can influence the organization and functionality of accountability systems (for more detailed analysis of these types of accountability and shifts within them, see Erkkilä 2007). Recently, these two ideological trends have begun to merge in the search for good governance. They come together in the concept of transparency.

1.3.2   Transparency: performance and deliberation

Since the late 1980s, traditional state-centric types, or mechanisms, of accountability – such as political, bureaucratic and personal accountability – have lost some of their capacity to control public administration, whereas the mechanisms of professional accountability have become more central, due to the increasing complexity of the tasks of government (Erkkilä 2007). This development has perhaps diminished openness in decision-making, in both bureaucratic and political spheres, and enhanced expert authority. This has meant a shift from hierarchical means of control towards a more result-based oversight of public institutions. This, in turn, has influenced the conceptualization and organization of the different types of accountability, such as the traditional types of political, bureaucratic, personal and professional accountability.

An overall shift can be identified towards ideas favoring accountability through performance. Though deliberation is often seen as balancing the performance demands of NPM reforms, it is worth noting that transparency has been a central part of the NPM doctrine (Blomgren and Sahlin 2007). There is also an apparent ambivalence in contemporary social-scientific thought on transparency. The cognitive aspects of policy discourse are likely to be based on social-scientific assessments (Schmidt 2002, p. 214), and social-scientific paradigm shifts are thus relevant to institutional developments.

Many scholars of political science, administrative studies and international relations see transparency as a new means of bringing about democratization. In the political-scientific literature on deliberative democracy, the notions of consensus, collaboration and trust have become new democratic virtues (Cohen 1997; Habermas 1996; Young 2000; Dryzek 2002; compare Mouffe 1999).[16] This has brought the 'openness' and 'transparency' of public institutions to the core of contemporary political theory (see Kelly 2004), and as a result many scholars discuss transparency in the context of democratization and democratic government (Chapman and Hunt 2006; Roberts 2006; Lord 2006).

What political scientists often fail to see, however, is the role that transparency plays in contemporary theories of economics and management studies. Scholars of international political economy and economists perceive it as a means of enhancing efficiency (Best 2005, p. 141; Wintrobe 2007). Also, many analyses of public-sector reform currently see transparency in relation to budgetary processes as an element of performance management – an heir of New Public Management (see Blomgren and Sahlin 2007; Blomgren 2007). According to Stiglitz (Stiglitz 2002, 1998), a new economic paradigm has brought information asymmetry and the availability of information to the core of theoretical discussions of market efficiency. Stiglitz argues that 'it has been shown that in the presence of imperfect information or incomplete markets, the economy will not be Pareto efficient; in other words, there will always be some intervention by which the government can make everyone better off' (Stiglitz 1998, pp. 3–4). Consequently, within the field of economics, transparency has come to be used in reference to perfect market information and lower transaction costs (Kono 2006; Libich 2006; Breton 2007). Furthermore, political-economic theory sees transparency, low corruption, compromise and consensus as guarantees of efficiency (cf. Best 2005, pp. 28, 57; Lambsdorff 2007; Jenkins and Kuo 2007).

Some scholars have argued that the economic performance of countries is determined by their institutional evolution (North 2005). The above sketch of current research in economics points clearly to shifts in the understanding of efficiency in the discipline: democratic public institutions are no longer seen as a potential hindrance to efficiency, but instead as its guarantee (Skousen 1997; Stiglitz 1998).[17] This reduces democratic institutions to their economic aspects, expressed in terms of economic variables.

Jessop has criticized the governance research for being dismissive of the classic dichotomies on which the social sciences have traditionally relied. In this sense, 'governance' serves as the 'missing third term', allowing us to re-evaluate and bypass these dichotomies (Jessop 1998, p. 31).[18] This view illuminates some developments in contemporary political concepts. Like 'governance', *transparency* has the potential of being a mechanism of both democracy *and* (economic) efficiency. The debates on performance and deliberation both hold up 'openness' and 'transparency' as keys to better governance (see also Hood and Heald 2006). This implies that we can do away with either-or dichotomies, and have a system of governance that is both democratic *and* efficient, both public *and* private, merging the spheres of market and bureaucracy (hierarchy).

'Deliberation' is no longer conducted merely in the sphere of the democratic state, but is increasingly becoming an operative logic for markets and performance management. In a form of market transparency, states are assessed by external actors for their various qualities of governance – whether their eligibility for credit, perceived corruption or policy choices. And within the states, public institutions are monitored for their budgetary performance, a process known as 'budget transparency' (Blomgren and Sahlin 2007). Consequently, there is now a strong consensus on the need for openness, transparency and access to public information. The political and democratic nature of this newly emerged institutional design should be analyzed critically, to establish whether the new information strategies of the state are aimed primarily at promoting enhanced democracy or, rather, performance. Moreover, the way in which good governance is defined and organized is an inherently political question (Mouffe 1999, p. 752; cf. Somers 2005 and Zanotti 2005).[19]

Alongside these developments there has been an increasing demand for quantifiable information – merging scientific evidence into public policies, introducing market principles into government, integrating markets and polities, and trying to cope with geographic aspects of governance (Espeland and Stevens 2008, p. 402; Porter 1996; Power 1999; Miller and Rose 1990; Hummel 2006; Hopwood and Miller 1994). According to Espeland and Stevens, 'quantification facilitates a peculiarly modern ontology, in which the real easily becomes coextensive with what is measurable' (Espeland and Stevens 2008, p. 432). In presenting what they call the 'ethics of quantification', they claim that such ethics 'should strongly reject any conceit, scientific or otherwise, that measurement provides privileged or exclusive access to the real'.

The new ideas on transparency in governance are in many ways entangled in a process of quantification – whether in new forms of accounting, performance management or country rankings. This construction of social 'facts' may create political realities that are so captivating that actors no longer perceive a reality outside them. The empirical observations concerning transparency that I deal with here are mostly made in relation to governance measurements: on a national level, in performance management; or in global governance indices and country rankings.

1.3.3 Transparency in country rankings and governance indices

Since the late 1990s there has been a surge in the international production of country rankings and governance indices. Measuring the 'pulse' of public institutions leads to a reflexivity in the way public institutions are able to function in different countries.[20] Governance indices are perhaps the most apparent attempts at defining a universal normative codification of 'good governance'; since such figures are mainly issued annually, this results in an almost contemporaneous evaluation. The issues measured cover practices as diverse as economic competitiveness (monitored by the World Economic Forum), the performance of primary education systems (OECD PISA), or the perceived amount of corruption in a country (Transparency International). These measurements themselves constitute a new type of transparency.

Numerical governance assessments of this kind have implications for institutional openness and transparency in two senses: first, they are a form of (market) transparency, rendering visible the institutional structure of a state; second, they often build on a shared set of social-scientific presuppositions, holding openness and transparency to be preconditions for certain causal effects. They therefore echo current shifts in social-scientific conceptions of efficiency. Solid and long-standing institutions have also come to be viewed as an explanatory factor in economic competitiveness (North 2005; Fukuyama 2004).

Furthermore, these instruments of governance have become increasingly relevant for policy-making, entailing technical implications for those wishing to implement the policies that the rankings endorse. Moreover, the technical implications have geographical and temporal aspects, rendering national institutional trajectories visible. The numbers also have democratic implications: they define the virtues of good governance, but may also create a perception of a new external audience to whom civil servants are now perceived as being responsible, in addition to their domestic constituencies.

Some scholars have discussed globalization as a race for better economic competitiveness, investment and economic wealth (see Drezner 2004; Garrett 1998). In taking part in this race, states arguably have to adopt strategies in organizing their institutions to suit the processes outlined above. This can lead to a streamlining of standards in labor-market policies, taxation and environmental regulation, resulting in a 'race to the bottom'. On the other hand, it may lead to an attempt to institute firm institutional practices – for instance, reducing corruption and performing well in education policies, leading to a 'race to the top' in institutional performance. The perception of competition is most apparent in relation to governance rankings.

Geographical considerations are fundamental to an understanding of the new global economy, rendering the state a unit of analysis in itself (Moisio 2006, 2008). This is slightly opposed to the general argument in the literature on governance, which tends to downplay the importance of states. But the revival of states is only apparent, since attention towards state institutions also amounts to their reorganization. Interestingly, the means of quantification that allowed modern states to seek sovereign power are now used by various international actors to measure states. Censuses, cartography and statistics made the modern state possible – and, more importantly, governable (see Rose 2000, p. 147; Sheehan 2006). Governance indices are currently making global governance possible; states themselves are becoming governable entities by means of such measurements. Numerical measurement can problematize certain aspects of governance, such as transparency.

But political dimension of the many underlying causal and normative beliefs remains tacit as the beliefs – and even data – are shared by the participants in these processes .

The diffusion of 'neo' or 'market' liberalism is widely viewed as a substantial ideational shift that is now triggering institutional changes (Simmons et al. 2006; Peters et al. 2005; Harvey 2005; Boltanski and Chiapello 2005; Blyth 2002). Analytically, however, one should separate economic from democratic notions of liberalism (Brown 2003). This is empirically challenging because the new perceptions of institutional and informational economics use concepts that have democratic overtones. The external assessments and country rankings pay particular interest to state institutions as drivers of *national competitiveness* (see Sum 2009). One subject of these institutional assessments is the state of transparency in a given country. Moreover, the figures themselves make the states transparent to external examiners. So the notion of transparency is a presupposition of the measurements, and justifies the activities of those who produce the measurements; but transparency is also an aspect of governance that is being measured.

The global market has built increasingly on transparency (Best 2005), but this no longer relates only to market actors, but also to sovereign states. Governance indices often measure 'governance' in market-relevant terms (Erkkilä and Piironen 2009). The current governance indices reflect a departure from previous social-scientific attempts to compare countries. Whereas the large country comparisons were previously made by academics, such measurements are now increasingly being made by international public institutions concerned with economic development, or even by private institutions. The subject of measurement has also shifted. Whereas previous academic assessments were organized around the notion of democracy, the current country comparisons focus on the effectiveness of governance. It is important to note here that, while democracy still remains a highly disputed concept, as is clear from the plurality of ways in which it is measured, there seems to be a firm consensus on what constitutes *good governance* among those who produce the relevant data (Erkkilä and Piironen 2009, pp. 130–2).

Many previous assessments ground the notion of good governance in market-liberalist and efficiency-seeking perceptions of institutions advanced by international organizations concerned with economic development (Zanotti 2005; Drechsler 2004; Seppänen 2003). On closer examination, the indices of good governance appear to be more suited to measuring performance than the democratic merits of institutions. A previous study shows that the findings of both Transparency

International's *Corruption Perception Index* and the World Bank's *World Governance Index* correlate more strongly with the World Economic Forum's *Global Competitiveness Index*, a country ranking of economic performance, than with Freedom House's *Political Rights and Civil Liberties* assessments that measures democratic rights. The *Corruption Perception Index* and *Global Competitiveness Index* also correlate only weakly with the *World Governance Index*'s 'Voice and Accountability' component that assesses citizens ability to hold their government accountable (for a fuller analysis, see Erkkilä and Piironen 2009, pp. 137–9). The above results indicate that the ideational core of the better-known indices of good governance focus on the economic performance of public institutions, while the democratic aspects of governance are given less emphasis.

These indices are also part of the political imaginary of global governance (see Larner and Walters 2004). They make a claim concerning the present situation, describing it as a competition between states. By naming and measuring selected items of governance and competitiveness, they have come to dominate the policy agendas of many countries. Moreover, measurements tend to entail an idealization of what is being measured (Husserl 1970, pp. 34–5). While the figures neatly fit the present understanding of global economic competition, by measuring different elements of it, they also set policy goals for countries, either to maintain or improve their position. Their top ten rankings largely coincide, comprising Anglo-Saxon countries, Nordic countries, a few Central European countries and some economically advanced East Asian countries.[21]

Transparency has come to occupy a central position in the belief systems underlying governance indices (see for example Lopez-Claros et al. 2006, p. 6).[22] Still, few governance indices or rankings actually measure transparency or openness, which is partly an indication of their poor measurability. Nevertheless, particularly in developing countries, the policy ideas of 'transparency' have mainly been diffused through the presence of international financial institutions and NGOs such as Transparency International (West and Sanders 2003; Ivanov 2009, pp. 149–50).

1.3.4 Institutional engineering and perceptions of history

The number of countries with information-access laws has increased rapidly in the last two decades, and now includes developing countries. This development often has instrumental motivations. For instance, many African countries have recently adopted legislation on accessing government information in order to attract foreign direct investment (Azubuike 2008, pp. 89–92). The outcome of adopted or exported governance ideas and practices might bear only remote similarities to those of the institution in its 'original' context, or the outcome might be wholly contradictory (see Przeworski 2004). In extreme cases, the democratic qualities of openness, apparent for instance in the Nordic context, might go missing completely if the emphasis of reforms is solely on economic performance.

A good example of this is presented in an account of the transparency reforms of Singapore and Malaysia in their battle against the Asian financial crises of the late 1990s: the reform and increased transparency of public institutions helped to secure foreign direct investment without significantly furthering the democratization of these countries (Rodan 2004).[23] On the contrary, Singapore has been criticized for its censorship and the suppression of information (Hood and Margetts 2007, p. 41; cf. Sriramesh and Rivera-Sánchez 2006). This underlines the context-dependent nature of institutional principles and practices, and the consequent difficulty in exporting them (Przeworski 2004, p. 540).

One could argue that increased transparency, even if motivated by economic gain, is always beneficial to democracy. But one should be cautious not to overemphasize its importance (Fung et al. 2008). Without proper political rights, civil society organizations and citizens may make little use of transparency (see Rodan 2004); the importance of related civil society institutions and political rights is often overlooked. Freedoms of speech, of the press, and of political activity are indispensable if transparency and openness are to play a role in democratic control of government. Democratic practices may have contextual variations, however, that are difficult to gather under any single definition of transparency. The Nordic ideas concerning the consensual mediation of interests through openness can be seen as just such a contextual peculiarity.

The new institutional geography of country rankings renders visible the temporal aspects of governance – in particular, long-term institutional developments such as the conventions for government openness or secrecy. The Nordic countries have enjoyed a long history of institutional openness that allows citizens access to government information. Even if administrative laws around the world might be moving towards increasing openness, the Nordic countries continue to stand out in this respect (Harlow 2006, p. 193). The existing research literature makes a strong argument that the development of institutional openness in some European countries and, on the other hand, of long prevailing government secrecy in others is historically bounded. Equally, accounts of national attitudes to personal privacy reflect historical trajectories that play an explanatory role – often drawing lineages going back to the Second World War, or even to the of eighteenth century liberalism (Newman and Bach 2004). Diverging cultural and historical trajectories of nation-building have shaped varying conceptualizations of the public sphere as a cultural form (Eder 2006). This fact is largely ignored in the ahistorical representation of governance presented in country rankings and indices.

These constant country comparisons focusing on transparency have also led to a new appreciation of institutional history in those countries where there has historically been institutionalized public access to state information, such as the Nordic countries. As I will show, the ideational shift from publicity to transparency is also ongoing in these countries, though it may take more subtle forms than in developing countries. History thus becomes an important reference point, making the changes appear part of an administrative tradition that is nevertheless undergoing change as a result of such reflexivity. As the democratic institution of accessing government information is now held in high regard for its positive effects on economic efficiency and competitiveness, these new ideas have been added to the historical narrative on the openness of governance without general notice.

In rendering diverse institutional trajectories comparable and pointing out issues of concern, governance indices in their own right also represent an instance of a policy discourse on transparency and openness. It remains debatable, though, whether transparency always yields the results that it is presumed to deliver. In particular, the idea that it would make everyone better off (Stiglitz 1998) may be too optimistic, as it overlooks the path-dependencies and political ambiguities of each context. Some scholars have taken a critical stance towards the very notion of transparency, claiming that, instead of leading to the rational management of social problems, it may in fact bring about paradoxical results that make societies less governable (Tsoukas 1997; Strathern 2000; Hood 2010). These unexpected effects might be dependent on context, as developed countries may develop different pathologies of transparency from developing countries (Kolstad and Wiig 2008). Country comparisons also have implications for accountability, since states' responses to the figures they contain has strengthened the emphasis on accountability through results in preference to accountability through rules-based government, process accountability. The most pressing problem for the idea of accountability through transparency is *to whom* and *for what* actions the civil service is perceived to be accountable. Paradoxically, the drive for transparency might render public administration less accountable in a democratic sense (see Hood 2010, pp. 1006–7), as the new economic connotations of transparency tip the balance in favor of performance.

1.3.5 Transparency: paradoxes, unintended consequences and trade-offs

There are certain *paradoxes* in the emerging practices of transparency (see Hood and Peters 2004). There are also *unintended consequences* and *trade-offs* for the reforms in the name of transparency (Hood et al. 1996; Elster 1978; Baert 1991). Baert identifies *counter-finality, sub-optimality* and *structuration* (or *duality of structure*) as types of unintended consequence (Baert 1991, pp. 207–9; cf. Elster 1978, pp. 106, 122). 'Counter-finality' refers to the fallacy of composition: what might be possible and beneficial for one is not necessarily so for all (Baert 1991, p. 207).[24] Moreover, counter-finality allows unanticipated consequences. Sub-optimality refers to a situation in which actors are aware of the negative

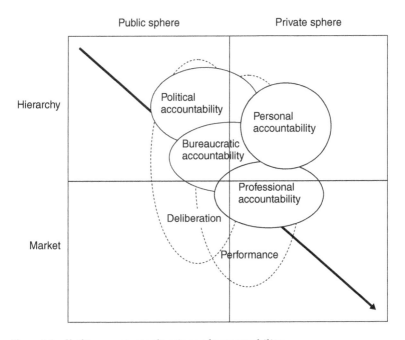

Figure 1.1 Shifting conceptualizations of accountability

aggregate effect of their actions, but nevertheless choose to pursue them to their own benefit (Elster 1978, p. 122).[25] The third type of unintended consequence in Baert's typology – structuration (or duality of structure) – refers to the fact that even reflective and self-conscious activity tends unconsciously to reproduce routine practices (Baert 1991, p. 209; cf. Giddens 1984; see also Marcussen 2000, p. 17).[26]

In relation to accountability, deliberation and performance are often seen as being either counterposed or complementary. The existing literature on political accountability mostly assumes that deliberation balances out performance-seeking public-sector reforms, most notably the NPM. As I will demonstrate in this study, however, the ideas of deliberation and performance strongly overlap in current thinking on transparency. Deliberation and the allocation of information become parts of the performance-management framework. Nevertheless, as has been discussed, neither deliberation nor performance themselves provide a mechanism for accountability (Mulgan 2000; Dubnick 2005).

The shifts in the conception of accountability are presented in Figure 1.1, which is based on the typology presented in Table 1.2. The categorization follows the Weberian division between market and hierarchy, and the Habermasian public–private dichotomy (Weber 1978; Habermas 1989).[27] The *public–hierarchy* field incorporates public political discussions and deliberative elements in bureaucratic or professional accountability, such as parliamentary debates and the deliberative structures of participatory bureaucracy. The *private–hierarchy* field points to those processes of governance that, for various reasons, are confidential or secret – either in the name of the public interest, or for reasons of personal privacy. The *public–market* field incorporates the transparency and public accounting, to which market actors, but also states, are exposed. In the related deliberative processes, even states assume responsibilities for giving an account of their performance to market actors and international financial institutions. The *private–market* field represents commercial confidentiality, which has come increasingly within the sphere of the state, as a result of the business-based processes introduced to into public administration and the state's collaboration with private companies.

The arrow indicates the direction of the shifting conceptualization of the traditional types of accountability that are now complemented through market-based mechanisms and rationalities (Erkkilä 2007). There are general calls for 'output legitimacy' through results and regulative effectiveness (Majone 1997; cf. Scharpf 1999, p. 6).[28] Political actors now declare responsibilities towards market actors, legal hierarchies have been loosened, and new means of performance management have arisen. Civil servants are increasingly involved in a processes of expert scrutiny or verification of their work – through auditing, peer review, or the exchange of ideas between policy experts, now also taking place transnationally through the OECD or the EU. Administrative ethics have also been explicitly linked to performance (OECD 1996).

There has been some success. Access to government information has come to be openly acknowledged as a citizen's right almost globally. Codifications of privacy have also been strengthened. In economic terms, countries with transparent government are performing better than most other countries (Lopez-Claros et al. 2006, p. 6; OECD 2003b). But the re-description of openness in government information as a mechanism of performance contributes to an emphasis on *results* rather than *processes*. In the long run, however, results do not compensate for lack of process accountability (Scharpf 1999, pp. 26–7; Skogstad 2003, p. 962; Papadopoulos 2003, p. 484; Van Kersbergen and Van Waarden 2004, p. 158).[29] As I will argue here, the ideas of deliberation and performance are inherent in the traditional types of accountability, but as tacit ideological elements. Deliberation has increasingly been promoted in the quest to enhance the performance of governance.

As the aspirations towards democracy and efficiency overlap, the civil service is consequently exposed to new expectations regarding openness that are difficult to separate from each other either analytically or in everyday practice.[30] While transparency is perceived as a definitive mechanism for accountability (Mulgan 2000), it is now expected to deliver both democracy and efficiency. This has caused a dislocation between deliberation and performance in the public–market field, indicated in Figure 1.1 by the dotted line; deliberation and performance increasingly overlap, but citizens are no longer necessarily seen as the forum of accountability.

Hall and Soskice identify institutions of deliberation as a component separating the liberal market economies from coordinative market economies (Hall and Soskice 2001, p. 11). As in the liberal market economies, there is now a tendency for public administrations to produce market-relevant information on their activities, reaching out to the public–market field. This indicates a shift in the political economy away from coordinative deliberations, for instance in the labor market. On the other hand, as my analysis of foreign political information will show (see Chapter 5), there are attempts to remobilize deliberation as a means of allocating information between strategic actors in state policy-making, under the pressures of economic globalization. All the same, deliberation has recently been favored as a mechanism to promote economic performance.

A trade-off can be observed here. While expanding the understanding of the openness in governance to cover active communication, civil services are now making a significant amount of information available to citizens and businesses (see Chapter 3). But this has also made openness an instrument for enhancing performance. Deliberation and performance now overlap (in the public–market field). Though information services are likely to increase citizens' trust in public administration, the information services do not provide a direct 'mechanism' of accountability (see Mulgan 2000).[31] In fact, the strategic communication now expected from the civil service is shifting the institution from process accountability to results-based accountability.

This is most apparent in the case of performance management, where new demands for transparency have led to the production of standardized and numerical information on the effects of government. Even if the mechanism of accountability in performance management is transparency (see Chapter 3), the public service is now held responsible for its performance, not for the processes of governance themselves. By replacing the principle of democratic accountability with that of economic performance, a general shift in the accountability system has been produced. Formerly, openness constituted an element of the application of accountability through democratic processes. As it is becoming a commonplace that the dissemination of government information, or its wider societal use, is favorable for economic performance, the locus of accountability seems to have shifted. These tensions pose a problem for democratic control. Though for any individual actor this might seem like a slight shift, its aggregate effect on democratic accountability may be more extensive.

Furthermore, the social contradictions and unintended consequences of the reforms have created situations in which the responsibilities of an agency are contradictory and plagued by trade-offs (Hood et al. 1996). Even the discourse of transparency in transnational policy has various modalities. On the one hand, it emphasizes freedom of information as a civil right – the 'right to know' – but on the other, there are calls for new forms of collaborative governance in which transparency is seen to enhance public trust, thereby also rendering governance more effective. Transparency is now also an economic concept, referring to market and budget transparency, and implying the availability of information on the performance of organizations and states. In other words, the promotion by the discourse of transparency of very divergent rationales explains its current appeal. However, these rationales can be contradictory and lead to unintended consequences.

For instance, performance management and budget transparency may create incentives for public organizations to charge for their data – an institutional development in the European Union since mid 1990s (European Commission 1998; Economist 2010a). Paradoxically, the new forms of budget transparency may lead to the closure of state information from the public through high pricing. Government agencies may also be under pressure to sell the private information of their citizens to meet the financial demands of performance-management schemes (Economist 2010a). This can cause difficult trade-offs between the tasks of state agencies, which will act as sellers and regulators of the same information. This is most apparent in the case of the census information I examine below, and which the civil service in Finland is supposed to sell for the purpose of maintaining privacy. Moreover, privatizing public information may cause it to become a costly resource, with a negative influence on the cohesion of the state administration, and more generally on economic development through transparency. This can be seen as a counter-finality or sub-optimality in terms of efficiency; commercializing activities can be highly beneficial for the agencies that engage in them, while their overall economic results may be negative.

In the received international jargon, transparency is also often linked with increased trust in government and consensus through deliberation (OECD 2001a, 2003a, 2005b). The democratic control of government, however, builds on the idea of conflict in state–citizen relations, and even of mistrust in government. Paradoxically, access to government information and deliberative forms of governance might have a negative effect on the very foundations of political accountability. Moreover, the consensual traditions of governance might allow a wide circulation of information without its necessarily becoming public. This is also linked to (economic) globalization, in which civil services are increasingly urged to promote national economic interests, thereby leading to the circulation of information within a closed system of trusted partners, including private companies.

Hence, while openness and consensus might support cohesive tendencies, they can also have limiting effects on democratic accountability, public debate and public scrutiny (compare Mouffe 1999; Tiihonen 2003, 112).[32] This is troubling for theories of deliberative democracy that posit openness as a means of reaching consensus – a normative goal as such (Habermas 1996). The drive for transparency leads to attempts at information-sharing among policy actors, but thereby runs the risk of making these deliberations non-public. As various social actors are included to the governance process as experts or stakeholders, there is less need for the government to give public accounts on its activities. The trust-based sharing of information and participatory governance can be termed democratic through representation, but this link requires a clear structure of representation, which is seldom present in contemporary governance that emphasizes ad-hoc expert groups. Moreover, as the voluntary sharing of information is not a legally defined institutional practice, there are informal hierarchic relations of power in the processes of inclusion and exclusion. The mechanism of accountability effectively becomes the means of governance.

In the area of accountability, governance indicators provide a whole new agenda, often highlighting the perception of economic competitiveness. Good rankings are thought to help in attracting international companies and investment; the subject-matter – the functionality of governance in a society – is put aside, and the instrumental value of the interoperability of institutions is highlighted. In the realm of foreign affairs, a country's good placement in the rankings is thought to attract an educated workforce and tourism, and also to provide a country with greater credibility in the international arena.

To appreciate the political potential of these figures, it is important to understand the normative and instrumental nature of such assessments. Contextually specific institutional practices are difficult to assess by means of a too general conceptualization of certain phenomena, let alone measure against an international standard. The international discourse of good governance has shifted from assessments of democracy, and the new governance measurements have depoliticized the concept of good governance, and paradoxically diminished the sphere of ethics and politics in transnational policy coordination (Erkkilä and Piironen 2009, p. 142; Husserl 1970).[33]

There have been some alarming shifts in perceptions of accountability: civil servants and politicians increasingly see themselves as being responsible to economic actors 'out there'.[34] As will be shown in the empirical part of this study, transparency and openness are now named as competitive advantages; sometimes it is even acknowledged that this no longer represents a democratic understanding of openness. Though the mechanism might be dissemination of information about activities, the current pursuit of 'economic gain through democracy' is problematic for the economic instrumentalization of democratic institutions.

Moreover, new ideas of performance management that traverse different levels of governance might dissolve legal hierarchies; but in seeking to increase the coordinative powers through accounting, they construct a bureaucratic hierarchy of calculative logic (see Weber 1978, p. 975) – a paradoxical outcome for a post-bureaucratic reform.

The reflexivity on different national models has intensified through the country comparison process. The numerical data create a political horizon of competition, and also claim to have a solution for it, and thus to have self-enforcing qualities. The competition that takes place with respect to the quality of governance has a normatively appealing form. Yet, what seems to be a race to the top in institutional quality might appear somewhat differently when one looks behind the figures that are used, and in particular the conceptualizations that the measurements imply. The new policy discourse on transparency may become entwined with ideas that are problematic from the perspective of democratic accountability. It is also worth asking to whom the actors producing the governance indices might be accountable, for what, and how. The concrete accountability mechanisms involved are often still weak with regard to international financial organizations, international NGOs and research institutes (Slaughter 2004; Kahler 2004; Tiihonen and Tiihonen 2004).[35]

There is also a very strong emphasis on measurable, public results for the activities of administration. This even steers organizations towards altering their activities in such a way that their core functions are seen as less important if they are not easily quantifiable, which undermines functional efficiency (Espeland and Stevens 2008; Hummel 2006). As institutional economistic ideas of competitiveness are embedded in the prevailing thinking of government, the economic re-description of democratic activities can be unconsciously reproduced (Baert 1991, p. 209).

Structuration as a type of unintended consequence also touches upon the adoption of international policy discourses, such as transparency, as the actors at the national level tend to produce culturally shaped variants of policy ideas (see Baert 1991). This is often unintended, and may lead to actors remobilizing old institutions for new purposes without appreciating the changes that are at hand. History is also a paradoxical element in the above process, as long-term institutional developments come to justify short-term reforms. As will be evident in the empirical section of this study, a long tradition of access to government information may in fact accommodate significant ideational changes, by making them seem part of that tradition: new economic ideas around transparency become entangled in the previous practices of government openness without being generally noticed. This ideational change can be observed in information-intensive public organizations such as agencies responsible for registry keeping and cartography, but also in the foreign service – all aspects of the core functioning of the state.

These shifts in the conceptualization of accountability entail trade-offs and unintended consequences in both the economic and democratic senses. This need not be inevitable, but more often than not there are trade-offs and limits involved in attempts to 'improve', 'reform' or 'modernize' administration (cf. Hood 1998 and Hood et al. 1996). There are general trends observed in the new ideas of public-sector reform, but the ideational input is translated differently in each context. The NPM reforms are said to have entered an 'age of paradox' (Hood and Peters 2004); the outcomes of transnational governance and attempts to coordinate national policies through rankings and indices are likely to be no less prone to paradoxes and unintended consequences.

So far, I have suggested that there has been an economic reframing of institutional openness in the form of transparency, which reflects the shifting ideas of accountability, now emphasizing performance. I will now propose that these ideational changes can be studied by analyzing policy discourses and their conceptual constituents.

1.4   Transparency and institutional change

1.4.1   The process of change

The administration of state information tends to have significant historical continuity within each country but differing trajectories between them. According to current research, institutional practices with substantial histories tend to change at critical junctures or in moments of crisis, where the context of governance and ideas around it can change rapidly (Peters et al. 2005; Krasner 1984). The context for general institutional change is often one of ideational uncertainty, in which the underlying norms of the state are being rethought (Schmidt 2002, pp. 225–7; Marcussen 2000).[36]

This process of change, though entailing political conflict, mainly takes shape in ideational terms (Schmidt 2008; Peters et al. 2005; Blyth 2002), facilitated by new ideas on public norms and narratives of the state (Somers and Block 2005; Somers 1995; Rothstein and Steinmo 2002; Schmidt 2002, p. 217 and Heiskanen 1977; cf. Douglas 1987, March and Olsen 1989). Moreover, the emergence of this new policy discourse indicates an innovation or a 'revolution in world view' (Bacchi 1999; Schmidt 2002, p. 222). The new policy discourse on transparency has driven the paradigmatic change in accountability described above. The ideational core of this discourse consists of the new social-scientific perceptions of governance and of institutional and information economics.

Despite the long historical trajectory of public access to government information in, for example, the Nordic countries and United States, I judge this norm to have been broadly acknowledged as a virtue of transnational governance in the mid 1990s.[37] Often preceded by a long but stagnant history, in terms of both legislation and – at least in some cases – institutional practices, this shift seems to have came about through a process in which previous ideas around governance were being rethought along the lines of a new model in the early 1990s. This juncture was brought about by various factors, including some global processes. The end of the Cold War, economic recessions in the 1990s and related public-sector reforms, European integration and globalization – both in terms of ideational transfer and economic competition – were critical contextual factors (cf. Christensen and Lægreid 2001; Sahlin-Andersson and Engwall 2002; Mittelman 2004; Schmidt 2006a). New digital technologies made information easier to transfer and commodify, but difficult to control.

The international drive for transparency has come about due to an ideational change at a time of discontinuation in the conduct of governance in nation-states, as well as a shift towards new governance models. States have found themselves in a new situation, where coping with the demands of efficiency and competitiveness has become mandatory. At the same time, it is often acknowledged that many long-lasting institutional practices that have developed over time are now giving certain states a competitive advantage as national economies (see North 2005; Hall and Soskice 2001).

Discussion of national models is indicating a shift to a national competitiveness paradigm, in which states compete against one another in the new global economy (Sum 2009). The discourse of national competitiveness often comes with reflexivity over a long institutional trajectory that has assured favorable economic development (see Kettunen 1999). In relation to the openness of public institutions and access to public information, one of the main ideational shifts has been the economic reframing of these features of governance. Because of this, ideas of national competitiveness, efficiency and enhanced public performance are increasingly making their way into the conduct of public information management, and debates around it. Here, too, the traditional institutional practices of accessing state information have come to be rethought and reformed. These ideational changes often take the form of small reforms, and are not easily discerned.

1.4.2   Policy discourse, actors and the diffusion of ideas

Policy innovations are increasingly claimed to be part of transnational governance (Mahon and McBride 2009, p. 85), a process of policy diffusion and transfer in which members of different policy communities interact (see Meyer et al. 1997; DiMaggio and Powell 1983; Dolowitz and Marsh 2000).[38] Though the most coercive policy diffusion tends to be directed at the 'weak', 'developing', or 'newly industrialized' states, these developments have also created a motivation and perceived need for the 'advanced industrial societies' to adopt new policies (Simmons et al. 2006).[39] Managerialist discourses are often seen as legitimizing the public-sector reform (Lee and Strang 2006; Radaelli 2000). In order to pursue policy innovation, policy actors need a shared discourse in which to communicate and discuss their new ideas (Schmidt 2008). This is also a prerequisite for reaching consensus over a set of policy ideas. Policy actors involved in the process of adoption are often seen as forming epistemic communities, which act on the basis of the normative and causal beliefs inherent in the new policy discourses (see Haas 1992; Schmidt 2002; Cogburn 2005).[40] Furthermore, the use of new policy discourses and political concepts facilitates institutional changes (Schmidt 2008, 2002; Skinner 1999).

These new discourses and concepts also legitimize new practices of governance (Schmidt 2002, p. 211). Talk of openness and transparency works to legitimize shifts from traditional forms of governance to a new governance environment. The commendable concepts in this field now include 'openness' and 'transparency' (cf. Skinner 1969, 1989, 1999). New policy discourses can also leave important institutional transformations unnoticed (Somers 2005; Berman 1997) or block other concerns from reaching the policy agenda (Bacchi 1999). In Europe, the commercialization of public information has not been publicly debated; nor have the possible unwanted consequences of increasing performance-management or budgetary transparency reached the agenda. Moreover, the contextual limitations of institutional openness are also seldom discussed, such as consensus seeking corporatist tradition in the Nordic countries that can diminish public debate.

Schmidt's work on policy coordination describes the spread of policy innovation in transnational governance (Schmidt 2006a, p. 254). Of particular importance is Schmidt's division of 'coordinative' from 'communicative' discourse (Schmidt 2002, pp. 230–1). The purpose of coordinative discourse is to explain and disseminate new policy ideas to members of a policy community, helping them to construct and agree upon a policy program. The purpose of communicative discourse is to explain and legitimize the policy program more widely. This discourse takes a simple form, translating the policy program into terms that are suitable for public debate. Moreover, it is rhetorically appealing, legitimizing the new policy program among the general public.

These sub-discourses tend to emerge at different points in the process of policy change and involve different actors. In the coordinative stage, such actors mostly consist of government participants (civil servants and politicians), but representatives of interest groups and private companies may also be involved (Schmidt 2002, pp. 232–4). The composition of this 'epistemic community' is largely dependent on the existing national political culture, being more inclusive in countries with a strong corporatist tradition, such as the Nordic countries (see Schmidt 2002, p. 233). During the communicative stage, the political actors communicate the policy program to the general public, giving it a 'sense of orientation' in terms of the country's present and future circumstances, effectively legitimizing government's policy (Schmidt 2002, p. 235).

The two discourses also have different ideational cores (Schmidt 2006a, pp. 251–2). The coordinative discourse tends to base itself on social-scientific knowledge, making a cognitive argument. The communicative discourse tends to focus on normative argument that articulates with the narratives, values and collective memories that are either newly endorsed or have prevailed for a long time in the national context.[41] The public narratives accommodating and mediating the institutional ideas should therefore be assessed within the relevant political and temporal context (see Somers 1993; Somers and Block 2005; Neustadt and May 1986; Douglas 1987, pp. 40–1; Rothstein 2005; Rothstein 2000). Moreover, reflexivity over national institutional history may itself provide a mechanism of policy diffusion (Kettunen 2008, pp. 124–6).[42] It embeds new institutional economistic ideas in social action and, through assimilation, may also lead to a convergence of institutional practices (Hamilton and Feenstra 1998, pp. 171–2).

Arguably, this has led to institutional isomorphism on a European and even global scale, which has come about through a convergence of institutional ideas and practices (Meyer et al. 1997; DiMaggio and Powell 1983; Radaelli 2000), such as transparency.

1.4.3 Country rankings and governance indices as policy discourse

Governance indices also operate as a new source of policy discourse. This interpretation slightly differs from the way in which Schmidt describes the policy process, since there need not be any contact with the actors developing and using the indices. The ideas are communicated through their public representation, and are apparent to the general public. Miller and Rose have described this in Foucauldian terms as 'governing at a distance' (Miller and Rose 1990). The new ideas on governance being circulated internationally are being formulated into governance indices, with countries ranked in order. The figures raise issues of governance (corruption, competitiveness) and offer goals for administrative or policy reform. The figures also contain recommendations: the definitions of good governance, sound institutions, low corruption, competitiveness, and so on, entail the means for achieving these goals.

Like to the more traditional means of transnational governance (Mahon and McBride 2009), governance indices also convey communicative and coordinative policy discourses. Governance indices have *scientific* implications that build on social-scientific methods and practices of verification (Haas 1992). Such numbers also have *political* implications, defining concepts such as transparency, corruption and competitiveness (Skinner 1999). Finally, the figures also have *symbolic* implications, whereby governance indices and country rankings function as a communicative discourse that makes a claim about a nation-state. The positive rankings may be locally very appealing for national self-identity. Whereas early statistics acted as a mirror of the monarch (Desrosièrères 1998, pp. 26–7), current governance indices have become mirrors of nations.

These new codifications of good governance and the international assessments of enhanced performance through transparency have hastened the diffusion of ideas on governance concerning the openness of public institutions. The process that makes countries adopt policies implied by the governance indices requires specific attention. As states are altering their policies based on these external assessments, there is a need to reconsider the process of policy diffusion described by Schmidt (2002; 2006a), Haas (1992) and Marcussen (2000; 2002). Governance indices reach policy actors and the general public alike, leading to reflexivity on the part of the subjects of measurement, who tend to alter their behavior according to the norm expressed in the figures (Erkkilä & Piironen 2009).[43] This type of policy transfer does not build on contacts between actors, such as policy experts, but instead functions through the public mediation of the measurements. The coordinative discourse is implicit in the numbers (concerning what is being measured, how and why). It is defined by their producers, and further echoed by the users of the numbers.

The rankings also imply commending concepts (Skinner 1999), such as transparency and competitiveness which often are uncontested. Who, after all, would want to oppose transparency or the fight against corruption? And for countries that fare well in the rankings, the message is even more appealing. Through their normative character, governance indices also function as a communicative discourse that serves to obscure their political character. The numbers used chart a course for the reform of national administrations in order to adjust to the pressures of globalization, and also provide an assessment of the present situation, a goal to strive for, and the means of achieving it – all in a single package (see Erkkilä and Kauppi 2010). This makes them seem like a reliable reference point in times of change. Moreover, the wide international coverage that such indices attract is likely to increase their value for decision-making in a transnational context, where they are likely to serve as a basic body of knowledge shared by most actors.

Country rankings portray the world as an arena of competition between nations that now also incorporates domains such as administrative ethics. The practical side of the assessments is seldom addressed – such as the questions of why these figures are being produced, by whom, and how. The concepts that the numbers express are rarely critically assessed. Since many producers of the numbers largely share a common world-view, normative goals, causal beliefs, and even data, there are seldom conflicts between the different sets of figures (Erkkilä and Piironen 2009). Consequently, their political character often remains tacit. The political horizon of competition now also involves the transparency of public institutions, which is seen to lead to better economic performance, national competitiveness, and an ability to attract foreign direct investment.

No matter how policy discourse is represented, whether in text or figures, it has to resonate with shared public narratives in order to be adopted. We can now turn to the role of narratives and concepts in policy discourse and the means of studying them.

1.4.4   Narratives and concepts in policy discourse

The end of an ideational cycle of government (Marcussen 2000), or the beginning of another one, is signified by the arrival of a new policy discourse (see Schmidt 2002, 2006a; Bacchi 1999) and concepts (Skinner 1989; Koselleck 2004 [1979]). The use of new concepts also generates concerns about the 'governable' features of governance (Miller and Rose 1990; Rose 2000). This policy innovation is also advocated and legitimized by reference to national values, narratives and traditions (Somers and Block 2005; Kettunen 1999). In addition to the literature on institutional change, we need to pay further attention to the means for analyzing ideational change.

In order to understand the force of ideas, one should open up the very notion of ideas in institutional analysis, whether 'schemas', 'labels', 'categories', 'scripts' or 'templates' (Peters et al. 2005; Schmidt 2008, Douglas 1987; Marcussen 2000, p. 17; Rothstein and Steinmo 2002, p. 5; Cambell 2001, p. 166).[44] In order to study political ideas, we should also analyze their carriers: political concepts. The process whereby they are formed, adapted, communicated, adopted and legitimized should be scrutinized. In other words, in order to assess analytically the ideas of contemporary governance, they need to be identified and contextualized, and located within a belief system (see Skinner 2002a).

The central ideas in the policy discourses on transparency are drawn from debates on public-sector performance and democratization. These ideas are not static, but constantly in flux. In order to uncover the ideational shifts in a policy discourse, its conceptual changes should be examined (cf. Skinner 1999; Skinner 2002a; compare Schmidt 2002, 223): Are there changes in the concepts that are used in the discourse and, if so, what added value or contradictory terms do the new concepts introduce? And if there is a sudden increase in references to an old concept, what semantic changes can be observed (see Koselleck 2004 [1979])? This not only allows us to examine evolving belief systems, but also the political innovation and communication around new ideas of governance.

Furthermore, because historically inclined scholars argue that 'history matters', they come to highlight its importance in two different ways. First, they point to a complex web of interdependencies, unintended consequences, unstated processes and knowledge structures, as well as contextual and structural peculiarities that guide institutional developments (Steinmo 2008; Thelen 2004; Pierson 2000b). Second, they stress how history is inherent in decisions and the beliefs of actors (Rothstein and Steinmo 2002, 17; Marcussen 2000, 17; Rothstein 2000). History is relevant not only for institutional continuity, but also for institutional change.

To understand new political concepts and the causal beliefs they embody, one must discover which story they are a part of, and what rationalities and beliefs they build upon (Schmidt 2002, 2006a, 2008; Skinner 2002a; Palonen 2003). At the same time, numbers tell their own stories (Erkkilä and Piironen 2009), making truth claims about states of affairs, goals to strive for, and means for attaining those goals. Moreover, numbers such as governance indices express political concepts such as good governance and transparency.

Policy discourses have both cognitive and normative features, which are often difficult to distinguish from one another (Schmidt 2002, p. 214). This task should be attempted, however, in order to outline the ideational core of the policy discourse and to uncover the mechanism through which new policy ideas are adopted. For, just as new policy discourses and concepts signify political innovation, they also signify (and cause) shifts in public values and narratives (Somers and Block 2005). At the very least, the adoption of policy ideas is facilitated by their resonance with national values and narratives.

In examining the coordinative and communicative forms of the policy discourse on transparency, I will explore the narratives and concepts used by the actors involved. They both have a special relationship to history: narratives make claims about history (White 1987), while concepts are always used in a historical context, and thus make references to and claims on both the past and the future (Skinner 1969; Koselleck 2004 [1979]). I will pay particular attention to the cognitive and normative aspects of policy discourse, and possible contradictory terms between them. What are the problems that lead to the emergence of a policy discourse (Bacchi 1999)? What political concepts does it involve? Moreover, what is being done with the political concepts (Skinner 1969)? With regard to institutional outcomes, the contradictory terms present in the various policy ideas are likely to lead to the unintended consequences of the reforms, which are also shaped by contextual factors.

1.4.5 Politics, path dependencies, and unintended consequences

The economistic framing of openness – the shift from openness to transparency – is likely to have significant institutional consequences, though the robustness of existing institutions should not be underestimated (Olsen 2009; Thelen 2004). Despite the theories explaining the process of change and stressing punctuated equilibrium, a revolution in world-views and shifts in belief systems (Marcussen 2000; Blyth 2002; Schmidt 2002, p. 222; Bacchi 1999), the actual institutional impacts might be more gradual in nature (Thelen 2004; Streeck and Thelen 2005).

The current thinking around institutional change emphasizes the centrality of destabilization so forcefully that the gradual nature of institutional change is often overlooked (Thelen 2004, p. 35; Streeck and

Thelen 2005, pp. 4–6). In relation to the policy recasting (Schmidt 2002, p. 222), the impact on institutions is likely to be more gradual and evolutionary than the ideational shift would lead one to expect (Thelen 1999, pp. 399–400). As we have seen, several forces of continuity and change run concurrently, which explains why existing institutional constructs can absorb new ideas or function as a prism through which the policy ideas acquire diverse outcomes in different contexts (Olsen 2009).

In functionalist accounts, institutions exist and evolve because they serve a function or a social virtue – they 'do good' (Thelen 2004, p. 25). For example, Konstari has described the Nordic *principle of publicity* in similar terms, arguing that, though the (official) control function of this institution was limited, it has served an integrative function for Finland (Konstari 1977). In understanding this institution, it is important that its interdependencies are understood, which include interest-mediation and consensus-formation, as well as other related institutions of accountability. The impacts of the new ideas of transparency are thus channeled and layered through existing institutional practices. Furthermore, the conceptual variations and conflicts of rationalities between different institutional ideas also influence the outcome of reforms. We should therefore analyze the ideational changes in an institutional context, just as one should place institutional changes in an ideational context.

Fundamental changes such as the liberalization of political economies still tend to come about gradually (Painter and Peters 2010; Streeck and Thelen 2005, p. 30). According to Streeck and Thelen, gradual change can take different forms, including the displacement, layering, drift, conversion or exhaustion of institutional practices (Streeck and Thelen 2005, p. 31). In this analysis I assume that the institutional changes resulting from the recasting of states' information strategies are best understood as forms of *conversion* and *layering*, meaning that old institutions are redeployed to new purposes, and that new ideational elements are attached to existing institutional practices, resulting in their gradual change, or at least in the coexistence of old and new institutional practices (Streeck and Thelen 2005, p. 31). As we have seen, there has been a shift from the democratic understanding of institutional openness towards an economic one.

The reflexive examination of national institutional practices that results from international country comparisons translates into a mechanism of institutional change. Awareness of the virtues of a certain (historical) aspect of governance leads to active attempts to promote it. This is also in line with Thelen's view of institutional change: institutions are subjects of *ongoing political negotiations* (Thelen 2004, pp. 34–5). Institutions are thus constantly being recalibrated and renegotiated by political actors (ibid., p. 35) – a process that tends to become heightened in times of crisis. This also allows institutions to abandon their (functional) roots: through conversion, the institutions may, over time, begin to serve different ends than they did in the initial context (Thelen 2004, p. 36). Accordingly, an information-access law can be adopted as a democratic reform but later redirected to serve other ends, such as economic competitiveness.

Since institutionalist thinking now stresses ideological change and political conflict, it should perhaps more actively try to detect their presence. Political conflict that paves the way for institutional change can be observed in the different uses of certain concepts (see Palonen 2003; Skinner 1969). Various political aspirations aimed at 'openness' or 'transparency' suggests new political horizons and possible developments that often conflict with one another. Conceptual analysis can therefore render visible the political conflicts of a policy, and can enhance our understanding of policy failures.

But we should exercise some caution in relation to the generally appealing arguments for grand processes, such as 'new' public management, the information society revolution, modernization, globalization, and isomorphism (Hood 1998, pp. 208–19). There is often no single rationale to such processes. Instead, many different ideas and aspirations become entangled with one another, often producing side-effects, or even reverse-effects, of acts of modernization in public administration (Hood 1998, p. 211). These effects are also echoed by the cultural context in which the new ideas are adopted.

Every attempt to make something a subject of conscious reform or politicking also disrupts continuity, opening the possibility of counter-finalities and unintended consequences (Palonen 2003, pp. 171, 184; Sartre 2004, p. 196; cf. Peters et al. 2005). The power to master the results of such disruptions is not in the hands of any single actor, but is rather the prize in a game involving many players. In institutional analysis, the concept of unintended consequences refers to the fact that the actions that actors take are often compromises, limited by contextual path-dependencies (Thelen 2004; Streeck and Thelen 2005; Hood and Peters 2004; Hood et al. 1996; Baert 1991; Elster 1978), and that governments rather seldom make 'everyone better off' (see Stiglitz 1998).

As a perspective on institutional change (Hood and Peters 2004), unintended consequences connect with institutional principles concerning what aspects are promoted and what are less favored or neglected. This has implications for accountability, as the various reforms carried out in the name of transparency might in fact have paradoxical effects for the system of accountability. With the help of discursive and conceptual analysis (Schmidt 2002; Skinner 2002a), we can see that, behind unintended consequences or limits of design, there lie deliberate actions that are distorted by the adversities of politics, by institutional contexts, and by the limits of the political imagination of the actors involved. Outcome can thus diverge radically from those that were intended (see Weber 1978, p. 994). Moreover, as Weber points out, politics represents the ultimate means of escape from and resistance to instrumental rationalities of governance. Disclosing the ideational elements of a policy discourse can also open the possibility of its critique and change. The notion of unintended consequences thus helps us to understand the trade-offs and compromises that are inherent in attempts to reform institutions.

1.5   The research design of this study

The Nordic countries have a long legal history of open access to government information, acknowledged constitutionally as the principle of publicity (see Chapter 1, Section 1.2). This principle can be associated with the high level of trust and consensual traditions prevailing in these countries. Moreover, Nordic countries exercise comprehensive registry-keeping, and citizens' trust in government allows exhaustive use of registry data in governing the welfare state. While there are contextual peculiarities in the Nordic countries, their long history of public access allows an analysis of the change from a democratic understanding of government openness to the more economically driven understandings of openness and transparency.

Konstari described the principle of publicity in functionalist terms, arguing that along controlling government (control function) it has served an integrative function for Finland, allowing broad participation and consensus-building (Konstari 1977). Referring to the work of Thelen and Streeck (Thelen 2004; Streeck and Thelen 2005), I will propose that access to government information now also has an economic function, and that the previous trust-based understanding of this institution is increasingly being complemented by economic rationales.

This institutional tradition has changed significantly over the last decade, beginning at the turn of the 1990s as the equilibrium of Finnish practices of governance was disrupted by several external factors, including the end of the Cold War, public sector reforms during and after economic recession of the early 1990s, Finnish accession to the EU, and the tightening of global economic competition and globalization (Tiihonen 2006; Raunio and Tiilikainen 2003; Raunio and Wiberg 2000; Väyrynen 1999; Pollitt et al. 1997; Pekonen 1995b).

It is my view that the openness of Finnish governance became a policy problem in the 1990s, which saw the rise of a policy discourse of Nordic openness, discernible also in changes to other related political concepts. The core of this discourse consists of new social-scientific perceptions of transparency, drawn particularly from institutional and information economics. State information strategy and related institutional practices have now consequently changed.

I will argue that key ideational changes have occurred since, or were initiated by, a critical juncture in Finnish governance during the 1990s. The structural changes and new perceptions of state information led to the emergence of policy problems relating to state information strategy. During the uncertainty attendant upon Finland's economic recession of the early 1990s, and surrounding Finland's access to the European Union, the adoption of policies from other countries became indispensable in the identification and resolution of domestic problems.

I will argue that the policies adopted are being communicated within a nationalistic discourse on Nordic openness, which has both communicative and coordinative variants with differing normative and cognitive elements, whether addressed to the general public or to policy experts (Schmidt 2002, 2006a). The ideational changes caused by this discourse are also apparent in conceptual shifts from publicity to openness and transparency (Skinner 1989; Skinner 2002a; Koselleck 2004). These changes are accommodated by the new public values and narratives shared by the Finns, which now see Finland as a progressive Nordic country and a senior participant in globalization.

I expect to find evolutionary changes within institutions (Thelen 2004). These are generally likely to emerge as new layered elements attached to existing institutional practices, and also as recalibrations of the old practices of information access (Streeck and Thelen 2005, p. 31). In this, also, public discourses and narratives are likely to play a role in mediating the institutional structure, also influencing its public use (Somers 1993). However, particularly in the organizational cases (the Population Register Centre and the Ministry for Foreign Affairs), we may even observe the conversion of institutional practices (Streeck and Thelen 2005). Paradoxically, these institutional changes are accommodated by the discourse of Nordic openness, reflecting an institutional tradition. This conversion is also likely to lead to unintended consequences of the reforms (Hood and Peters 2004; Hood 1998). I will pay particular attention to the institutional outcomes of the redeployment of openness for economic ends concerning accountability.

The research design of this study aims to establish a general direction of institutional change and evolution between 1998 and 2007, using several points of observation (see Rueschemeyer 2003; Mahoney 2003, pp. 360–8). I have combined interviews, textual analysis, and statistical time-series data to analyze ideational and institutional changes in the following contexts:

Central steering mechanisms and institutional developments

1. Political steering: government programmes and government bills, publications of the government's Economic Council, and strategic documents of selected government programmes; political debate in the Finnish parliament on the 1999 Act on the Publicity of Government Activities; Public material on the Finnish EU Presidency (2006), and selected public speeches of politicians.
2. Normative steering: background material of the 1999 Act on the Publicity of Government Activities and related acts; expert interviews and additional government documents.
3. Financial steering: government documents on administrative ethics, budgeting and accountability reform, and initiatives on public hearings; expert interviews.
4. Institutional developments at central government level: statistical time series regarding the judicial system, communication and information services, and performance management.

Organizational level

5. Population Register Centre (census information): expert interviews, selected policy documents, and statistical time series.
6. Ministry for Foreign Affairs (foreign political information): expert interviews, selected policy documents, and statistical time series.

I conducted a total of thirty-one interviews, of which twenty-eight were with civil servants and three with non–civil servants, in order to collect background information. The interview material is used in the general narrative in this book, along with official documents and time series.[45] The data were collected mostly in late 2006 and during 2007, and a few of the interviews were conducted in early 2008. Political strategies are studied in light of government programmes, government bills and the publications of the government's Economic Council. The government programmes provide a corpus that allows transhistorical comparisons over some ninety years. In recent years, the government programmes have gained strategic importance at a contractual level, becoming part of the new information strategy of the state, thus increasing the predictability of policies to be pursued within the following four-year term of government. The economic connotations of openness and transparency, which first appeared in government programmes during the 1990s, are contextualized with reference to the publications of the government's Economic Council (1998–2007), thereby opening up the economic ideational core of the policies. Some material on political steering is also referred to in assessments of normative and financial steering mechanisms and organizational cases.

The normative and financial steering mechanisms have undergone major ideational changes, apparent in the legislation adopted in late 1990s and early 2000s and in efforts at governance reform throughout the period 1998–2007. These provide essential insight for understanding the general trends of development, as well as the organizational cases. In analyzing the policy discourse on openness, I identify the normative and cognitive dimensions in its coordinative and communicative variants (see Schmidt 2002, p. 214). The identification of policy problems is important for understanding the cognitive dimensions and causal beliefs underlying a particular discourse.

The organizational cases – the Population Register Centre and the Ministry for Foreign Affairs – were chosen because both of these organizations are knowledge-intensive: they collect, manage, produce and allocate information as their primary task. From the perspective of performance management, both the Population Register Centre and the Ministry for Foreign Affairs must comply with the new demand for quantifiable results. These commonalities apart, the cases differ sharply, allowing general observations of large-scale shifts in the state's information strategies. Moreover, the general context of change – a shift from traditional government to a new governance model – can be used as an argument for selecting these cases, since both organizations now act in a completely different environment than they did ten or fifteen years ago. Finally, both organizational cases provide a longitudinal perspective.

Concerning change, I will argue that there are commonalities in the above contexts, pointing to a larger layering – coexistence of old and new institutional forms – and partial conversion of institutional practices between 1998 and 2007. Though the critical juncture of Finnish governance was the early to mid 1990s, the ideational shifts and consensus formation came later. Hence, the starting point for my analysis is 1998, when the legislation for openness in government information was being redrafted and the government made the first decision on good governance. The end of the time-span under examination, 2007, represents the start of the international financial crisis, in which the economic connotations of transparency are also becoming evident. Therefore, the period from 1998 to 2007 covers both an era of post-crisis consensus-formation and an entry into another crisis, marking a potential new juncture of governing.

The structure of this study corresponds to the theory and research design outlined above. Part II explores the ideational and institutional changes in the drive for transparency in central steering. Part III explores the institutional transformations and unintended consequences produced at an organizational level. Conclusions chapter contains my findings, and proposes some explanations for how the changes have been possible, and what institutional transformations can be observed in the central government, organizational cases and in the accountability system.

Part II
Transparency and Central Steering

2
Transparency and Ideational Changes: Nordic Openness as a Policy Discourse

2.1 Introduction

Transparency has become one of the key concepts of contemporary politics. It is also a newcomer to the political language both in the Anglo-American world and outside. There are, in addition, liberal market notions bound up with the term that are making their way into national political contexts. This is perhaps most apparent in developing countries that are dependent on foreign direct investment and development aid (Relly and Sabharwal 2009). But also countries with a significant institutional history of openness, such as the Nordic countries, are exposed to the new implications of transparency. International policy discourses often tend to take nationalist forms (Schmidt 2002, p. 211), and this chapter explores the policy discourse of 'Nordic openness' in Finland. Even if openness is at present discussed as a tradition of Finnish governance, there is an apparent conceptual reframing of institutional practices. Access to government information is no longer merely an issue of democracy and political accountability but is becoming a policy concern to do with (economic) performance. The above discourse is therefore a national variant of the wider transnational policy discourse on transparency.

Following the analytical framework presented in Part I of the book, I will show how access to government information became a policy problem in the mid-1990s, when Finnish governance reached a critical juncture due to economic crisis, Finland's entrance to the global economy and accession to the EU. In explaining the rise of the policy discourse of Nordic openness and its communicative and coordinative forms, I will build on the work of Marcussen (2000), Bacchi (1999) and Schmidt (2002, 2006a). In assessing the conceptual shifts that took place, I will use the conceptual historical framework of Skinner (2002a), with insights from Koselleck (Koselleck 2004 [1979]).

The changes in the rhetoric of governance – the arguments for its justification – are not only a reflection of the institutional state of affairs but also carry the potential for institutional change. Such changes can be seen as representing changes in the perceived responsibilities and goals of government. In institutional theory, 'ideational life-cycle' is often seen as consisting of periods of consensus (on the term see Marcussen 2000), interrupted by an external shock or ideational uncertainty during which change is possible or necessary. Once the ideational and normative consensus is again sought, for example as ideas become embedded or institutionalized (Somers and Block 2005), another stable period follows (Marcussen 2000, pp. 14–15). In order for ideational change to come about, it has to fit into the existing narrative of the state or be coupled with a new one, replacing the old narrative (Schmidt 2008; Somers and Block 2005, p. 280).

In Finland, 'openness' has become a part of the contemporary narrative of the Finnish state, starting from the 1990s in the context of Finland's accession to the European Union. It has also appeared later in the EU context, where Finns were active in promoting openness. International country comparisons, such as the country rankings of Transparency International, have tied Finland's low corruption to the transparency of its public institutions. This has created a narrative of Nordic openness, a perception of Nordic institutional tradition that separates Finns from other nationalities. This narrative also offers the Finns a new self-image bearing connotations of progress and modernity. It also draws a distinction between Finland's Cold War past when it was a gateway between east and west.

The policy of the virtuous circle has been seen as a normative standard for the Nordic countries (Kettunen 2008, pp. 142–5; Kettunen 1997), emphasizing the values of efficiency, solidarity and equality, and binding together economics, politics and ethics (Kettunen 1999, p. 123; compare Tiihonen 2003). The Nordic countries have grown to depend largely on exports, which has been balanced with planning, welfare state and labor market policies, premised on the broad inclusion of actors (Kettunen 1999, p. 129). In institutional economics, the notion of the virtuous circle is now used when referring to economic competitiveness, resulting from tightly interlinked institutional developments (Garrett 1998). In the accounts of the international financial institutions, the Nordic countries have been seen to have entered virtuous circles where various institutional factors reinforce their increasing economic competitiveness; openness and transparency of these societies has been named as one factor in this development (Lopez-Claros 2006; World Economic Forum 2006).

Kettunen has referred to this discourse of national competitiveness as a 'coercive circle' that diminishes the sphere of politics and democracy (Kettunen 2008, p. 12). Erkkilä and Piironen assess similar potential in the governance indices, using the Weberian term 'iron cage' (see Erkkilä and Piironen 2009; Weber 1978). As we shall see in the following, the drive for transparency is closely linked with the new demands for national competitiveness. Consequently, there is a shift in the ideas of accountability, as the government is increasingly perceived as being responsible for its economic performance through transparency and openness.

I will first analyze the conceptual changes in linguistics, and in government programs and the publications of the Economic Council of Finland. I will then explore the communicative aspects of the policy discourse of Nordic openness in Finland, in parliamentary debates over the Act on the Publicity of Government Activities in 1998–99 and in the historical accounts of the mid-2000s, when openness was also a theme for the Finnish EU Presidency (2006). I conclude that the 'virtues' of good governance that are circulating internationally, seek historical reference points in the Finnish policy discourse. Yet, the cognitive aspects of this discourse point to political innovation and reassessments of accountability. The second part of the chapter analyzes the ideational changes in the normative and financial steering, based on interviews. Also here, the economic ideas of transparency that circulate internationally have entered Finnish thinking on governance.

2.2 Ideational changes in political steering

As I hypothesized above, the general notion of 'openness' became a political innovation during the 1990s juncture in Finnish governance (cf. Skinner 1989, p. 20; Farr 1989, p. 25). This point of change allowed new institutional practices and ideas to be introduced to the Finnish model of governance (cf. Marcussen 2000; Peters et al. 2005). It is here that the vocabulary tends to change, as actors need to re-conceptualize the new environment (Koselleck 2004, p. 256).[1] Looking at the political concepts used in Finnish government programs (see below), neither 'publicity' nor 'openness', let alone 'transparency', have been traditionally part of the political vocabulary, but only started to appear in the 1990s. Moreover, political concepts are means for governance (Skinner 1969), bringing an issue to the centre of our political agenda, making it a policy concern or 'problem' (Bacchi 1999; Miller and Rose 1990).

In the following, I will analyze the notions of 'publicity', 'openness', and 'transparency'. Why do they appear in the government rhetoric at a given time and context? How are they conceptualized and what is seen as being achieved with them? We can begin by briefly looking at the ideational roots and linguistic bases of these concepts.

2.2.1   Ideational roots and semantics

In the Nordic context, the idea regarding the publicity of government records had been debated already in the eighteenth century. Anders Chydenius, a representative of the clergy in the Swedish Diet, is often credited for initiating legislation in 1766 in Sweden. There is now an international interest in his ideas (see Hood 2006, p. 8; Lamble 2002). In Finland, historians have drawn attention to the 'Finnish' roots of this 18th century thinker (Manninen 2006; Virrankoski 1986). Underlying Chydenius' views on freedom of print and the right to acquire information on state affairs was opposition to the mercantilist tradition of eighteenth century Sweden, embodied in Stockholm's trade privileges over the peripheries (Käkönen 1983, pp. 46–9; Manninen 2006; Patoluoto 1986; Virrankoski 1986). In order to understand the importance of the freedoms of information, speech and print to the political philosophy of Anders Chydenius (see also Chydenius 1929a), one needs only to look into his ideal of the state.

In his writings, Chydenius portrays the 'free state' or 'free nation', not as an enemy of libertarian freedoms, but rather as their keeper (Chydenius 1880a, p. 31). It was a privilege of every member of this community to seek prosperity free of coercion and unnecessary rules and constraints. However, this was to be done under the help and guidance of the 'highest power' and civil servants (Chydenius 1880b, p. 115). Perhaps Chydenius' most radical idea concerned the responsibility of rulers. The people were to follow their leaders but not 'blindly' (Chydenius 1880a, p. 31; compare Chydenius 1880b; 1880a, p. 25). This reserves a possibility for non-compliance. Chydenius also saw that rulers had to enjoy the people's trust and that they acted on a mandate. A nation was free, when not only those mandated were free to participate, but also those giving this mandate enjoyed this freedom (Chydenius 1880a, p. 47).

Chydenius argued for a widening of political inclusion, for which the information on state matters was a necessity. The state was to inform its citizens on both successes and misfortunes so that they would know the 'truth' and engage with debates (Chydenius 1880a, p. 31; Chydenius 1929b, p. 170; Chydenius 1880b). Information was critical for the search of truth, and all attempts to limit it had serious implications to the foundations of Chydenius' ideal state (Chydenius 1880a, p. 32; Chydenius 1929b, pp. 436–7; Chydenius 1880c, p. 93; Chydenius 1880d). To Chydenius, the freedom of print was the most valued property of a free nation.

Chydenius uses the terms *'stat'* [state], *'nation'* [nation], *'samfund'* and *'samhälle'* [community, society] somewhat analogously. There is the same collective and inclusive – social – emphasis linguistically (compare Kettunen 2003a, p.175; Kettunen 2003b). The Swedish term *'offentlig'* can be described as open (*'öppen'*) or accessible to everyone (Nationalencyklopedins ordbok 2004, p. 1150). Having its root in the older Germanic notion of *'öffentlich'* or *'offen'*, the Swedish notion (*'offentlig'*, *'öppen'*) bears a specific reference to the public sphere, similar to the German notion of 'öffentlichkeit' (Habermas 1989; Hölscher 1978). As a principle of governing, *'offentlighetsprincip'* carries in its general Swedish language accounts connotations of control over the use of power.[2] The Swedish noun *'publik'* refers to 'a public', an audience, whereas the adjective *'publik'* again is perceived synonymously with *'offentlig'*.[3]

In Finnish, the term *'julkinen'* (public) has been the key concept for describing access to government information (cf. Mäenpää 2008a). It was present in the first Act on the Publicity of Government Documents (1951) as well as in its constitutional form of *'julkisuusperiaate'*. Literally, the Finnish *'julkisuusperiaate'* should be translated as 'principle of publicity', which is the term I use in this study. The linguistic accounts of the Finnish *'julkisuusperiaate'* describe it as a principle, according to which common (public) documents are public.[4] This democratic principle is nowadays often translated to English as 'principle of openness', which comes closer to its Swedish variant *'offentlighetsprincip'* (as I will elaborate later, this is also part of a conceptual shift from 'publicity' to 'openness'). In Finland, the idea of government as a 'public' body or activity rose alongside parliamentarism and legalism (Pekonen 2003, p. 141). The dictionary accounts on *'julkinen'* (public) give it connotations of shared knowledge, experience or incident: for something to count as public it has to be shared by a community, preferably by everyone (Nykysuomen sanakirja 1978; Nykysuomen etymologinen sanakirja 2004).

In the Finnish context, the rise of the terms transparent (*'läpinäkyvä'*) and transparency (*'läpinäkyvyys'*) finds contrast in such terms as open ('*avoin*') and openness ('*avoimuus*'), and in particular in public ('*julk-inen*') and publicity ('*julkisuus*'). '*Avoimuus*' (openness) is often seen as a peer concept to publicity,[5] but it was first acknowledged in the 1999 Act on the Publicity of Government Activities. 'Transparency' is a new concept of governance not only in Europe but in the Anglophone world as well (Sanders and West 2003). Still, this optical term has received remarkable international attention in recent debates on power and society (cf. Hood 2006).[6] In Finnish and Swedish dictionaries 'transparent' and 'transparency' get only optical connotations.[7] This is telling in terms of their recent political use. Nevertheless, this notion has become one of the central concepts for contemporary politics since the mid-1990s.

In Finland, this has also drawn attention to the institutional history of 'openness', now discussed as 'Nordic openness'. I will next explore the evolution of this policy discourse and the above conceptual shifts in government programs.

2.2.2   Government programs: competitive and transparent state

In my analysis, I concentrate on the expressions of responsibility in the government programs (Finnish Government 2010a): *for what, to whom* and *how* is the government accountable? (cf. Mulgan 2000; see also Weber 1999) The classification presented in Table 2.1 shows that such ideas of responsibility have timely variations (see also Erkkilä 2010a). Also, concepts of governance are prone to change over time, both semantically and through the adaptation of new terms (see Hyvärinen 2003, p. 83; cf. Dunn 2006). The historical periods adopted in the classification roughly follow previous analysis of government programs (Koskiaho B. 1973; Kantola 2006) and Finnish political, administrative and legal history (Jansson, 1993; Heiskanen 1977; Stenvall 1995; Inha 2005; Jyränki 2006; Nousiainen 2006; Heiskala and Luhtakallio 2006).

The government programs contain a marked shift over time in the *locus* or bearer of responsibility (see Table 2.1). Until the late 1950s, the citizen was seen as having responsibilities to the state and government. Parliament is addressed with hopes for cooperation and common understanding. Towards the 1960s, the vocabulary changes and government's democratic responsibilities to parliament are addressed in the government programs. Thus the logic changes: the government increasingly admits its responsibility to parliament and to its electorate. The mechanism of accountability is the parliamentary confidence. Towards the present day, the vocabulary again changes, making the government responsible for its

Table 2.1 Ideational cycles of responsibility in Finnish government programs 1917–2007 (after Erkkilä 2010a)

Societal peace, civil merit 1917–1939	War, rebuilding and national unity 1939– late 1950s	Growth, welfare and parliamentarism, late 1950s–1980s	Competition and welfare, efficient and open govern- ment, late 1980s–2000s
Citizens responsible for their behavior. Citizens, parliament and civil servants should support and cooperate with the government.	Citizens responsible for their behavior. Government and parliament should work in common understanding.	Government responsible to the parliament (and to the constitu- ency) through parliamentary representation and cooperation.	Joint responsibility of citizens and government. Government responsible to the citizens and parliament, but also to the market.

performance. Throughout the 1990s the programs carried an ideational shift towards performance as a type of accountability.

Ideational shifts have occurred during obvious times of turmoil, such as the Second World War, but there have also been less momentous changes. The shift towards welfare state policies was undoubtedly the culmination of political activity, but it was not a result of great turmoil or crises. This view tends to leave the political aspects of the 'use' of concepts undervalued (Skinner 1999, p. 72; Skinner 1969). Still, the occurrence of concepts is difficult to fully explain. In government programs certain references to commendable concepts first appear in the time of their apparent paucity or when these features of governance are under threat.

For instance, the rhetoric of the welfare state changes during the late 1980s, when the structural changes in the world economy and politics were starting to be seen, as well as their challenges to the Finnish welfare state (cf. Kantola 2006, pp. 173–5). The welfare state becomes an issue of concern, a debatable and governable domain, which then remains topical in the government programs to follow. Competitiveness and productivity appear as the shared goals of Finnish government coalitions since the 1990s, irrespective of their political orientation (Kananen and Kantola 2009).

Though the concern over competitiveness appears in programs over time, there is a significant change in the mechanism through which this is seen to be secured (Kantola 2006). Whereas until the mid-1980s governments argued for planning as a means for achieving efficiency, the logic changes towards the end of the 1980s as the idea of market forces replaces planning, signifying Finland's rapid entry to the open market economy (cf. Alasuutari 2006; Heiskala 2006). The market is not only a site of economic competition by the state but also a means for organizing the tasks of the state. This makes national competitiveness a goal in itself, overriding several other concerns (cf. Kettunen 1999). National competitiveness becomes the means for upholding the welfare state, now stressing new responsibilities of the citizen as well as 'know-how' and 'innovation' (Kantola 2006, pp. 168–71, 174).

Whereas previously national competitiveness was a by-product or means of welfare politics based on equality, it was now increasingly becoming a goal in itself (Kettunen 1999, p. 135). A previous understanding of 'society' amalgamating civil society with state institutions is replaced by the new nationalistic notion of national competitiveness (Kettunen 2003a, p. 207). The spatial dimensions of statehood are also being re-evaluated, as nation-states are reduced by the economic environment (Moisio 2008). This ideational context is important in understanding the rise of 'openness' and 'transparency' as new concepts of government responsibility.

Internationally, the adoption of information access laws has been usually preceded by a political debate on the topic, often crucial for the adoption (Bennett 1997). The term 'publicity' does not appear in Finland's government programs at the time of adoption of the Act on the Publicity of Government Documents in the 1950s. There are hardly any references to 'publicity' or 'openness' before the 1990s. 'Public' is used in reference to public institutions, public companies or public funding, as a synonym of state bureaucracy and activities (cf. Pekonen 2003, p. 141).

The notion of 'openness' starts to appear in the government programs of prime ministers Harri Holkeri (1987–1991), Esko Aho (1991–1995), Paavo Lipponen (1995–1999, 1999–2003), Anneli Jäätteenmäki (2003) and Matti Vanhanen (2003–2007, 2007–2010). There is an apparent confusion between the concepts of 'public' and 'open' as the former, at the turn of the 1990s, refers to the public sector and government and the latter is understood in economic terms, as the 'open', unregulated, sector. References to public information also appear around the same time, encapsulated in the notion of the information society. The vocabulary then shifts, as the openness starts to get democratic connotations, as in 'openness of governance'. The economic connotations are then cropped under a new term, 'transparency'. This also introduces a new account holder, to whom the government is responsible, the market.

The government program of Prime Minister Harri Holkeri (published in 30 April 1987) contained no references made to 'openness' with regards to responsible rule, but a reference is made in relation to 'open labor markets', which suggests a perceived need for cooperation between government and labor market organizations, implying deliberation. Similar to the government program of Holkeri, the program of Prime Minister Esko Aho (26 April 1991) contains references to 'openness' in the context of economy and GATT negotiations, 'openness of world trade'. The notion of the open sector refers to private entrepreneurship and the market, distinct from the public sector and public finance that refer to the domain of the state. Remarkably, in the early 1990s, 'open' acquires connotations of 'non-public'. The government program of Paavo Lipponen (published 13 April 1995) names itself 'The government of employment and joint responsibility'. Skilled people, functioning labor markets as well as labor market agreements are mentioned as the keys to success. The 'open' labor market deliberations become an element of national competitiveness (cf. Kettunen 1999; Pekonen 1995a; Hall and Soskice 2001, p. 11).

The democratic connotations of 'openness' first systematically start to appear in 1995 and in the context of European governance (Finland joined the EU in 1995). The first government of Lipponen states that Finland will 'enhance the openness of the decision-making of the European Union'. The Finnish mission to open up the decision-making processes of the European Union becomes a legitimizing argument for the Finnish accession to the Union. Moreover, Finland becomes depicted as the advocate of openness in the European Union. Openness remains a topic of Finnish EU politics in the program of the second government of Paavo Lipponen (15 April 1999). Increasing the openness of EU institutions was also on the agenda of Prime Minister Anneli Jäätteenmäki's program (17 April 2003), now coupled with the notion of 'good governance'. The 'openness' of the European Union remained an issue for Matti Vanhanen's two government programs (published 24 June 2003 and 19 April 2007), both as a general remark on the running of administrative processes and as a remedy to the citizen critique.

Since Paavo Lipponen's first government program from 1995, references to public sector reform highlight efficiency, functionality and service orientation – the citizen inclusion and publicity of governance emerge to balance these. In the second program of Lipponen (1999), there is another reference to openness of international actors in relation to global economics and free movement of capital. 'Openness' and access to information are also addressed in the section on the Information Society, which addresses the availability of information from the perspective of the innovation system. Here access to information is still coupled with the notion of 'rights', though the focus is shifting to national economy. In 1999, transparency appears for the first time in the vocabulary, as 'transparency' of pricing and financing in domestic politics.

Four years later (17 April 2003), Anneli Jääteenmäki's government names its program as 'Towards resurgence with work, entrepreneurship and joint responsibility.' Openness also remains with reference to the market economy and 'open markets', of which Finland is to benefit. This is seen as being realized providing that Finland remains competitive and provides a good location for companies both in terms of infrastructure and taxation. 'Openness' is also referred to in the managing of public-owned companies and ensuring market trust in the state's shareholder policies – the government hence expresses its responsibility to the market. 'Openness of the use of law' is mentioned concerning renewing legislation on the publicity of legal proceedings. 'Transparency' is mentioned four times, again in the domestic context, with connotations of market or financial transparency, referring to the 'clarity of a process', coupled with 'effectiveness'.

The government program of the second government of Matti Vanhanen (published 19 April 2007) states that with regards to welfare the distinction between individual responsibility, joint responsibility and the responsibility of society has to be clarified, marking a shift in the ideas of accountability.[8] The program makes references to transparency in pricing, state funding, trade and services. 'Transparency' has six mentions, four of which carry explicit market connotations and two in reference to the 'clarity' of processes or 'system', implying external scrutiny.

To conclude, increasingly, statements of government responsibility have been given greater expression, albeit in more abstract ways. Responsibility has been the main heading of three government programs, though referring to 'joint responsibility'. The omnipotent role of the state still present in the programs in the 1970s and early 1980s has diminished and 'planning' has been replaced by the market as a means for achieving goals. The 'openness' that was first also used as an antonym of 'public', with reference to the market economy, is later replaced by the term 'transparency', a newcomer to Finnish political vocabulary.

Despite the long institutional history of the 'principle of publicity', this first becomes an explicit policy problem in the 1990s (Bacchi 1999). We can detect a related conceptual shift over time: the government discourse shifts from the semantic field of democracy towards the market. The first step is the emergence of the political concept of 'openness', which gets economic and (later) democratic connotations, unlike 'publicity', which belongs solely to the sphere of democracy. In the government rhetoric, openness also appears as a state tradition that is defended in the EU. Approaching the present, the economic connotations are cropped under the notion of 'transparency', also a newcomer to Finnish concepts of governance. According to Koselleck (2004), new political concepts tend to arise when there is too great a gap between past experiences and future expectations. As the previous democratic semantics of publicity become complemented with new liberal market connotations, talk turns to openness. The concept of 'transparency' further propels the shift towards an economic understanding of access to government information.

The two debates around 'openness' and 'transparency' – Finland's exceptional openness in the EU context and the economic potential of transparency – meet within a nationalistic discourse of 'Nordic openness'. Finland's concern over the secretiveness of the EU in the mid-1990s initiated a narrative of openness as a Nordic tradition of Finnish governance, separating 'us' from 'them'. The national competitiveness, to which openness or transparency is increasingly seen as a remedy, is also debated under the same logic of inclusion and exclusion: 'our' competitive edge over 'the others'.

The coupling of efficiency and performance with openness is somewhat a novel and perhaps not so readily apparent idea. This conceptual change in government vocabulary points to a political innovation due to a paradigm change in economics and governance, where the ideas of efficiency increasingly build on transparency. This also marks a shift in the responsibilities assumed by government. Now aware of a new external audience, government increasingly assumes responsibilities towards market actors for its performance.

2.2.3 Publications of the Economic Council of Finland

The ideational core behind the new economic perceptions of institutional openness and transparency can be identified in the ideational input provided to the governments (compare Schmidt 2002; Marcussen 2000; Haas 1992). One site of relevant ideational exchange is the Economic Council of Finland. Chaired by the Prime Minister, the Council aims to facilitate cooperation and dialogue between government, the Bank of Finland and key interest groups. By definition, the Economic Council discusses 'economic and social issues that are of central importance to the success of the nation' (Economic Council of

Finland 2010). The Council calls for broad-based analytical discussion prior to economic decision-making being a forum for constructing consensus over economic policies and sharing information. The monthly meetings are confidential but the background studies on which the discussions are based are made public.

These publications offer a social scientific context where the ideational change around 'openness' and 'transparency' can be better understood in the timeframe of 1998–2007. The ideational addendum to this coordinative discourse draws on institutional economics and public management theorizing (cf. Schmidt 2002). Despite a wide range of topics, the publications have a commonality in cherishing 'openness' and 'transparency' as elements of national competitiveness. This social fact gains substance over time (cf. Bacchi 1999). Also, we find that the dialogue on public (sector) information (*julkinen tieto, julkisen sektorin tieto*) crescendos in the Economic Council's publications. This is an echo of the 'new economy' theorizing of the 1990s, but as I discuss later, it is also linked with the drive for transparency (Chapter 4).

In the early 2000s publications of the Economic Council, 'openness' (*'avoimuus'*) appears as a concept of economic competition or a condition to accustom to an 'open' economy and open labor market (Valtioneuvoston kanslia 2000b; Valtioneuvoston kanslia 2001b, pp. 11, 23; Valtioneuvoston kanslia 2001c). As with the government programs, 'open' refers to an open market sector, as opposed to state regulated or the 'public' – as in public service (*julkinen palvelu*), public finances (*julkinen talous*) or public sector (*julkinen sektori*) (see, for example, Valtioneuvoston kanslia 2002b, p. 100; cf. Rodrik 1998). Economic openness thus refers to diminished regulation and low protectionism (cf. Glatzer and Rueschemeyer 2005). The term 'transparency' also appears with reference to finances and in estimating cost efficiencies.

A policy document by the Ministry of Finance published in 2002 (Valtiovarainministeriö 2002), aimed to identify the elements of national competitiveness, defining it as the ability of a national environment to support entrepreneurial activity (cf. Rouvinen 2002, p. 90). Public institutions are addressed in terms of democratic stability and trust but only in terms peripheral to the ideational core. The focus is still on policies. It is remarked, however, that international rankings of national competitiveness also name transparency, low corruption and a consensual political culture as Finland's strengths (Valtiovarainministeriö 2002, p. 100). An academic commentary on the document criticizes the Ministry of Finance for addressing institutional aspects only indirectly, and it highlights equality, social cohesion, low corruption and openness (Rouvinen 2002, p. 91).

In the early 2000s, 'openness' was understood as exposure to international trade in the debate on the scope of government. Since then, institutional economics have also been a rising topic in economic policymaking (cf. Pagano 2004; Rodrik 1998). Accordingly, shortcomings in the transparency of governance and information start to feature prominently in the publications of the Economic Council (Valtioneuvoston kanslia 2002b, pp. 17, 21; cf. Rothschild and Stiglitz 1976; Stiglitz 1998). Big government is seen to correlate with exposure to international trade ('openness'), complementing it (Rodrik 1998). Public institutions are seen as bringing private sector gains (cf. Stieglitz 1998; Hall and Soskice 2001). The texts cite mainstream thinking in political economy at their time: theorizing on relations of the open market and information (Rodrik 1998; Iversen 2001) and the role of the state as an enabling structure for market activities (Stiglitz 2002).

In 2004, the government published a strategy document entitled 'Finland's competence, openness and renewability', which was a final report of the project Finland in the Global Economy, launched by the first government of Matti Vanhanen (Valtioneuvoston kanslia 2004). This document seeks to outline the challenges posed by economic globalization and measures to tackle them. The motivation for this is said to have been the economic strengthening of China and other emerging economies. The main Finnish proposals concern adjustments to education and innovation policies and proposals for the running of the labor market and market goods and of the civil service.

Overall, the report proposes the 'opening of the society' as a remedy to stimulate competitiveness. Openness acquires economic connotations, referring to small and open economies, such as Finland, Denmark and Ireland (Valtioneuvoston kanslia 2004, pp. 6, 63, 83). The global economy is termed 'open', leading to investments running geographically to those locations that are most favorable for making profit (Valtioneuvoston kanslia 2004, p. 108). 'Public' refers to public sector organizations or public funding. 'Transparency' appears in the strategy too, as it discusses the transparency of financing (ibid., pp. 81, 112).

The 2004 globalization report also discusses access to information as a matter of national economic competitiveness: private companies should have greater access to government data and further have the right to develop it into new knowledge products and use it in digital service provision (Valtioneuvoston kanslia 2004; see also Zysman 2004; Ottaviano and Pinelli 2004; cf. Sitra 1998; Kuronen 1998; Valtioneuvoston kanslia

2006a). Though the regulatory system is acknowledged as being key for national competitiveness, the public sector is mostly seen as being opposed to the market activity, causing disturbances to the market (cf. European Commission 1998). The economic perspective is focused on the wellbeing of Finnish private companies.

However, in related commentaries a low level of corruption is already named as being an economic advantage for Finland, implying an institutional history (Brunila 2005, p. 32). Geographically, countries are players in a global relocation of economic activities (Ottaviano and Pinelli 2004). This also links to the ensuing discussion of national 'models', comparing and learning among countries amid global economic competition (see also Valtioneuvoston kanslia 2005a, p. 14; Valtioneuvoston kanslia 2005b). The Nordic Model is reduced to a choice over key elements of national competitiveness (cf. Kettunen 2008; Pelkonen 2008).

A 2005 document on productivity and employment credits 'transparent administration and low corruption' as a key element for economic competitiveness (Valtioneuvoston kanslia 2005b, p. 81). Furthermore, Northern Europe is seen to have a competitive advantage (over Southern Europe) in their 'transparent societies', clear administrative structures and rule of law, leading to low corruption (Valtioneuvoston kanslia 2005b, p. 83). The talk of different models intuitively shifts the focus to the differing historical trajectories of countries, now explaining their economic competitiveness (cf. North 2005). Consequently, (democratic) institutions are reduced to factors in institutional analysis, with corruption a transaction cost (cf. Lambsdorf 2007) and the rule of law the feature of a firm business environment. The institutional history of a country is elementary to national competitiveness (cf. North 1998; North 2005; Hall and Soskice 2001).

This new economic geography imposes new economic responsibilities on the state (Moisio 2006; Moisio 2008; Harvey 2006): since foreign direct investment and private corporations are on the move, states have to create institutional conditions that appeal most to market actors. Consequently, a shifting perception of 'accountable to whom?' is to be seen. The state is increasingly seen as being responsible for economic performance and maintaining an appealing economic environment for market actors. This also has ramifications for the understanding of politics.

In 2006, the Council of State released a memo on the program management within the Finnish government. It describes the policy programs as a tool for an efficient resource allocation in governance

(Valtioneuvoston kanslia 2006a, p. 16). In assessing the efficiency and effectiveness of the programs the notion of indicators appears. In the programs of the Economic Council this calculus of government activity extends to measuring democracy and civic engagement (Valtioneuvoston kanslia 2006a, p. 62; see also Oikeusministeriö 2006; cf. Setälä 2006, p. 9). Interestingly, the English translation of the memo on program management has a different background section than the Finnish and Swedish versions, and presents the Finnish system to an external audience (Prime Minister's Office 2007). This is an indication of a new type of deliberative process in the domain of political accountability, where political steering mechanisms are reviewed internationally. The steering capacity of the Prime Minister's Office is the primary concern of the document (cf. Tiihonen 2000; Tiihonen 2003; Bouckaert et al. 2000, pp. 11–12). Rather than a conflict-based process, politics is seen as a hierarchical action that produces measurable outcomes (Prime Minister's Office 2007, p. 13). Consensus is seen as a key element for the success of above strategic governance – it is designated a Finnish tradition (Prime Minister's Office 2007, p. 22, 24).

In 2007, some Economic Council publications still refer to the dichotomy of the open and state-regulated market, and in others transparency receives both democratic and financial connotations, while openness is strictly a democratic concept (Valtioneuvoston kanslia 2007a; Valtioneuvoston kanslia 2007b, pp. 24, 131; Valtioneuvoston kanslia 2007c). Economic geography is again prominently addressed in the document on the Baltic Sea region as an economic environment for Finland (Valtioneuvoston kanslia 2007d), building on international country comparisons, such as the World Economic Forum's Global Competitiveness Index and Transparency International's Corruption Perception Index. Public institutions and (low) corruption are also measurable elements of competitiveness. Transparency becomes a precondition for economic success (Valtioneuvoston kanslia 2007d, p.15).

The Economic Council's publications provide a social scientific context for the market connotations of openness and transparency, which also appear in government programs. Access to government information is actively being reframed as market activity. As I have argued, the conceptual changes are part of a discourse on Nordic openness, emerging in the mid-1990s in Finland. This discourse has communicative and coordinative aspects that stress either democratic or economic aspects of institutional openness. We can now look at the communicative aspects of this discourse and at the gradual entrance of economic ideas in the communicative discourse of Nordic openness in Finland.

2.3   Communicative discourse of Nordic openness

The communicative discourse between political actors and the general public has emphasized normatively more appealing aspects of openness, stressing its democratic qualities. I will analyze the construction of the legitimizing discourse of Nordic openness in the parliamentary debates on the Act on the Publicity of Government Activities in 1999 and in the theme of the Finnish EU Presidency in 2006. This was important for legitimating policy changes, but we find that the coordinative discourse on openness shared by the policy experts similarly seeks historical reference points. The communicative discourse of the late 1990s describes openness as a democratic institution, but moving towards the mid-2000s economic ideas are already tangled in the perceptions of Nordic openness.

2.3.1   Perceptions of a tradition: parliamentary debates in 1998–99

Laws to grant access to government information, such as the 1999 Act on the Publicity of Government Activities (enforced 1 December 1999), are particularly complicated, due to the numerous conflicts of interest that converge in the law. Because the Finnish law is a general one, regulating the handling of information in all issues processed by public bodies, the Act potentially covers almost all imaginable social interests. It is a problem to debate such a massive issue constructively, and when the draft law on the publicity of activities of government was presented to parliament in 1998 the actual debate was somewhat unfocused, targeting mainly the schedule of the proposed law or certain of its features. Still, we can make observations regarding the discourse of the political debates on the government draft on the Act on the Publicity of Government Activities in the Finnish parliament in 1998 and 1999. (I will elaborate on expert views on the adoption of the 1999 law later in this chapter.) In these debates, openness was cherished as a Nordic tradition of Finnish governance.

The government draft law also echoed the discourse on institutional history, describing the principle of publicity as a long standing Nordic and Finnish tradition. The bill claims that the principle of publicity has prevailed in Finland since the 18th century, even though the first law dates from 1951 (HE 30/1998). This apparently builds on Konstari's view that the principle of publicity survived the tsarist era as a guiding principle of organizing administration in Finland that was later revived and received legal status as a norm (Konstari 1977, pp. 52, 58).

The government bill further describes the institution as a Nordic democratic tradition of governance that has allowed everyone equal access to information on government activity.[9] This tradition is seen as being embodied in the controlling function of the law. Information rights are also seen as a crucial balancing element in the use of power and its control.[10] This was used as an argument for expediting the passing of the legislation: access to government information was an acknowledged basic right since 1995, but the law to grant this right dated from 1951. This marked a new emphasis on the idea of rights and on certain demands that this made on general legislation.

The Nordic roots of the institution are also mentioned in the debates, implying reasoned public debate, democratic control and inclusion.[11] Openness is seen as a precondition for democratic participation.[12] The tradition of the principle of publicity is seen to be the clearest proof that Finland belongs to the sphere of Nordic culture.[13] There were also references to legislative history, mentioning the drafting of the current law in the 1930s, its passing in the 1950s and failed attempts at revision in the 1970s. The historical narrative presented in the government bill is, by and large, reproduced in parliamentary deliberations.[14] Finally, it was the much-delayed task of parliament to pass the legislation at the end of the twentieth century.[15] The legislative history, presented in detail in the government draft, becomes a continuum, described as a 'process' of over half a decade. History and the narrative over it thus pose a demand for action: after such a long process, something had to be done (cf. White 2005, p. 338). Moreover, seen in terms of continuity, the big questions of the legislative process are downplayed (see the section on normative steering in this chapter). Why was this legislation not passed before? What were the disagreements in the earlier debates in the 1970s? And, how has the world changed to the extent that this law should be passed now? Ironically, after arguably more than 50 years of preparation, the major critique of the 1999 law in the parliamentary hearings was the perceived haste in its drafting, which was used as an argument for postponing the law.[16]

Reflexivity over the administrative systems elsewhere appears in the parliamentary deliberations – the new law would stand up to 'international comparison'.[17] This points to the reflexivity over what other countries were doing in the same domain, which was also stressed in the government draft. Another, similar comparison over different models is the concern expressed about the influences of Finland's EU accession on publicity.

'The model of the European Union stands in opposition to the open, democratic model of the Nordic countries, and in this there is now a certain degree of controversy over which model will prevail – the secrecy of the European Union or Nordic publicity.' MP Kankaanniemi (16 February 1999)[18]

The EU was seen as a secretive opposition to Finnish governance, which is described as 'Nordic' and 'open'.[19] The new law is seen as a protection against the secretive EU.[20] Though most likely a truthful assessment of the quality of the openness of the European Union at the time, it also makes a claim for Finland's status as an 'open country'. This perception of 'openness' makes it a monolithic national character that knows no variations between levels or sectors of administration. The concerns of openness in relation to Finland's EU accession were also addressed in my interviews with civil servants.

Interestingly, EU politics also provides a benchmark for Finnish domestic governance. The Finnish government had demanded increasing openness in the European Union, as Finland's own access legislation dated from the 1950s. Also the activities of the European Ombudsman, Jacob Söderman from Finland, are referred as a positive example of the demand for more openness.[21] Moreover, the adoption of a new law in Finland is seen as a matter of national credibility following Finland's calls for increasing the level of openness in the European Union.[22] In the Finnish parliamentary debates of the time, the European Union appears as a secretive entity that the Finns are intent on opening up, but the Union is also depicted a reference point for national reform.[23]

Altogether, the concept of publicity is more dominant in the debate than openness as such. In this context, the two terms are used somewhat synonymously.[24] They are seen to belong solely to the domain of democracy.[25] Public power is seen as belonging to the citizens and to be controlled by laws.[26] The publicity of administrative process is stressed.[27] The different modalities of 'public' appear – public institutions, public duty and public sphere. These are also seen as merging: public administration should be public. The Act on the Publicity of Government Activities is perceived as an instrument of democratic control, assuming an underlying conflict between government and citizens. This is also explicitly stated. The media is also seen to be in conflict with civil servants.[28] Secret appears as a counter concept to public, and the choice between the two is seen as a matter of democracy and power.[29] Also openness appears as a counter concept of secrecy, as a quality of a 'modern Nordic country'.[30]

The law is seen to be enhancing the exchange of information between public bureaus, which implies efficiency, though this too is presented from the perspective of the citizen.[31] The same idea of interoperability is touched upon in MPs' complaints about the secret documents of the

European Union that have entered the Finnish parliament.[32] Yet, the principle of publicity is seen to belong to a domain of social critique and democratic control where there prevails the potential for conflict between the government and civil society. The integration function of this institution was not addressed in the debate, nor are its contextual forms allowing the wider political inclusion of social actors.

Economic concerns are rather low key in the parliamentary debate. Some MPs are positive about the publicizing of income and tax information that was to come. A remark was made on the perceived diminishing of budgetary secrecy and new national economic adjustments, but the point is not developed.[33] The notion of good governance is also referred to, again stressing the perspective of citizens.[34] In some accounts, the citizens are named as customers as part of a new service paradigm.[35] The new economic value of public information and the problem of pricing are referred to. It is seen as a democratic problem that has consequences for citizens and that potentially limits access to information.[36]

There are few references in the parliamentary debate to transparency, coupling it with the increasing complexity of government and decision-making, and to Finland's EU membership. It is also used as a parallel concept of 'public' as opposed to 'secret'. Transparency and public are also used synonymously, making a firm claim for better government.

'One can say that the more transparent the administration is, the more public it is, the better it is too.' MP Tiusanen (23 April 1998)[37]

Transparency seems to set a demand for action. It has to be increased and the result of this is (unquestionably) better governance. The optical connotation of permeating light is used with reference to economics, functioning markets and abilities to conduct finance politics, but the assumed audience is made up of citizens and the rest of society.[38] In the parliamentary debates of 1998, transparency is thus still perceived in terms of democratic control.

The notion of quality also features in the debates. The government bill draws a link between the increased 'quality' of decisions that will result from the openness of policy drafting. The public debate that would ensue about openness is seen as leading to well-reasoned policies. The claim was made that public deliberation is efficient:

'This legislation aims at the deepening of democracy, which is of course important for individuals and citizens. In addition, an interesting contradictory principle has been brought to light, which I agree on and find interesting. Namely, the government sees it in [the background document of the draft law] that the quality of decision-making can be enhanced with this law, because the public debate can in some issues bring to attention such points of view that have been overlooked in the policy preparations. This is a very interesting concern, and I hope this will also happen, but so that the issues won't be delayed because of it.' MP Pohjola (23 April 1998)[39]

A remarkable point about the above quote is the outspoken connection between publicity and efficiency. According to the earlier understanding of openness and publicity, they belonged to the sphere of democracy and public debate, and are at odds with efficient decision-making. This highlights the bipolar view of democracy-efficiency. Yet, by presenting publicity here as a potential conduit for efficiency the shifting perceptions of publicity (and efficiency) are accentuated.

To summarize, the discourse used in the parliamentary debates stresses the democratic, legal and ethical connotations of publicity, which is the concept mostly used. Publicity is seen to entail conflict between the government and citizens and government and the media, and to provide the means for democratic control and inclusion. Openness was used somewhat interchangeably with publicity as a strictly democratic concept. The sporadic references to transparency were also framed in democratic terms.

Publicity and openness are also cropped in the construct of Nordic governance. The coupling of publicity and efficiency is an odd novelty in the parliamentary debates. Economic perceptions are more prominently expressed in the government programs and the documents of the Economic Council of the same period and shortly after.

But when we turn towards the mid-2000s, the communicative discourse of Nordic openness starts to acquire economic constituents. This is particularly evident in relation to transnational governance.

2.3.2 Transnational governance and Nordic openness

One effect of transnational governance has been the steepening practice of country comparisons. This has resulted in nationalistic collective positioning in terms of policy choices and administrative culture (cf. White 2009). Since the 1990s, openness and transparency have remained on the agenda, becoming part of the new narrative of the Finnish state and shifting to its new European identity. The governance rankings, which have appeared since the late 1990s, have been of great symbolic value to Finland.

While previously the Finns perceived themselves as hard-working citizens of a small nation, a non-aligned gateway between east and west, a nation existing on forestry, the current self-perception is shifting towards a nationalistic narrative of Finland as a winner of globalization and a top dog of innovation (Pakkasvirta 2008, pp. 23–8). This element is also present in the numerous debates concerning globalization and Finland's response to it (cf. Kettunen 1999; Kettunen 2008). Many of the winning qualities that the Finns now find in themselves are based on historically shaped public institutions. For a scholar of the economic dimension of historical institutionalism this comes as no surprise, but for the wider public to become aware of this is another matter. Openness, in its variations, increasingly seems to become a metaphor for a national survival strategy in a new global economic competition. It is also becoming the subject of nationalist prestige (Weber 1978; see Chapter 5).

In the mid-1990s Finnish-EU relations became a key site of reference where the nationalistic talk on 'openness' emerged. Openness has been a mission statement for both of the Finnish EU presidencies held in 1999 (see Raunio and Tiilikainen 2003, ch. 6) and 2006. In the EU context, Finnish MPs and civil servants have joined countries such as Sweden, Denmark and the Netherlands in promoting more open practices of governance (Stasavage 2006, p. 171). Individuals such as the first European Ombudsman Jacob Söderman and MEP Heidi Hautala, have gained a reputation for promoting openness in the EU. This is particularly well-received in Finland where openness has become a part of the political profile of these actors. In a way, they have also become concrete examples of Finnish openness.

The design of the logo for Finland's 2006 EU presidency (Figure 2.1) was chosen so as to highlight the key agenda of the presidency – how to make a more transparent Union. The transparent motifs in the logo of the Finnish presidency were said to symbolize 'the Finns' open and direct way of going about things' (EU Presidency 2006a). The core problem of the EU was perceived to be its 'diminished legitimacy in the eyes of its citizens'. The mission statement of the Finnish presidency claimed that 'the best way of demonstrating the need for the EU is through effective legislative work and efficient management of the Union's other business.' In accordance, the objective for the Finnish presidency was defined as 'a transparent and effective union' (EU Presidency 2006b). The union of transparency and efficiency indicates the embedding of the idea of public acts of governance as being efficient.

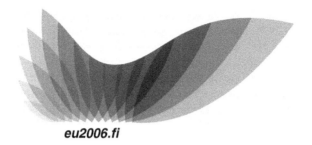

eu2006.fi

Figure 2.1   The transparent logo of the Finnish EU presidency in 2006
Source: Prime Minister's Office[40]

During the 2000s, the perception of openness as a historical trait of the Finns seems to gain weight in the communicative discourse of Nordic openness. The Finnish positive outlook in the governance indices provides social scientific proof for the narrative adopted earlier. There has recently also been a renewed interest in Anders Chydenius and particularly in his ideas regarding the freedom of print and free trade (Anders Chydenius Foundation 2006). Since the early 2000s, Chydenius has also cropped up in the speeches of Finnish politicians (Halonen 2005 [delivered in 2003]; Söderman 2006a, 2006b; Brax 2007). Swedish politicians too have staked their claims for this thinker, whose ideas they now think of as an 'export product' (Helsingin Sanomat 2009; Manninen 2006, p. 13).

Chydenius' interest in accessing information on government affairs arose because he wanted accurate information on the sales that mercantilist rule in Stockholm made at the expense of tar producers. The uprooting of corruption was also seen as playing a role in this (Virrankoski 1986). In political oratory this now provides an apt analogy to contemporary globalization (Halonen 2005). The advent of new printing technology in Chydenius' time provides a fitting metaphor for today's new information technology and the internet. Chydenius's ideas are seen to be relevant in the contemporary context, especially when analyzing the global transformations in trade and democracy, where openness or transparency are coupled with ideas of low corruption, the rule of law, democracy and competitiveness.

Chydenius stands as a historical reference point in a time where the relations of centre and periphery were being rethought (cf. Skinner 1969; Skinner 1989). A vigorous opponent to mercantilism, Chydenius is easily brought into debates where notions of (neo) mercantilist and (neo) liberalist viewpoints converge. Even the Finnish narratives of openness involve the dialectic of democracy (open) and efficiency (direct). Though the storyline is not always fully explicit, there are references to global markets and globalization and the role of information in organizing them. The references to institutional history become part of the communicative discourse of Nordic openness, which now accommodates the new ideas on transparency that we find diffused internationally.

We see, therefore, that the policy discourse on openness has resonated particularly well with the Finnish institutional context, where legislation on accessing government information and the principle of publicity has existed for a long time. The cognitive aspects of this new policy discourse tap into the social scientific perceptions of governance, and institutional and information economics (cf. Schmidt 2002, p. 214). The normative, legitimating discourse of Nordic openness resonates with Finland's institutional history. The discourse of openness has appeared in Finnish government programs and bills since the mid-1990s, in policy documents and strategies, the speeches of politicians and narratives told by civil servants. We also read it in newly emerging governance indices and their interpretations.

The shifting belief systems among policy actors carry new cognitive aspects, though this is largely tacit in the normatively appealing talk of openness. Because institutional openness has a long history as a virtue of the Enlightenment, the Nordic welfare state, and liberalism, the new connotations of transparency find a seemingly ideational root in these philosophies. In the era when the Finnish welfare state was built, the exchange of information and negotiations between various groups were an underlying and unspoken norm of governance (Kettunen 1999). Entering new transnational governance, 'openness', 'public sector information' and 'transparency' become political and economic concerns that are actively governed.

Though the above developments in political rhetoric are seemingly interdependent with institutional affairs, they converge in the rationalities and mechanisms of change. The shift in the political rhetoric and concepts of governance not only reflects institutional change but also propels it. In terms of accountability, the shift in conceptualization reframes a mechanism of government control. This also points to new external demands and audiences to whom civil servants are responsible. Somewhat paradoxically, the reflexivity over a democratic trajectory marks an opening for its reframing in economic terms.

The historical perceptions are also prominently present in the coordinative discourse shared by policy actors. I will next look at the ideational changes in normative and financial steering, including an analysis of oral accounts, concerning how the consensus over new policies of openness was reached in Finland in the late 1990s.

2.4   Ideational changes in normative steering

I will now look at the emergence of a new coordinative policy discourse (Schmidt 2002) of openness in the late 1990s in Finland, and how it created a firm understanding among the policy actors that 'openness', democratic qualities aside, is a national economic virtue. In the interviews with civil servants, on which the rest of this chapter is based, the above process of communication was elaborated. Many interviewees referred to key moments, venues and actors as a process of learning, where institutional openness shifted to a new conceptual domain of efficiency and national economics (cf. Haas 1992). While the interviewees mostly discussed openness as a tradition, the core of the narrative concerned the changes around the issue of institutional openness as it shifted towards economic notions of transparency.

The communicative discourse of openness and its coordinative variant therefore meet in the idealized perception of Nordic openness, depicting Finns as open, progressive and competitive. This was apparent from the accounts given by the interviewees and from the official documents analyzed below. Despite the heavy referencing of a tradition of Nordic openness, this tradition is now changing and there are even deviations from it. Finnish legislation to regulating access to government information (Act on the Publicity of Government Activities, Personal Data Act, and Administrative Procedure Act) initially had a Swedish model when it was first adopted. But when renewed in the late 1990s and early 2000s, ideational influences were increasingly sought elsewhere, leading to a policy recasting (cf. Schmidt 2002, p. 222).

There are changes within central steering and in the accountability system that can be linked to the ideational cycles in government responsibility. Access to information and deliberation are no longer only related to legality and the reliability of the administrative process. They are now also seen as being relevant to the performance and outcome of the process, and of national economic significance. There are new ideational addendums to the Nordic legal tradition, such as openness as strategic communication and public information as a commodity. In the sphere of financial steering, new economic ideas are coupled with public hearings and publishing performance information on government activities. Hence there is a shift in the perception of accountability from process accountability to accountability through results.

2.4.1 Ideational change and policy programs

Following the turmoil that affected Finnish governance in the mid-1990s, Finland's information access legislation was completely revised in 1999 after several decades of minor revisions and apparent resistance to change. The information services of public bureaus became active after the new law. In the mid-1990s, openness also made its way into public sector reform, and work in the fields of administrative ethics and service quality and productivity now uphold openness as a virtue. The right of access to government information was also reframed as an element of a macroeconomic perception of good governance. Finally, new numerical measures of transparency have merged to assess the performance of public bureaus both domestically and internationally.

What increasingly seems to link all these cases is the realization that openness and the transparency of the public administration are favorable features of governance in terms of economic competitiveness and performance. Though implied in the efforts at increasing central government's steering capacity in the information society (Tiihonen 2000; Holliday 2001), this shift has become most apparent in attempts at imposing new practices of accountability that are based on measures of budgetary transparency and also in the attempts to allow for the reuse of public information for economic activity. Finally, it has also extended to the planning of legislation in the notion of better regulation.

The coordinative discourse of openness that has diffused among Finnish policy actors since the mid-1990s carries connotations of both democracy and efficiency. The ideational core and the cognitive aspects of this policy discourse are more inclined towards an economic and performative emphasis than the communicative discourse of political actors, which stresses the democratic connotations of openness. There is an observable dissonance in the legitimizing talk of government and the coordinative policy discourse of policy actors.

Figure 2.2 presents the timeline of the major reforms and debates concerning the openness of the public administration in Finland between 1998 and 2007. Though the division into political, normative and financial steering is at times artificial, these provide an insight into the evolution of ideas in different contexts. Moreover, the picture also reveals the different aspirations that are grouped within 'openness'. In terms of timing, the changes in normative steering (law), have mainly taken place in the late 1990s and early 2000s. Initially, the legislative changes

Political steering

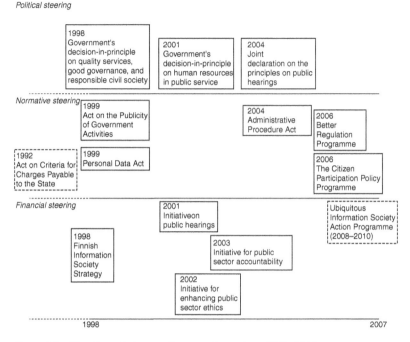

Figure 2.2   Timeline of changes in central steering, 1998–2007

were attempts to speed up the legal updates in response to the changing governance environment. Subsequently, the relevant legal reforms have addressed mainly administrative procedures and good governance (Administrative Procedure Act). Within the sphere of financial steering the new ideas of transparency were mostly adopted from the OECD, mainly under programs concerning public hearings and administrative ethics. The OECD also had an impact on the initiative on public sector accounting (accountability reform) and new forms of budget transparency. This was a continuation of policies on accrual charging, which had been launched already in the early 1990s. In relation to this, the information society strategies and policies on the pricing of public sector information became topical. The European Union had a major ideational influence on these policies.

Historically oriented institutional analyses, particularly when tracking change, often tend to follow changes in legislation (see, for example, Somers and Block 2005; Béland and Hacker 2004). The key pieces of legislation to regulate state information in Finland have a Nordic root: the principle of publicity and the Act on the Publicity of Government

Activities (translated into English by the Finnish Government as the Act on the *Openness* of Government Activities) have their ideational antecedents in the Swedish law on the freedom of printing. The Finnish Personal Data Act (Henkilörekisterilaki 1987) considered the Swedish Datalagen (enacted in 1973) as a model, and the first Finnish Administrative Procedure Act (*Hallintomenettelylaki* 1983) carried a reference to the Swedish Förvaltningslag (1972). However, at the end of the 1990s and during the early 2000s they became influenced by other ideational sources. I will next highlight certain relevant changes that have occurred in the legislative framework, beginning with a brief legislative history.

2.4.2 Stagnant legislative history

Looking at Finland's legislative history of the law on accessing government documents, it becomes apparent that this legislation has enjoyed remarkable continuity after it was issued in 1951 (see Table 2.2). In fact, the legislative history appears stagnant, with a law drafted in the late 1930s that remained somewhat resistant to revision until the 1990s. The first attempt to create a law on accessing government information in Finland was in 1939, but the Second World War interrupted it. The 1939 law was revised slightly in 1945, but the draft maintained the form of the 1939 version. It was not until 1951 that the legislation was first adopted (Wallin and Konstari 2000, p. 73). K.J. Ståhlberg,[41] both an academic and political figure committed to liberalism (Inha 2003), was largely responsible for the making of the first law. There was very little public debate on the decision to adopt the law.

This lack of public debate was an apparent feature in adopting democratic institutions in newly independent Finland. After Finland gained independence in 1917, such institutions were largely copied from Sweden

Table 2.2 Historical reference points in negotiating access to government information in Finland

1930s–50s		1960s–80s		1990s–2000s	
1939: First Law Draft on Publicity of Government Documents	1951: Act on the Publicity of Government Documents	1970–75: Information Systems Committee	1983: Administrative Procedure Act 1987: Personal Data Act	1999: Act on the Publicity of Government Activities (renewed) 1999: Personal Data Act (renewed)	2004: Administrative Procedure Act (renewed)

and their function was often not publicly mediated, reflecting the rather patriarchal public sphere in the country (cf. Nieminen 2006, p. 200). This was particularly apparent in the 1919 adoption of the Ombudsman, another institution of public accountability of Swedish origin that only later gained popular recognition (Hidén 1970, pp. 2–3). Similar to the adoption of the Ombudsman, the law on the publicity of government records was not a result of civil society pressure (cf. Schulz-Forberg and Stråth 2010). At first glance, the revisions to the legislation on the publicity of government records appear rather to have proceeded in times of relatively low social conflict in Finland. This has also been a domain of policy experts where the general public has had limited influence.

There were attempts at revising the legislation before 1999 and the interest in the openness of administration peaked in the 1970s, leading to the appointment of a state committee to handle the matter.[42] The general social atmosphere was also evident in the selection of members. The committee, named the Information Systems Committee, became a terrain of debate between young leftist members and representatives of economic interests. After five years the committee was abolished. The last and only report, or rather the differing opinion that some of the members wished to include in it, points to a major obstacle in the work: the left-wing members of the committee wanted to broaden the principle of publicity to cover the activities of private companies, which was unacceptable to their opponents on the committee, who consisted mainly of representatives of banks and credit agencies (Tietojärjestelmäkomitea 1974). The scope of the committee's work was also seen as being too broad, as it tried to draft legislation on publicity, data protection and crediting all at once.

A remarkable feature of the 1974 Information Systems Committee report is the idea of openness as something that should not be applied in the sphere of private economic activity. When we compare this to contemporary ideas about market transparency, it becomes apparent how big the ideational shift in the sphere of economy has been. The legislation on stock market activities alone has entailed significant reporting duties to private companies since the 1970s. According to one legal expert interviewed for the study, the current Limited Liability Companies Act largely contained amendments to the publicity of private companies that the Information Systems Committee wanted to add. By the late 1990s, when they were exposed to increasing demands of corporate governance, private enterprises were already accustomed to the idea of transparency.

However, in the 1970s, access to information held by key economic actors was seen as a question of power in society. The Information

Systems Committee report refers to a broadening of the publicity of private sector actors as an important question for the use of power in society (Tietojärjestelmäkomitea 1974, p. 38). Altogether, the reason for expanding institutional openness was seen as a priority because of the societal planning and politics (Tietojärjestelmäkomitea 1974, p. 2; cf. Kettunen 2003a, pp. 169, 194). This indicates the key problem of publicity as perceived by the members of the committee: how to control power and plan societal activities. In the context of political tensions the adoption of a draft on a new law was simply not possible. This also highlights the potential for political tensions that this institution bears.

In the interviews I conducted, the Information Systems Committee was described as controversial and one legal expert called its abolition dramatic, since this was not a customary measure in Finland. Another respondent thought that the reform ideas were simply 'put aside to cool off' and that both the reform and the committee died out along with it. The political tensions in the committee were apparent and openly expressed but the committee was, nevertheless, described as an arena for both resisting social critique and absorbing it, as we see in the account of a legal expert:

'Young boys, radicals, were on the move. I don't know if it raised much concern. It was thought that come in here [to the committee] to let off some steam.' (Legal expert)

The work of this abolished committee did, however, bear fruit some twenty years later. The law that it tried to enact in the 1970s formed the basis for the law that was subsequently drafted in 1999 (Wallin and Konstari 2000, p. 77). Also, the laws on personal data and credit information that the committee tried to have enforced were enacted in 1999 and 2007.[43] One respondent noted that in the late 1990s and early 2000s these draft laws were dug out from the 'fox-holes' of the 1970s. The world was seen to have changed and the structural changes in Finland's governance called for a new law to replace the one that had been already drafted in the late 1930s. There was also a new interest in public information. Most importantly the political tensions around the issue had dissolved. These had set in motion the long process of revising the law:

Q: Why did it take so long [to bring about the law]?
A: It was not a simple matter. It is demanding from a technical procedural point of view. And legislatively it went to the hub of various social interests. The distribution of information to different

directions and setting limits, that's the core of societal policy. (Legal expert)

In previous accounts, resistance to revising the law was seen to have stemmed from economic institutions, such as the Ministry of Finance and the Bank of Finland (Hynninen 2000, p. 39). In these accounts the issues of openness and economic interests have been seen as opposed to one another, which led to lukewarm attitudes towards revising the law. This issue was by no means forgotten or dormant, but rather remained pending while not being actively promoted. It progressed in the preparations within administrative ranks that lead to partial revisions of the law, but the big step for the law revision to proceed was a political readiness for reform.

Even when discussing resistance to a revision of the law, the interviewees did not stress the role of actors. Rather, the political climate in the country was said to have changed significantly. While the publicity of government information was still a politicized issue in the 1980s (Takala and Konstari 1982), the collapse of the Soviet Union drastically changed the ideological climate. Also the economic recession that hit Finland in the early 1990s was mentioned in the interviews as a factor that had dissolved the political confrontations and made cooperation mandatory. The consensual practices favoring a wider representation of societal groups that had prevailed in the country were seen to depend on the circulation of information. This inclusion was also seen to be threatened in the process of Finland's EU accession, leading to the stressed importance of openness, for instance in government programs and parliamentary debates.

On a general level, the adoption of the law and its revisions came about as a result of an expert-driven process of consensus formation on the necessity of 'openness' in response to a felt need for change within the administration (cf. Schmidt 2002; Haas 1992). The interviewees saw this as being a somewhat natural course of development, since the legislation on the whole covered all spheres of state regulation and, as such, required a high amount of expertise. A public debate on the matter was seen as counterproductive and one legal expert stated as a personal opinion that 'one cannot discuss publicity in public'. Looking at the drafting of the 1999 law and the developments preceding it, it becomes apparent that the concern over the 'openness' of public institutions was not triggered by pressure from civil society but became topical within the administration as the world was changing.

The technical means for storing and processing public information were also in flux for most of the 1980s and 1990s, which caused delays to revisions of legislation (Hynninen 2000, p. 39). As the 1990s approached, the law that had received its main outlines in the 1930s was rapidly becoming outdated. The newly-expressed concerns that were seen to demand a new regulatory environment were largely related to the shifts into a new governance environment (Pekonen 1995b; Pollitt et al. 1997; Pierre and Peters 2000; Pierre 2000): changes in public sector tasks and their organization, new relations to citizens, organizations and media, the shifts in basic rights, internationalization of governance and EU integration, and the development of information technology (Wallin and Konstari 2000, p. 74).

Looking at the legislative history in Finland, it becomes apparent that the ideas of controlling government, present still in the 1970s, were pushed to the back and the tacit integration function of the access to government information became appreciated amid the pressures of globalization and open economy. Moreover, the institution was now appreciated in terms of effectiveness and economic performance. There are several important shifts in the understanding of the institution that I will next outline. These by and large included the ideational elements discussed internationally under the umbrella of transparency, referring to citizens' right to information, trust-based collaboration and effectiveness, and economic performance. The new information services required of civil servants were added to the 1999 law. However, what is particularly interesting in the context of this study are the new perceptions of institutional openness as an economic virtue or a key element of public sector performance. I will begin with the emphasis on citizens' rights.

2.4.3 Ideational shifts: citizens' rights

Tracking the ideational changes in the new Act on the Publicity of Government Activities (621/1999), there are new perceptions that could be seen to have resulted from the diffusion of 'liberalism' (Simmons et al. 2006; Peters et al. 2005; Rose 1999; cf. Skinner 2003), such as understanding transparency as a 'right to know'. Most notably, there has been an emphasis on citizens' rights, which can be seen as an addendum to the Nordic tradition of universalistic rights. Openness as a norm of governance was reinforced in the 1990s, and not only in the act on the openness of the activities of government.[44] The principle of publicity and the right to privacy were acknowledged in the 1995 reform to legislation on basic rights. The constitutional law of 1999 formulated the principle of publicity or the right of access to information: 'documents and recordings in the possession of the public authorities are public, unless their publication has for compelling reasons been specifically restricted by an Act.'[45] The same idea is expressed by the 1999 Act on the Publicity of Government Activities.[46]

In 1995 access to information was promoted as a 'basic right' of each citizen (Konstari 1999, p. 943). This was related to a wider reform of basic rights that was executed in Finland in 1995. The key feature of this reform was the inclusion of the notion of human rights in Finnish national legislation. Until the 1980s, Finnish ideology of basic rights saw them as distinct from the conception of human rights, which were seen as belonging to the domain of international agreements (Viljanen 1996). The Finnish legal tradition of basic rights was somewhat closed from external influences and remained resistant, until the 1995 reform, to ideas of human rights that were of foreign origin. A broader reform on basic rights was attempted in the 1970s, after which partial revisions were sought, but these were rejected due to political tensions in the 1980s (Viljanen 1996, p. 788).

One of the most obvious features of the reform of basic rights was the merging of the viewpoints on 'basic' and 'human' rights. This also meant that many notions derived from international jargon, such as 'fair trial' and 'respect for private life' made their way into Finnish legislation. According to Viljanen, access to public information as a basic right was ideationally of domestic origin (Viljanen 1996, p. 791). However, there is an apparent similarity in the international jargon of good governance and the new addendums to the 1999 law, such as the notions of 'openness' and 'good data management practice'.[47]

Perhaps most important here is the use of the notion of 'rights' altogether. Other institutions of public accountability such as the Ombudsman had already adopted the issue of 'human rights' as a domain to defend in the 1980s (Hidén 2000, p. 70; Viljanen 1996, pp. 797, 812). Even though the legal roots of the principle of publicity lie in citizens' ability to control the activities of government, there is also a widespread interpretation of publicity as a practise of governance. The basic rights reform reinstated the conceptualization of access to public information as a political right. The right to privacy also became more prominent. The 1999 Finnish Constitution acknowledges this and the Personal Data Act was amended in 1999, which also gave this citizens' right a more pronounced role.

Requirements for information services were added in the 1999 law, making civil servants responsible for them. Here the notion of openness enters the legal language.

2.4.4   Openness as strategic communication

Along with the concept of publicity, a new concept of 'openness' appears in 20§ of the new law, referring to the new *obligation* of civil servants to produce and hand out information, that is to provide information services (Valtioneuvoston kanslia 2001a, p. 34). Openness had already appeared in government programs as a new legitimizing concept (see above). Ideationally, this comes close to the international codifications of transparency and openness, such as the often cited OECD's (2002a, p. 3) definitions, understood as 'availability of information' and 'listening' to citizens and businesses. Openness received a particularly prominent role in the European Union's attempts to define European 'good governance' (European Commission 2001, p. 10).

Following the 1999 Act on the Publicity of Government Activities and a specific act on communication services (2002),[48] the Prime Minister's Office published a Recommendation for Central Government Communication in 2002. Seeking to direct the administration 'towards open, trustworthy and efficient administration' (Prime Minister's Office 2003, p. 6), the Recommendation merges the idea of openness and efficient and goal-oriented governance. The information provision therefore becomes a deliberate tool of governance (cf. Hood and Margetts 2007). Moreover, it endorses a trust-based understanding of the institution, which also seeks to increase the participatory forms of governance (Prime Minister's Office 2003, p. 8).

The Recommendation frames communication as an inherent part of the democratic rule of law and the Nordic welfare state, but also of goal-oriented 'management'. It discusses the state's new information services as a citizens' right, including now the duty of civil servants to produce and share information (Valtioneuvoston kanslia 2002a, p. 10). It is noteworthy that when the Finnish version of the Recommendation discusses the institution from the perspective of democratic control it refers to the concept of publicity (*julkisuus*) and the 'principle of publicity' (Valtioneuvoston kanslia 2002a, p. 6), whereas 'openness' is understood as the communication and provision of information. This also involves strategic aims of effectiveness:

The increased importance of communication within society, combined with notions of efficiency and profitability, place new expectations on governmental communication. For that reason, communication must be target-orientated, systematic and applied both in management and implementation. [...]But communication is not just a responsibility; it also represents an opportunity for each authority to perform their functions effectively. (Prime Minister's Office, 2003, pp. 6–7)

This poses the perceived responsibility of public authorities differently. They are not only expected to give out information on demand, allowing control of their activities, but through communications-based 'openness' they are also seen as responsible for optimizing the effectiveness of their operations. The Recommendation for Central Government Communication also refers to 'transparency' when describing the essence of its communication and information services (Valtioneuvoston kanslia 2002a, p. 14). It is worth noting that since the late 1990s, the government's (unofficial) Finnish-English legal translations no longer refer to 'publicity'. The 'principle of publicity' is instead termed the 'principle of openness' and the act to define it is translated as the Act on the *Openness* of Government Activities.[49] The above perception of openness shifts the principle of publicity from its control function towards a proactive government that informs citizens from its own strategic needs. This is a new ideational addendum to the principle of publicity.

There was also a consensual understanding of openness stressed in the interviews. The Nordic consensual practices of governance were addressed as a result of a wider sharing of information, which was also one of the major reasons why the issue became topical in the 1990s.

2.4.5 Openness as consensus and collaboration

The law emphasizes the control function of the institution, but previous assessments regarded the overall understanding or function of the institutions in different terms, depicting it as a principle of governance with an integrative social function (Konstari 1977, pp. 7–8; cf. Thelen 2004; Tilly 2004, pp. 24–5; Seligman 1992, pp. 9–10). This was also referred to in the interviews where the 'openness' of administration was seen to allow information to be circulated widely among policy actors. In contrast to the idea of citizens' rights to control government, the above conceptualization of the Finnish tradition of openness made the circulation of information appear to be a strategy of governance. This also highlights the contextuality of the institution. The interplay of the Nordic consensual tradition and corporatism had formed institutional practices where the institution appeared as an enabling structure, allowing information to be shared and conflicts to be prevented.

The conflict that the laws (and the parliamentary debates) assumed had perhaps not been necessarily the functional core of the institution in Finland, and, moreover, there was an increasing awareness of this among the policy actors. According to one interviewee closely involved in the process of drafting the 1999 law, the general feeling about the revision of the law revision was positive, even enthusiastic. Even though the law revision was not primarily targeted at the possible problems of Finland's EU accession, it was one of the reasons that had sparked an interest in the revision of the law. The Finnish consensual tradition was mentioned as a reason for adopting the law. The harsh economic realities of the recession of the early 1990s were also linked to this:

> As a lawyer I could imagine that the consensus thinking had prevailed strongly for a long time, for instance, in the tripartite agreements of labour markets. That these have worked to the same direction, so that you cannot reach such compromises, after which you remain in good relations, if someone withholds information. [...] [I]n a way it is related to how a small country fares. We have had hard times; still in 1995 we had these [expenditure] cuts. The strength is that we do things together and trust each other. In that way [openness] has deep roots in everything that Finland does. (Legal expert)

The above quote subsumes access to public information within the practice of consensus, often grouped with the Nordic tradition of governance (Rainio-Niemi 2008; Kettunen and Kiviniemi 2006; Kettunen 1999). Moreover, it portrays Finland as an actor that does things in a unitary way. Kettunen has pointed to a trend of reflexivity in Finnish institutional practices in the labour markets amid economic globalization (Kettunen 1999), where the importance of consensual institutional practices of tripartite agreements is stressed – now only in terms of national competitiveness.[50]

Openness as a Finnish tradition of governance was described differently in the interviews and in the official documents. The logic of consensual inclusion was addressed in many interviews, regardless of the organizational contexts. In the views of civil servants, 'openness' becomes described as a grey area, where the extended circle of policy actors is able to exchange information without it becoming public. 'Openness' thus becomes a 'third term' of governance, blurring the dichotomy of public-secret, public-private (cf. Jessop 1998).

Moreover, the interviewees saw openness as a Nordic and Finnish tradition, of which there was a particularly long history. Compared to the differing accounts of the administrative traditions in Sweden, Norway and Denmark, or certain aspects of Finnish governance, this monolithic view might be somewhat idealized. Also the term 'transparency' emerged in the interviews at the initiative of the interviewees. The international context tended to reduce the administrations to models that were units small enough to think and pass judgments on (below also the interviewer is guilty of this reductionism):

Q: How did the international debate that went on around the issue of transparency appear through the Nordic principle of publicity?
A: In these matters we've led [the rest of the world] in all respects. Certainly, there was nothing to be ashamed of globally or by European standards that we and the Swedes could afford to pose as advocates of openness. (Legal expert)

The core of the tradition seemed difficult to characterize. On the one hand, the tradition was seen in terms of consensual decision-making and, on the other, of accounts of democratic control. There is an apparent tension between the two. If we perceive openness as a trust-based institution where information can be circulated among different members of politico-administrative networks, it does not necessarily contribute to the publicity of current policy issues. Instead, these are likely to remain to some extent uncovered, while there is no need to make public demands for information. In the interviews, the consensual root of the institution was mostly seen in democratic terms. Nevertheless, both can be still be framed democratically, as democratic control or representation. But several interviewees pointed to the fact that members of the media were often included in the informed networks, making them partially involved in the circle of trust forming, entailing even a potential for censorship. Moreover, in some accounts this trust-based circulation of information was reframed as efficiency (see also Chapter 5).

The accounts that pose openness in terms of efficiency and national economic gain are part of the new mindset of governance, where open and transparent become efficient. The 'quality' of governance has become a synonym for efficiency-seeking programs in public administration (Hautamäki and Mäkipeska 1994), now also covering openness.

2.4.6   Perceptions of quality, productivity and market transparency

In 2003, the new Administrative Procedure Act (*hallintolaki*) was passed. Coming into force on 1 January 2004, it replaced a previous law (*Hallintomenettelylaki* 1983) that had its antecedents in the Swedish Förvaltningslag from 1972.[51] In the government bill the new law was grounded on notions of good governance and rule of law, coupled with new notions of quality and productivity.[52] The arguments for passing a new law also by and large comprise descriptions of shifts into a new governance framework. Changes in the regulatory environment, the number and type of actors involved, and the new demands of good governance and efficiency were given as reasons for comprehensive reform of the legislation on administrative process.[53] Also the shift towards customer and service orientation is mentioned.

Good governance appears also in the government bill's section on international developments. Referring to the European Commission's White Paper on European Governance (COM 2001/428), the government draft cites the five proponents of good governance: openness, participation, accountability, effectiveness, and coherence (compare European Commission, 2001).[54] Altogether noteworthy in the law drafts of the 2000s is the comprehensive country comparisons, which are presented in detail.[55] From the perspective of democratic control, the Administrative Procedure Act, and the government bill in particular, highlight the administrative process and its reliability from the perspective of the citizen. Yet the draft law stresses the performative aspects of the process. The government is not solely responsible through the process but, increasingly, for the swift running of the process.

The new concepts of governing, such as governance and good governance were mentioned in the interviews as normative principles that demand openness and transparency:

A: Yeah, but then it's good to separate publicity and openness. And transparency. These are not the same things in their contents.

Q: How do they differ?

A: You can characterise them thus in that when we speak of publicity we mean the traditional publicity of documents, the publicity of parliament and the courts. This is so that we receive information on processes, documents and procedures. Openness is more than this, not just the availability of information. One main difference is that officials have to give reasons for their decisions. This affects the practice of the law on publicity. Transparency is international jargon, appears in the documents of international actors, and there is also the organization Transparency International. It can be characterized even more broadly in that it concerns structures and that the structures of the public administration are open. [...] It's very foggy, rather like governance. Not government. More than government. And then in the business world you can have 'corporate governance'. [...]In that way transparency and governance are aligned. (Legal expert)

The above excerpt points to the three different concepts of public: publicity, openness, transparency. Publicity is termed as traditional access to documents, and information on process, documents and procedures. Openness is more broadly defined. It also removes the issue from the mere process but also requires active measures of account-giving in justifying their actions. Transparency is deemed an alien term coming from international policy circles. It makes the administrative structures visible. The respondent uses the notion of 'fog' to describe the term, which further points to the active blurring between public and private categories. Publicity can be seen as a well-formed political concept with a clear counter concept, secrecy, but since openness and transparency lack explicit counter concepts in the present political jargon they remain somewhat ambivalent.

The 1998 government bill of the Act on the Publicity of Government Activities contains an early reference to the responsibilities of state in the face of market transparency, resulting from the liberalization of the world financial markets:

The liberalization of the money and capital markets has led to a growth in the importance of official information, and the markets may react to the release of information from documents in the possession of certain authorities. The acquisition of such information on market activity ahead of others would harm confidence in the markets. (Finnish Government Draft Law, HE 30/1998)[56]

Though the state assumes responsibilities towards market actors, its responsibilities still seem to be indirect. Exceptional discretion is called for in issues related to state finances. This underlines the subtle nature of the public exposure of financial matters. The economic recession of the 1990s is likely to have raised the awareness of this.[57] As a result of these calls for discretions, new practices of standardized information releases on the state finances were adopted in the government's Recommendation for Central Government Communication, published in 2002 (Valtioneuvoston kanslia 2002a, pp. 32–3).

Since then this perception of the markets' trust in the state has appeared in Finnish debates and the awareness of the interplay of the functionality of market actors and the access to government documents has deepened. The perception of openness as a keeper of national economic competition becomes self-explanatory in the 2006 Better Regulation initiative of the second government of Matti Vanhanen (Valtioneuvoston kanslia 2006b). 'Openness' and 'transparency' become part of an institutional framework for economic success, with references to international models and similar programs of other countries (Valtioneuvoston kanslia 2006b, pp. 12–14). As one of its ideational inspirations the document cites the studies on economic history that have revealed that the national economic advantage is an outcome of favorable institutional developments (Valtioneuvoston kanslia 2006b, p. 92).

In the outline of the Finnish Better Regulation program (Valtioneuvoston kanslia 2006b; see also Valtioneuvoston kanslia 2006c), 'trust' is used to describe the citizens' confidence in state institutions, but more emphases are put on the market actors' trust in the state. The references to openness and inclusion as underlying characteristics of the Finnish system make a generalization of this characteristic of administrative culture (Valtioneuvoston kanslia 2006b, p. 92). Moreover, these democratic principles are moved to the category of economics. The perspective is no longer that of domestic actors. The state is being observed from afar by global economic actors. The 'openness' of the public administration is seen as a low transaction cost, as a keeper of trust, and operability of private companies. The legal system of a polity becomes a regulatory environment, creating and maintaining market conditions (Valtioneuvoston kanslia 2006b, p. 92).

Political accountability is defined as responsiveness through results (Valtioneuvoston kanslia 2006b, p. 162), not as responsibility towards a constituency. Moreover, with reference to the political room to maneuver, there is a remark on the limited nature of national political initiatives. In pointing to the global harmonization of national regulatory frameworks, the sphere of effective national politics in economics is seen to be limited. The extent to which government is to draft its own regulations is also subsumed within competition. In other words, adopting the international regulations is proposed as a norm that should be abandoned only if the national regulation leads to competitive advantage (Valtioneuvoston kanslia 2006b, p. 110; cf. Majone 1997).

The above ideas travel to legal institutions. For instance, transparency and competitiveness appear in the Supreme Administrative Court's Annual Report of 2006, celebrating the 100th anniversary of universal and equal suffrage in Finland:

> In Finland last year was the 100th anniversary of universal and equal suffrage, i.e. of the basis of à democratic state ruled by law.

A functioning democracy requires access to justice, whereas transparency and broad participation are needed to create a common experience of justice. These are basic components of Finnish society, welfare and of competitiveness. (Supreme Administrative Court 2007, original English translation. Note: the Finnish version talks about openness, which is translated as transparency: Korkein hallinto-oikeus 2007, p.4)

As noted earlier, the above perception of market transparency has made its way onto the agenda, especially during the 2000s. In the late 1990s, the focus was on exploiting registry data for value-added digital services.

2.4.7   Public sector information as a commodity

In 1998, economic concerns were present in two different ways: as a general idea of transparency and as raw material for value-added digital services. In the late 1990s, during the drafting of the new information laws, there was a vocal a discourse on the new economy. The government bill of the 1999 access law refers to the European Union's policy work on information economy, noting that the proposed law might enhance economic activities in digital service provision.[58] In the interviews, the European Commission's Green Paper on Public Sector Information of 1998 was cited as a source of ideas that was included in the legislation (European Commission 1998 / COM(1998)585). This was described as a learning process.

> Q: As the economic interests have stepped in, was the 1990s discourse of information economy of relevance [when drafting the law]?
> A: Yes, when the EU's Green Paper on Public Sector Information came, we were humble students. A section of law was written on it. Nobody noticed it or wished to remove it. There it is [in the law]. (Legal expert)

This learning process and the Green Paper on Public Sector Information was also reflected in other interviews conducted for this study (see Chapter 4). The economic perspective on registry data was even more emphatic in the Personal Data Act. The Act has been criticized for being rather centered on the economic exploitation of registry data (cf. Korhonen 2003). Altogether, there has been a clear shift towards a new economic perception of registry data, personal data and census registries included (Korhonen 1997; Korhonen 2003; cf. Chapter 4). As one interviewee noted, the law on privacy (Personal Data Act) now also had a strong legitimating function for the commercialization of activities. The Act on the Publicity of Government Activities now acknowledged private sector exploitation of public data, based on 'good data management practices' (Pakarinen et al. 2002). Also the Personal Data Act was strongly influenced by the idea of the wider private use of data managed by the public administration.

Some interviewees acknowledged that there was firm pressure from the private sector to allow for the further economic exploitation of data. Also, though the EU initiatives at the time seem detached from Finnish politics, it is worth noting that the EU Commissioner in charge of the Green Paper and the directive (2003/98/EC) to follow was Finland's Erkki Liikanen. Yet the whole debate on public sector information can be fully understood only against the developments in financial steering. Though the interest in the economic exploitation of public sector information had grown since its digitalization, the policy problem was a result of the high pricing of public data, due to accrual charging and budget transparency. I examine the perceptions of registry information as a commodity in more detail in Chapter 4.

Even if the economic exploitation of public data is directly linked to economic competitiveness, apparent in an initiative such as the EU's Lisbon strategy of 2000, there has since been a shift towards a more abstract and macro-level assessment of the efficiency-enhancing aspects of the principle of publicity. The integration function (Konstari 1977) of the institution was realized to ease the shift to global governance and economic competition. Alongside this lessening of societal conflict, now understood as efficiency, access to information was also seen to make the state more attractive to private companies. Framed in economic terms in the sphere of general administrative reform already in the early 2000s, the legislative aspects first came under scrutiny in the mid-2000s.

Ironically, the radical idea of the 1970s – that publicity belongs to the sphere of economics – had become generally accepted in the late 1990s. Since then, the economic framing of the principle of publicity has become even more outspoken. This is most visible in the programs on 'better regulation' and 'public sector information' but has evolved in different domains of normative steering as well. Despite the emphasis on citizen rights, the historical concept of 'publicity', implying democratic control, is now complemented by a more vague notion of 'openness', and market-oriented notions of 'public sector information' and 'transparency'. I will next turn to the issue of parallel developments in financial steering.

2.5   Ideational changes in financial steering

In this section, I outline the key changes in the financial steering mechanisms of the Finnish public sector that are of relevance to public information. I discuss the commercialization of public sector information (PSI) against the NPM reforms conducted in Finland since the turn of the 1990s. Moving on to the work done among public hearings and ethics, I explore how openness has been reframed in cooperation with the OECD. I also explore the ideational shifts in the means of accountability from legal hierarchies and normative steering to accountability through performance favoring (budget) transparency. The OECD had an important influence in this.

NPM reforms and good governance doctrines have had a major impact on the industrialized countries (Christensen and Lægreid 2001; Sahlin-Andersson and Engwall 2002; Marcussen 2002; Peters et al. 2005, pp. 1292–6; Zanotti 2005; Shore 2006; Drechsler 2004; Seppänen 2003; Pollit et al. 1997; Lane 1997; Lane 2000). These reforms have taken different shapes in different national contexts (Pollitt and Bouckaert 2004), but they do have a common ideational root in reassessing the role of the state. The relation of NPM and the shifting strategies of public information management have been scarcely studied. The relation of performance and openness and transparency becomes of interest in terms of the role they play in public sector reform and new paradigms of performance management.

In the sphere of financial steering in Finland, the early 1990s recession not only set many reforms in motion but also set the course for further developments. The severe recession had caused a shift in power relations, making the Ministry of Finance more influential than ever (Temmes 1998, p. 443; Kantola 2002). While the actions taken amid the recession were not highly elaborated or planned, but rather an ad hoc repertoire of crisis management, the policies that followed have been more intentional. Moreover, they have been drafted in an environment, where the Ministry of Finance has a strong position in the overall design of steering.

2.5.1   Public sector information and New Public Management

As we have seen, the economic interest in the registry information of the state, now in full digital format, has been a policy issue since the mid-1990s. However, the whole dispute over 'public sector information' can be understood as a by-product of NPM and performance management, endorsing budget transparency. In the early 1990s the bureaus were given more autonomy in their finances (Pollitt et al. 1997; Temmes 1998; Tiihonen 1999), on which the law on accrual charges was issued. When Finland sank into economic recession shortly after, the bureaus were encouraged to find alternative sources of funding, and it was here that the new information services proved lucrative. The policy debate on the pricing of public sector information was a response to the increased charges on the data released by the state bureaus, now acting on a partially self-sufficient financial basis.

The change coincided and was partially caused by the adoption of new information technologies and the rise of the ideas on the so-called New Economy. This interplay framed public information as a key resource of production in the future information economy. Digital public information became the desired raw material of informational products and trading-good of value-added digital services (Koski et al. 2002, pp. 99–109). Altogether, 1998 has been seen as a juncture in information society policies, shifting towards globalized strategies where Finland was now seen as a forerunner and model country for others (Nevalainen 1999, p.18; cf. Pelkonen 2008). The Finnish information society strategy, published in 1998, calls for cooperation between the public and private sectors in order to exploit the economical potential of public information resources through commodification (SITRA 1998). The NPM reforms in Finland resulted in the commercialization of public information resources. This change came about as a result of a straightforward budgetary shift due to accrual charges, which in Finland was termed 'net-budgeting'.

One remedy for the shrinking budgets of government departments amid the economic recession was seen to be accrual-based charges about which an act was presented in 1992.[59] The user charges were also proposed or imposed on key departments in public data management, which started to compensate their budget cuts with profits from their own activities. The overall outcome of this single reform was not fully seen at the time, or it was not given much thought. The country was in grave economic difficulties and extra funding for public services was sought wherever possible and individual bureaus were given a clear message to charge for their service if only possible.

The commodification and commercialization of public information did not as such cause much public outcry. During the worst of the recession it went mostly unnoticed. The bureaus responsible for public information management started charging for the use of the information resources that they maintained. The interviewees considered this to have been the unintended consequences of policies adopted to counter the economic recession. The problems of this activity came to the sur-face in the mid-to-late 1990s, due to the digitalization of these informa-tion resources and the rising 'New Economy' and 'Information Society' debates, marking increased interest in knowledge-based services of state and other service providers wishing to use public information (cf. Valtiovarainministeriö 2003b). Non-commercial actors, such as the aca-demic community, were also interested in utilizing public information for their work. But public information proved to be an expensive com-modity. The pricing of public information first became a policy issue when private companies who wanted to use public data complained about its high price. The debate, ongoing for some 15 years, had again become topical during the time I conducted my fieldwork, discussed in detail in Chapter 4.

2.5.2   Macroeconomics of openness in public hearings

The beginning of the 1990s is seen in the interviews as a critical junc-ture in Finnish public administration. The perceived stagnation before it was contrasted with rapid changes after the collapse of the Soviet Union and the economic recession of the 1990s and the opening of financial markets. As one respondent stated, the public sector that had been grown with domestic knowledge was now to be cut and reformed. To accomplish this, international influences and management ideas were seen indispensable. The source of this ideational feed was twofold: the OECD and the domestic private sector knowledge centers on service quality as well as external consultants. Work on the public hearings was more inclined to international peers in seeking new policy solutions and assessing the existing practices. Previous assessments of the Finnish NPM have seen it as having been led by senior civil servants, rather than politicians (Temmes 1998, p. 443). The same ideational domin-ance was echoed in the accounts on the reframing of openness.

Concerning new perceptions of public hearings and citizen govern-ment relations, a new belief system was communicated among the members of a wider international network of policy actors, perhaps best understood as an epistemic community (Haas 1992) or discursive policy community (Schmidt 2002). As for other potential sources of ideational feed, in the realm of public sector reform, the OECD was seen of greater importance than the EU. While the EU was perceived as a forum for daily routines, the OECD and World Bank were named as potential sources of ideational feed (cf. Marcussen 2002). Yet even if circulating through the international policy community, the ideational core of these policies can be traced back to the new social scientific debates on governance and, more importantly, to new ideas of information economy.

The previous debates on NPM and the quality of services brought a process view to the managerialistic input-output models of productivity. This favored such things as standards, auditing, benchmarking for the evaluation of public services and their productivity (Hautamäki and Mäkipeska 1994, pp. 36–38). It is worth noting that in the early 1990s the NPM doctrine, discussed under the theme of service quality, did not as such concern the general openness of the administration. One could see this as a new shift in administrative thinking, where openness and efficiency were now merging due to the perceived causality between these two.

In the general public sector reform work in Finland, the administrative openness made its way onto the agenda in the mid-1990s. The background for this was the perceived lack of citizen trust in ministries and government, later confirmed by an opinion survey (Harisalo and Stenvall 2001). The Ministry of Finance, responsible for governance reform in Finland, had first raised the issue in its work on administrative ethics, but the theme also became topical in the general administrative reform, expressed in the Decision in Principle of the Council of State on quality services, good governance and responsible civil society in April 1998 (Valtiovarainministeriö 1998). This was followed by a specific project on public hearings launched in 2000 (Valtiovarainministeriö 2000).

The concept of good governance has been pervasive in the jargon of internationalizing governance of the last two decades or so. The origins of the concept can be found in the Development Economics of the World Bank and other international finance institutions (Drechsler 2004, p. 389; Tiihonen 2004). The concept later spread from the context of development economics to wider use and has since become a concept of responsible rule in international and national levels of governance alike. Good governance defines the key concepts for administrative virtues and responsibilities. The actual virtues often carry market liberalistic connotations and can be linked with the NPM doctrines (Drechsler 2004; Zanotti 2005, p. 468). In particular, the concepts of accountability and transparency have been present in all codifications of good governance. The work of the OECD on the topic can be linked to this development.

In the OECD, the issue had arisen around 1998–1999 and has been present in the work done in the PUMA Working Group on Strengthening Government-Citizen Connections (1999–2002) and the Expert Group on Government Relations with Citizens and Civil Society (2001–2002) and, later, in the Public Governance Committee's project on Open and Inclusive Policy-making (OECD 1999; OECD 2001a; OECD 2001b; OECD 2005a; OECD 2005b; see also OECD 2003a). Concerned with what was perceived to be a general decline in trust in government, the initiative highlighted restoring citizen trust (see also OECD 2000). The use of emerging digital technologies was also a concern. Though the general rhetoric of trust has remained, there has been a shift towards a more comprehensive understanding of the economic potential of the institution.

In Finnish public administration the issue of openness made its way onto the agenda of public administration reform as a general way of organizing public administration, while in the sphere of public sector reform this was so particularly in relation to public hearings. Here, OECD meetings offered a site for country comparisons and exchange for ideas and practices, a site for learning (Marcussen 2002). When assessing the means available to the OECD for influencing national politics, attention is drawn to the informal nature of the organization: how can an organization that imposes no rules or policy directives on its member states influence their national politics? According to Marcussen, the OECD functions as a deliberative forum for the administrative elite of different countries, bearing similarities to a think tank rather than a decision-making forum proper (Marcussen 2002). This allows ideas to be exchanged and diffused among the members and member states of the OECD. This was also the case regarding openness of public administration.

> In the OECD the point of departure [for work on openness] was that because it is an organization for economic cooperation it was seen that those countries, such as Finland, in which publicity laws and administration are more open, were also more successful economically. In other words, there appeared to be a link between administrative openness and the economy [...] This is one reason why the Ministry of Finance is involved [in this]. Businesses, in addition to citizens, fare better in the sort of environment where they receive reliable information that is as timeous as possible. And [an environment] in which information is used as much as possible when consulting citizens, interest groups and businesses. There is this sort of economic aspect in this. This was the start, this sort of macroeconomic perspective. (Civil servant, Ministry of Finance)

In Finland, no publication on the topic was produced, though some internal memos were written. The issue had risen already within the ranks of the ministry, but the sharing of experiences and ideas in the OECD meetings played an important role in gaining further insight on the matter. Also, information attained through a Finnish senior civil servant visiting the World Bank in Washington was said to have given a new perspective on public governance. The issue was addressed by the Ministry of Finance in a 2001 publication on the matter, noting that the national competitiveness would also benefit from public hearings (Valtiovarainministeriö 2001, pp. 5–6). The issues of openness and public hearings became part of projects concerning quality and productivity. The Finnish perspective marked a point of difference to the work in the OECD, where the issue was seen in varying societal contexts. In the interviews this is largely seen to have resulted from different administrative traditions regarding the issue of openness: Finland had had a law on publicity of government information since the 1950s, whereas many other OECD countries did not have such legislation.

When we consider the OECD meetings as forums for exchanging ideas on governance, the Nordic model of openness was seen to have gained interest among the participants of the meetings. In this sense the small and open countries were able to promote or up-load their administrative models or ideas to the OECD agenda. The adoption of these ideas was seen to require a new frame of mind, where the causalities between openness and efficiency had to be rethought. This gives 'transparency' a mirror-like quality, perceived either as democratic or efficient, while both conceptualizations would be potentially available. The context of the OECD, where different national traditions of governance were compared and assessed (cf. OECD 1999), allowed participants to see through to the other side. It could be possible to enhance economic efficiency through democracy, or at least openness.

Q: Is this more a broadly politicized or societal question in other OECD countries?
A: No, or maybe to the extent that they have had to get the 'ahaa' experience that is something sensible from the angle of their success. It's been so that in them openness is not seen as a factor of competitiveness. Rather the opposite, in that if they are very open then it won't benefit them but will entail problems and burdens on the administrative machinery. [...] In the OECD those who carry out this work saw a correlation that in successful countries, such as Finland, there has long been a law on publicity. (Civil servant, Ministry of Finance)

This resembles the ideas of scholars of information economics, widely publicized at the time, which pointed to the virtuous relations of open and deliberative processes in contrast to secrecy (Stiglitz 1998). In this macroeconomic model the notion of consensus is promoted as an economic virtue, alongside its democratic qualities (ibid., p. 19). In the literature on international political economy, consensus and institutional openness have become part of the new market architecture built on transparency (Best 2005, p. 57). From the perspective of accountability, this opens up an interesting viewpoint. Bearing in mind the dichotomy between democracy and efficiency, and the general idea of performance and deliberation as reflections of this dichotomy, the above extract amalgamates ideationally these two, as openness and public deliberation become sources of performance and economic competitiveness. They both meet in the notions of openness and transparency. The above remarks also point to the actors involved in the process. The OECD provided an arena of comparison and institutional learning. The people working with the new ideas of transparency were seen as mentors in this process, where the participants of the OECD meetings were given the tools to see through to the other side: openness was not a hindrance to efficiency – on the contrary, it was an efficient and economically sound strategy to pursue.

Yet also, the role of the long 'tradition' of openness was seen as an asset. Since access to government documents was no novelty in Finland, and information was generally made available, openness and transparency caused minimal pressure on the public administration. Unlike in countries that were just opening up their bureaucracies, the Finnish system, from the point of view of civil servants, handles these pressures well, albeit due to other features of administrative culture, such as the consensus. The consensual practices concerning openness were also addressed in a Swedish account on the openness of the public administration, claiming that one can keep the curtains open as long as no one is looking (Larsson 1998). Here, the contextual perception of minimal conflict and integrative tendencies of openness emerged as a praised quality.

In its 2003 report on international investment perspectives, the OECD refers to a 'developing consensus among OECD countries and beyond' that the transparency of public institutions enhances public sector performance and enables countries to draw in foreign investments (OECD 2003b, 135, pp. 139–43). Linking transparency with economic performance and public sector efficiency, the democratic root of this institution becomes blurred or at least somewhat disregarded. The

OECD report points to transparency as the new architecture for organizing global trade and financial markets. The report also addresses the need for reform at national level throughout the OECD community and its potential obstacles (OECD 2003b, pp. 153–4).

Assessing the strengths' and qualities that make for economic advantages in a given setting is difficult and not always possible to predict. The question of how certain countries historically arrive at an economically more favorable position than others is also a matter of historical institutionalism, where path dependencies and differing historical trajectories matter a great deal (North 2005). However, institutions are highly dependent on endogenous factors (Przeworski 2004). In this sense it might prove to be difficult, if not impossible, to adopt institutional practices such as access laws to a new context and expect them to work exactly the way they have worked in another context with a significantly different institutional history.

Also policy discourses are highly dependent on the institutional context. The new discourse of transparency diffusing in OECD circles was easy to adopt by the Finnish policy experts because it resonated with the existing institutional design and concepts. Communicating this to other policy actors domestically was uncomplicated because it did not mean a complete rethinking of the administrative culture. Finally, the existing political concepts and narratives of state favored communicating and legitimizing these new policies to the general public.

This was also said to have been addressed in OECD meetings with reference to the UK. The British representatives were skeptical about granting access to government information, fearing it would result in a massive public demand for documents. This was not unfounded since when the Freedom of Information Act came into force in 2005 in the UK, the pressure for accessing documents was in fact very high (James 2006, p. 19).[60] Here again, it was not only the long awaited opening of the bureaucracy that exacerbated pressures but also several other factors, such as a vigorous media culture, are likely to matter a great deal in the public 'use' of the institution. This, and the Finnish experiences alike, shows the highly contextual nature of openness.

Even if the new economic reductionism of the institution would not be all encompassing, so that the policy measures would be a single-sighted aim for economic gains only, it is still worth asking, what the reforms strive for. Are they primarily to enhance economic competitiveness or democracy, or both, equally? At present, the macroeconomic perceptions of public hearings or the institutional openness dismiss several institutional conditions related to public empowerment. It might not be that straightforward to create a system that empowers both citizens and managers (Pierre and Peters 2000). Internationally, the big policy discourses of trust, social cohesion and social capital related to the debate on public hearings tend to have dismissed the institutional developments that have gone along with it (Berman 1997; Somers 2005).

Similar remarks can be made about the perception of accountability in organizing public hearings (cf. Bovens 2005). If citizens are empowered to enhance national economic competitiveness, then are civil servants still accountable to these very same citizens, or private entrepreneurs choosing a place for their functions, or international organizations making the assessments of the national competitiveness? The above questions have been barely addressed in the new guidelines and principles on public hearings in Finland (Valtiovarainministeriö 2005a; Valtiovarainministeriö 2005b). Also, the economic perceptions emphasized in the interviews have gained limited attention in the public documents. Openness is defined as equal access to information and, together with public hearings, as an 'essential part of democracy' (Valtiovarainministeriö 2005b). When discussed as citizen empowerment, openness and public hearings become a logical part of deliberative democracy. But the new economic frame, outlined above, leaves room for an alternative interpretation. At first glance this is unproblematic, but when seeking to answer the three core questions of accountability – to whom, for what and how the public service is accountable – the problems become visible.

While previous literature on accountability perceives deliberation as a counterforce to performance, these are merging in the current thinking among practitioners. Deliberation is no longer a counterbalance to the performance-seeking policies favored by the NPM. On the contrary, it is becoming a logical part of it. At least on the aggregate level, the deliberation is now being reframed in economic terms, also. Alongside this reframing, the perception of accountability is changing. Particularly, the notion of 'accountable for what?' is shifting from the democratic process to performance. As the administrative process, and public hearings as a quality enhancing part of it, is now understood in terms of performance, the civil service, while deliberating within it, is responsible for the outcome and not the process itself. Also, the query 'accountable to whom?' is in a state of flux.

2.5.3   Administrative ethics

In addition to public hearings, openness as an ethical norm became topical in Finland alongside the work done in the OECD. In the OECD context, the topic of administrative ethics, covering also inclusive and open governance, became topical in the mid-1990s. The OECD's Public Management Committee (PUMA), actively promoting New Public Management (NPM) in the late 1980s and early 1990s, regarded the work on administrative ethics of the OECD as the continuum of its work on managerial administrative reform – 'ethics' became the 'fourth e' after economy, efficiency and effectiveness (OECD 1996, p. 60).

This outlines the importance of ethics in maintaining public trust and building the legitimacy of rule, notions which embodied the work done within the organization in the 2000s. Moreover, NPM has had a negative influence on the ethical infrastructure of public administration, public values and sense of responsibility, which has also led to corrupt behavior, or, at least, made the government more prone to corruption (Maesschalck 2004; von Maravic 2007). The OECD names this denting of public accountability as an 'unintentional impact' of the NPM (OECD 1996, p. 24; OECD 2000; cf. Oulasvirta 1993, p. 3). The citation on the 'fourth e' points to the potential of ethics infrastructure as an instrument of productivity and economic efficiency.

In Finland, work on administrative ethics had become topical in the 1990s (Oulasvirta 1993; Moilanen 1999). It first proceeded domestically but then extended to international cooperation. International networks of expertise were found in the OECD and the Council of Europe's Group of States against Corruption (GRECO). A key document in the domain of Public Sector ethics in Finland was a 2001 Decision in Principle of the Council of State on human resources in public service (Valtiovarainministeriö 2001). Preceded by a 1997 Decision in Principle on the selection criteria of the higher civil servants, the 2001 Decision in Principle listed the following values: effectiveness and quality of activities, strong expertise, service orientation, openness, trust, equality, impartiality, autonomy and responsiveness. These reflected traditional values and newer, NPM-led values. Compared to the 1997 selection of core values, the emphasis on effectiveness, quality and expertise appear as novelties. Altogether, the general aim of the 2001 Decision in Principle is to enhance the competitiveness of public service and state (Valtiovarainministeriö 2001, p. 26).

The Decision in Principle on human resources in public service, stresses the new economic pressures where the state is operating, the need for attaining personnel (that is, being competitive in the job market) and remaining competitive in the global economy. Openness acquires two slightly different nuances. It is understood as an inter-organizational cultural feature, open and deliberative management, or as an administrative principle enforced by law, 'principle of publicity' (Valtiovarainministeriö 2001, p. 27). Though openness is merely a value among others, it is again being drawn to a debate on national competitiveness. The principle decision states that the 'public service values build on the democratic rule of law and on the Nordic welfare state model.' Yet, the outcomes of the strategy are single-handedly assessed in terms of competitiveness, effectiveness and efficiency (Valtiovarainministeriö 2001, pp. 26, 34–5). Democracy and the rule of law are the means for achieving these and are not goals themselves.

In the handbook that followed, openness, perceived as a traditional public service value, was defined according to the 'principle of publicity' and government-citizen relations; as an information need of the citizen (Valtiovarainministeriö 2005c, p. 9; cf. Valtiovarainministeriö 2004). The legalistic terminology emphasizes the public's ability to control the public service. Similar views were presented in the interviews, with reference to historical Nordic traditions now accommodating the new policy program.

In the new codifications of administrative ethics in Finland, responsibility has been defined as bureaucratic accountability, based on law and administrative hierarchy (Valtiovarainministeriö 2005c, p. 15). It is acknowledged, though, that 'in practice, performance is [an] ever more important form of responsibility' (ibid., p. 15). A proposed mechanism for this is performance management, the assessment and evaluation of results. The rhetoric emphasizes the legalistic notions of traditional bureaucratic accountability, but looking at the big picture the civil service is seen as being accountable for its performance. As already stated, this poses a shift on the part of the accountee (Bovens 2005), whether the general public or an external accountability forum of another kind. The above policies on budget transparency (accrual charging), public hearings and administrative ethics do not make up a coherent picture at first glance, though recently they have become more weighty components of the general framework of performance management.

2.5.4   Transparency and indicators in performance management

While the NPM reforms of the 1990s shaped the Finnish public sector remarkably, shifting the focus of responsibility of public bureaus towards responsibility through performance, a second wave of reform followed in the early 2000s. The issue of performance management can thus be separated into two phases, although these form a continuum. The first, in the 1990s, was characterized as managerialistic and based on NPM doctrines and work on quality, while the second contained elements of 'good governance' and 'corporate governance' together with ethical and social connotations.

In the early 1990s, the Finnish NPM reforms were carried out in a managerialistic manner, loosening the hierarchical steering of public bureaus. The reforms of the 1990s had brought about a decline in legal steering, where agencies were given strict normative rules about how to conduct their activities. This was changed together with the regulation of the spending of bureaus. Before, the budgetary funds were divided into particular moments that were keenly followed. This was reformed in the early 1990s, when the agencies were given significant budgetary autonomy. Internationally, the managerialistic reforms tended to make the heads of agencies accountable for the performance of their bureaus through performance contracts (Behn 2001, pp. 23–125). In Finland, the bureaus themselves, rather than managers, were made responsible for their performance (cf. Pollitt et al. 1997, p. 6).

The work on quality and the outcome of governance was tightly linked to shifting ideas of administrative responsibilities. The new term in this debate was 'accountability' (*tilivelvollisuus*), which marked a shift in the perspective of bureaucratic responsibilities, now naming responsibility for results as a new type of responsibility (Summa 1993, p. 5). It is worth noting, that the term 'accountability' is a newcomer to both Finnish vocabulary and European administrative vocabulary (cf. Harlow 2002). In Finland, it has thus far rather carried the connotations of accounting (cf. Meklin and Näsi 1994, p. 232; Myllymäki and Vakkuri 2001).

Initially, the market type mechanisms (accrual charging) and performance management were seen as two separate entities (cf. Meklin and Näsi 1994, p. 36). In Finland, these two 'models of financial steering' were separated until the early-to-mid 2000s. This separation was addressed as an underdeveloped aspect of Finnish budgeting by the OECD (OECD 1997, pp. 60–61; OECD 2002b, p. 22; see also Bouckaert et al. 2000, p. 37). Evolving from the early forms of net-based budgeting and accrual charging and from the use of performance targets thus far, the new accountability reform, started in 2004, aimed at bringing a shift towards central steering and political control. This ideational shift coincided with the trend of increasing the use of evaluation in studying 'effectiveness' of policies (Rajavaara 2007). The means for control were less based on bureaucratic hierarchies or law but on information steering (Pöysti 1999), where information on the performance of ministries and agencies was the means of control. Even though this can be seen as an attempt at revising the managerialistic shift of the 1990s, the mechanism for control remained the performance of the bureaus.

The fact that the bureaus were given vast autonomy in their use of resources had a mixed reception. One interviewee pointed to an apparent contradiction between the democratic control of bureaus and the trend of the 1990s by saying that parliament in particular was deprived of significant power since it no longer decided on how the resources were used. This was seen as being important to the politicians who had to demonstrate results to the electorate. Without being able to point out how resources were allocated due to their particular actions they were said to have lacked the means of convincing their constituency that they indeed had done a good job. The official documents of the Finnish government and the OECD refer to the weak link between the market mechanisms and performance information becoming a policy problem with regard to the role of the Finnish parliament (OECD 2002b; Valtiovarainministeriö 2003a).

It is worth noting, though, that the linking of performance management information and the actual process of budgeting is the ultimate goal of performance management thinking (Peters 2008, p. 8). Thus the second phase of the accountability reforms was initiated with the support of parliament that wished to have more say on how the budgetary resources were actually used, leading to a process in which a new model for budgetary planning was adopted (Valtiovarainministeriö 2003a; Valtiovarainministeriö 2005d; Valtiovarainministeriö 2006a). This also brought the concept of 'accountability' into the everyday vernacular of the Finnish public administration (Valtiovarainministeriö 2003a). As mentioned, the concept was used by some practitioners and academics already in the mid-1990s (Summa 1993; Meklin and Näsi 1994), but it first became institutionalized in the early 2000s (Valtiovarainministeriö 2003a; Ministry of Finance 2006; cf. Rajavaara 2007).

The process of adoption, again, saw a parallel work in the OECD. An OECD peer review provided ideational input on the possible aspects to address in the reform (OECD 2002b). The OECD document states in its conclusions that the further integration of the results information and financial accounts is necessary and that a more uniform reporting framework would have advantages to the present one (OECD 2002b, p. 25). Whether these guidelines were followed, or whether they merely echoed the ideas of domestic actors in Finland, is not apparent. Nevertheless, the peer review validates the policy choices adopted. The method not only provides new ideas but also strikes accordance with the shared notions of validity (Haas 1992, p. 16). The method of the peer review also implies expert accountability. Following the peer review and the domestic preparatory work an International Public Sector Accounting Standard (IPSAS) was adopted for Finland.

The adopted model was visualized as a triangular figure that in the everyday jargon of the civil service was called the 'outcome prism' or 'performance prism' (see Figure 2.3). The optical connotations of the term 'prism' tie it to the notion of transparency, which is the core model. Accountability, forming the one side of the triangle, is weighted against the operational performance targets, which makes the 'account-giving' an element of performance management. The model was implemented with very little legal adjustments. Instead, the logic functions on the concept of 'true and fair information' that the ministries and the agencies underneath them are supposed to produce on their activities (Ministry of Finance 2006, p. 32). This new measure of 'budget transparency' added an addendum to the perception of institutional openness, now referring to the standardized stream of performance information, preferably in numerical form (cf. Blomgren and Sahlin 2007).

What the ministries and agencies are accountable for in the new model is their policy effectiveness. This is measured against their operational results. Also under scrutiny are the operations and finances that were supposed to have affected the policy effectiveness. Actual performance management is done through outcome targets and operational performance targets. The model rests largely on performance

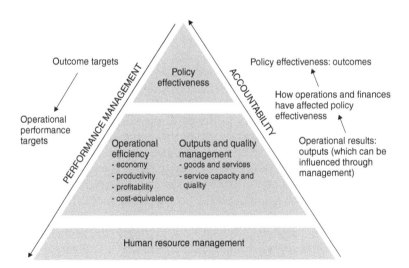

Figure 2.3   Basic performance criteria: true and fair information
Source: Ministry of Finance[61]

measurement. The logical parts of the model are presented in Figure 2.3. At the heart of the model is the provision of true and fair information, which is supposed to achieve a holistic picture of activities, and set goals and their attainment.

The budget transparency and the performance information that the model circulates are not the only links to the general discourse on openness. The model also covers public hearings as a part of the goal setting and operational efficiency and the emphasis of openness in human resources. They also become logical parts of the greater scheme of performance management and accountability through results. Because the model does not replace accrual charging but instead builds on it, the commercialization of public sector information is firmly part of the emerging practice, desired or not. Moreover, the new emphasis on numerical information and indicators – transparency in numbers – may have unintended consequences on the information strategies of bureaus. I will discuss these later in Chapters 4 and 5.

The new performance prism reduces governance to an input-output model that consists of the logical components of input, process, output, effect or outcome. The model differentiates efficiency (productivity) and effectiveness (impact or effects of outcomes). The process becomes the engine for efficiency, but in order to reach desired results (outcomes) the performance has to be managed through performance goals and measurements of their achieving. The performance measurement thus requires the quantification of the operational results. The information created in the new system is often (though not necessarily) quantitative indicator data. Here again, a new international trend of using indicators has gained attention, and a memo on the (global) use of indicators was produced in 2005 (Valtiovarainministeriö 2005e). The use of indicators was seen as a potential means for the quantification of operational activities in the performance prism. The issue of national competitiveness was a focus of the report, which also referred to the Finnish rankings in the international country comparisons on economic competitiveness (Valtiovarainministeriö 2005e, pp. 21–3).

Though the issue of performance management may seem like an alien addendum to Nordic openness, it has become an item of this tradition. Some interviewees treated it as part of this transforming model, but so have Finnish civil servants, who have endorsed this view in their international appearances, where the Finnish principle of publicity is seen as a foundation of the newly adopted performance management system (Valtiontalouden tarkastusvirasto 2007), which, at its core, is a public sector adaptation of the corporate accounting standard.

The above example basically describes the shift in the understanding of the principle of publicity that is at hand. Understood as active communication of result information, it shifts the perception of the access to information, now making citizens and parliament entitled to performance information of public bureaus – a position analogous to that of shareholders in markets. In terms of access to information and accountability, the emphasis is now on the outcome and not on the process. The actual process of governance, in the views discussed above, is merely an item in the input-output model: 'what' is achieved (outcome) has priority over 'how' it is being achieved (process).

During the 2006 Finnish EU presidency, Finland promoted its new performance management system in the EU context (see Ministry of Finance 2006). Also, the Better Regulation Programme was on the Finnish agenda (Valtioneuvoston kanslia 2006b). Thematically, the EU presidency held transparency as a key quality of Finnish governance that the European Union should also adopt (see above). The performance management system and Better Regulation Programme are apparently new ideas and their adoption in Finnish contexts was influenced by the OECD. Finland's high rankings in new governance indices, such as the Corruption Perception Index of Transparency International, also raise awareness of the Finnish tradition of institutional openness. The new ideas are not only of relevance in Finland but also internationally, as the Finnish system of performance management is presented abroad. Here, too, the policy discourse of Nordic openness carries the new ideas.

The production of performance information is often related with organizations' attempts to legitimize the activities of the organization. The functions of performance management for organizations tend to be culturally shaped, ritualistic and multifaceted, and the whole activity is therefore prone to unintended consequences (Hopwood and Miller 1994; Power 1999; Vakkuri 2001, p. 187; Hummel 2006, p. 75). These problems are apparent in the organizational cases, explored in Chapters 4 and 5.

2.6 Conclusions

The contemporary international interest in the topic of transparency has increased interest in the publicity of government in Finland, thereby making it a policy concern. This has also allowed the re-description of the institution: openness and transparency are now valued for their economic potential. Even though the concept of openness emerges in a discourse on Nordic openness it is nevertheless a novelty in the rhetoric of the Finnish governments. The policy discourse of Nordic openness is a contextual variant of the international discourse on transparency, and now emphasizes effectiveness through collaborative governance and efficiency through public information on performance. The conceptual shift from 'publicity' to 'openness' has introduced economic connotations to government vocabulary. 'Transparency' gives a name to the new ideas of enhanced (economic) performance through public scrutiny.

Consequently, the openness of government activities has become part of a new political imaginary of national competitiveness. There is a perceptible reassessment in the responsibilities of the government, marking a new ideational cycle (Marcussen 2000): Finnish governments now are increasingly responsible to market actors through openness and transparency. Though the democratic connotations of openness would intuitively imply greater government responsibility towards the citizens, the emergence of this discourse coincides with mounting demands for the citizens, now (jointly) responsible for their own wellbeing and Finland's competitiveness in an open economy. This is an indication of the change taking place in the accountability system, which now stresses performance over accountability through results.

Comparing the programmatic and policy-relevant government texts with the public speeches of politicians, one can identify cognitive and normative aspects in the discourse of openness that are in dissonance (Schmidt 2002), though economic aspects are also slowly entering the normative talk on Nordic openness. This is part of the new European identity of the Finns. The historical aspects are also prominently present in the coordinative discourse shared by policy actors.

There are observable ideational shifts in steering mechanisms. These shifts are also marked by conceptual changes concerning the economic connotations of transparency. New liberalistic emphases on access to information and privacy as citizen rights have also become more vocalized. The previous legislative history was stagnant, with minor reforms and little public debate on the ethical foundations of the institution. The politicization of the issue in the 1970s apart, access to government information has not been a domain of explicit social conflict.

Yet, there has been an *ongoing negotiation* of the institution over the years, which hastened in the last decade (cf. Thelen 2004, p. 35). This occurred after the juncture in Finnish governance when the country was shifting to a new governance environment, in which new concerns for global markets and digital government emerged. What is remarkable, still, is the shift in social tensions around the institution: the radical ideas of the 1970s were widely accepted in the late 1990s. The consensus over these ideas partially resulted from the general social atmosphere and the internationalization of governance, where consensus and the circulation of information in society were seen in new terms. Broadly speaking, the change was part of the new ideational cycle in government responsibility. The opposition of the economic actors was seen to have lessened and even shifted: access to government information had become an issue of economic importance.

Also, international attention on the issue of openness, economic exploitation of public sector information and transparency have influenced the Finnish policies, apparent in the keen referencing to 'lessons from abroad' in government bills, the narratives of civil servants and in policy documents. The aspirations for performance and economic gains, debated under several policy programs since the late 1990s, have been more tightly coupled with the access to government information. The coordinative policy discourse of Nordic openness has allowed the general understanding of this ideational shift to be communicated, debated and agreed upon by the policy actors. The communicative aspects of the discourse of Nordic openness are normatively appealing, highlighting institutional openness as a tradition of Finnish governance.

But this tradition is now changing through the policy recasting of the late 1990s and early 2000s. The Nordic roots of related administrative practices are partially dissolving, with influences now adopted from the EU, OECD and country comparisons. There are ideational addendums to the principle of publicity, such as openness as strategic communication, public information as a commodity, public hearings as effective governance and provision of public performance information. Furthermore, the narrative on openness as a tradition of Finnish governance not only accommodates the new policy ideas, but also allows their promoting internationally.

Though access to government information is still valued for controlling government and as an institution for conflict resolution (control and integration functions), the new coordinative discourse of openness has spread an awareness among the policy actors that access to information also has an economic function. This economic reframing builds on the ideas of market transparency, good governance and knowledge economy, where well performing institutions, citizen trust and reuse of information are now seen as components of national economic advantage.

I will next look at the institutional developments that have occurred alongside the ideational changes discussed in this chapter. First, I will describe the general institutional developments in accessing state information in Finland, pointing to the firm democratic core of these institutional practices, but also an emergence of new institutional elements.

3
Transparency and Institutions of Public Accountability

3.1 Introduction

The ideational changes discussed in the previous chapter have implications for institutional developments. This chapter discusses ideationally induced changes in institutions of public accountability (for the term see Bovens 2005) – that is, changes in the judiciary system on accessing government information and protecting privacy, the development of communication and information services, and performance management, a novelty in the institutions of public accountability. These developments reflect the shifting ideas of central steering (see Chapter 2), now stressing citizen information rights owing to the international debate on freedom of information as 'a right to know'. On the other hand, there are new initiatives on budget transparency that view the publicity of government activities as a measurable element of performance. The verbose public debate on Nordic openness is also reflected in the increasing activity of citizens and the civil service around the issue.

Information rights, like any other citizen rights, become effective through public mediation (Somers 1993). In light of the statistics presented below there seems to be a very low level of conflict in accessing information in Finland. But as a result of the public debate on the institution and the legislation adopted in the late 1990s there was a 'recalibration' (Thelen 2004) of citizen information rights, visible on the number of cases reported in the judiciary system. Institutional developments point to increased citizen activity in challenging the public service on accessing government information and maintaining privacy. On a general level, the policy discourse of openness and the legislative work seem to have strengthened the idea of access to information and privacy as citizen rights. In particular, privacy issues have become more pressing since the turn of the 2000s.

With regards to active communication, the public administration is at present producing abundant public information on its activities. There is, however, also a recasting of the institutional practices towards performance management. In the spirit of transparency, the civil service is also producing a new kind of performative information about itself and conceptualizing its activities in market terms. Therefore, while the communicative discourse of openness has increased citizens' awareness of their rights, the new performance ideas that are present in the coordinative discourse are reflected in the changing means of central steering and communication (cf. Schmidt 2002), causing institutional 'layering', a growth of new institutional practices on the edges of old ones (Streeck and Thelen 2005, p. 31). In terms of accountability, there is an observable shift towards accountability through outcomes focused on results. The policy discourse of Nordic openness seems to have a dual role in the institutional changes. The debate has stimulated an interest in citizen rights but on the other hand it has downplayed certain addendums to the Nordic administrative tradition, and even departures from it.

3.1.1   Rediscovering citizen rights: developments in the judiciary system

According to Thelen, institutions are constantly being renegotiated by political actors, leading also to their recalibration (Thelen 2004, pp. 34–35). However, this can be heightened in times of crisis or during other formative moments, where institutions receive particular attention. As has been argued so far, openness of public administration became a subject of political debate in Finland in the mid-1990s. The debate on openness focused public attention on the related democratic institutions. Altogether, as the debate has drawn on the Anglo-American discourse on 'right to know' and 'freedom of information', it is likely to have influenced the understanding of the principle of publicity, framing it more as a citizen right. Moreover, public mediation of the information rights and institutions safeguarding them has also had institutional effects, as the citizens and media have become more active in appealing to these.

In the Finnish judiciary system, appeals regarding denied access to public information are filed with the Supreme Administrative Court. The rulings of the Supreme Administrative Court under the previous law of 1951 were of particular significance as they created precedents that shaped the practices of administrative openness. Looking at the

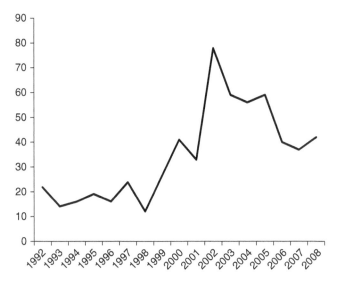

Figure 3.1   Number of appeals addressed to the Supreme Administrative Court regarding access to information, 1992–2008

number of appeals from 1992 to 2008, we see that the complaints are small in number (Figure 3.1). The overall small number of complaints, perhaps more than anything, points to the fact that the legislation is working and that access to information is a 'no issue' in Finland.

However, there is an apparent rising trend in the complaints filed with the Supreme Administrative Court since the 1999 act, which points to the increased interest in the issue and awareness of the exist-ence of the 'right to information'. The overall publicity that the issue of openness has received in Finland since the late 1990s has undoubtedly cumulated in court cases on situations where information has not been surrendered by the public institutions. But as the number of complaints is small, reaching a peak in 2002 (78 complaints), even the follow-up studies (see later) and occasional efforts by journalists who make a com-plaint in order to probe the new law, have an impact (see, for example, Hynninen et al. 2001).

We could also see this as the result of the communicative discourse of openness that has increased awareness of the right of access to gov-ernment documents (Schmidt 2002). All in all, use of rights requires existing public mediation of the related institutions (cf. Somers 1993). This is most apparent in the case of the Finnish Ombudsman, who has

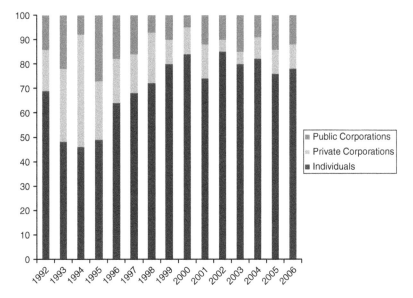

Figure 3.2   Supreme Administrative Court's cases regarding access to information by appellants (in percentage), 1992–2006[1]

received an ever-increasing number of complaints since the rise of this institution's public profile in the 1980s (Erkkilä 2008). Thus, the talk of Nordic openness and the media attention to the revisions to the Act on the Publicity of Government Activities and Personal Data Act have increased the use and functionality of the 'principle of publicity' as well as the appeals on 'privacy'.

When we look at who issues these complaints (Figure 3.2), we see that there has been a slight shift towards private persons and journalists – the category of Individuals – whereas the figure for Private Corporations, that is private companies and associations, has been declining slightly. The appeals made by Public Corporations, meaning bodies of public authority, have also diminished slightly. Although the changes are fairly minor, we could interpret these figures as indicating a slight shift towards the perception of the principle of publicity as a right exercised by individuals, allowing one to appeal to the Supreme Administrative Court, when information has not been given.

When it passed the 1999 Act on the Publicity of Government Activities, the Finnish parliament required that there be a follow-up study conducted on the functioning of the law. In the interviews conducted for this study, the experts generally estimated that the new legislation was working rather well. The previous law of 1951 was perceived as complex and difficult to apply (Wallin and Konstari 2000, p. 74). One legal expert estimated that no more than five people in the country knew all the exemptions in the previous law.

As mentioned, the follow-up studies on the new law indicated that it was working rather well. These studies mainly concentrated on the potential conflicts in the use and interpretations of the law, such as the numbers and types of complaints made to the Supreme Administrative Court and concerning its rulings (Konstari et al. 2003; Salovaara and Tala 2003). At the time there was also academic research on the topic, pointing to problems in the handling of EU-related documents in local administration and the possibilities of journalists to use the law (Hynninen 2000). A separate study on civil servants' actual knowledge of the law and their ability to use it was conducted, revealing a lack of knowledge on the details of the law in several sectors (Hynninen et al. 2001). The journalistic control function of the law was also probed in follow-up studies, which revealed no major problems (Mörä and Tarkiainen 2003). The journalists surveyed remained undecided about whether the law had brought about a significant increase in the openness of government activities.[2]

On asking the legal overseers, the Finnish Parliamentary Ombudsman reported that in 2000–2006 there were 69 cases concerning the right to access information. When we consider that the annual caseload of the Ombudsman in recent years has been about 3,000–4,000 complaints (in 2007 there were 3,857 complaints), the figure is low. The number of cases concerning privacy was also low, amounting to 80 cases from 1992–2006. The office of the Chancellor of Justice has no statistics on all filed complaints, but of the cases that led to resolutions (some 17–18 percent of all cases) there were 98 involving publicity of governance between 1988–2008. In the same time frame of 20 years, there were 21 references to privacy in the resolutions of the Chancellor of Justice. Overall, from the perspective of the legal overseers, the conflict over information seems to be rather limited.

The protection of personal data was also regulated by a new law in 1999. The citizen-driven cases and inquiries of the Data Protection Ombudsman, who is responsible for guiding and controlling the processing of personal data in Finland, have doubled over a ten-year period since the late 1990s (see Figure 3.3). In a follow-up study on the new privacy act this was seen to be a result of increasing awareness on the matter and due to the rapid technological development of the time (Muttilainen 2006, pp. 45–53). As Figure 3.3 shows, after the passage of the law, similar to the complaints to the Supreme Administrative Court (Figure 3.1),

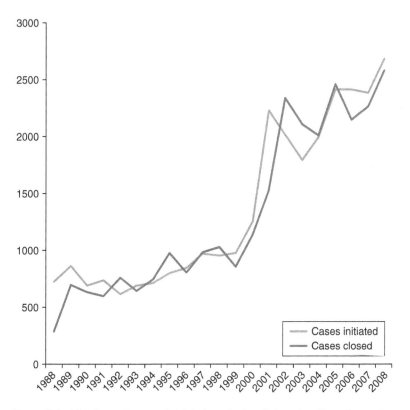

Figure 3.3 Number of cases initiated and closed by the Data Protection Ombudsman, 1988–2008

there was a sharp rise in the figure, totaling 2,233 cases in the year 2001. In 2004, the total amount of 1997 cases was initiated.[3] In a longer perspective, there is a significant rise from the early 1990s, when the total figure was still some 600–700 cases (see Figure 3.3). The rise started gradually in the mid-1990s measuring close to 1,000 in 1998.

Like the complaints regarding access to information to the Supreme Administrative Court, the complaints on privacy to the Data Protection Ombudsman also dropped to 2,000 in 2004. As the debate on the new law and the right to privacy withered away, there were also fewer complaints. There is, nevertheless, a sharply increasing trend in the caseload of the Data Protection Ombudsman that still continues. There are several things that partially explain this, most notably the increasing use of electronic media of various kinds that now include personal data, but one should also consider such factors as the accessibility of the Data

Protection Ombudsman. For example, the option of initiating cases by email has clearly lowered the threshold for inquiries.

Some 50–60 percent of the Data Protection Ombudsman's cases concerned the private sector. Issues related to work, health care and direct marketing were the three biggest in terms of the volume of cases. We should bear in mind, though, that the figures are not only citizen complaints but, in significant numbers, initiated by the office of the Data Protection Ombudsman. They also include inquiries concerning information, for instance by phone. Yet, the topic of privacy has undoubtedly become pressing in Finland in the last decade, and though the majority of cases concern the private sector, it is important to understand that the new forms of governance have created public-private partnerships and collaboration that might not be readily apparent. For instance, the third biggest category of cases that citizens brought to the Data Protection Ombudsman in 2004 concerned direct marketing (Muttilainen 2006, p. 52). While this is a private sector activity, the Finnish Population Register Centre is involved in the activity as the provider of personal information of citizens (this is discussed in the Chapter 4).

As the development in complaints to the Supreme Administrative Court, Parliamentary Ombudsman and Data Protection Ombudsman suggest, there was a sudden increase in the awareness of these institutions existing and of the citizens' rights on accessing or withholding information (see also Muttilainen 2006, p. 50). Hence the communicative discourse on openness (and privacy) as a citizen right had an effect on the number of complaints to the above institutions (cf. Schmidt 2002; see also Chapter 4).

Yet, for the Supreme Administrative Court, the figures on complaints on denied access have, since their peak in 2002, been in slight decline marking, perhaps, a return to the norm. Moreover, the perceived conflict in accessing information is quite low, supporting earlier remarks on the contextually unique use or integrative function of the institution (Konstari 1977). Still, it is worth noting that there has been an increasing conflict with regard to both information access and privacy.

Comparing the complaints filed to the above institutions, we can conclude that social conflict prevails in the appropriate level of privacy, more so than in citizens' access to information. The discourse on openness has a likely effect on the number of complaints. The figures were on the rise as of the turn of the 2000s, when openness became a policy issue. As time has passed the complaints have diminished, most likely suggesting a gradual fading of interest in the issue. But one should also consider the possible outcome of the collective memory and general understanding that Finland has a particularly open public administration, which might not spark a desire for challenging civil servants.

On the other hand, as discussed below, openness now also has a firm place in the values of civil servants, appearing in the working orders of government bureaus. For the above reasons, there seem to be few legal problems in accessing government information, but there are more tensions regarding privacy. Nevertheless, public mediation of the information rights of the citizen and the recalibration of the institutional practices (Somers 1993; Thelen 2004) has led to the citizens and media rediscovering their rights, and now more actively referencing them.

3.1.2   Communication and information services: something gained, something lost

There is now a layering of old and new institutional forms of openness (Streeck and Thelen 2005, p. 31), apparent in the understanding of 'openness' as active communication vis-à-vis the right to access information upon request. Openness has also become an expressed norm and value of governance, and has found its way into the working orders of ministries. As such, it has been not only been acknowledged as a norm but has also been established in the chain of responsibilities of these organizations. In many cases the working orders also outline the actors responsible for the decisions on the publicity of documents. For instance, the working order of the Ministry of Transport and Communication states that the ministry is open and interactive, the working order of the Council of State names the chain of responsibility for the publicity of documents, and similar acknowledgement is included in the working order of the Ministry for Foreign Affairs.[4] Also, surveys on the value base of civil servants and legislators show that openness is among the top-values for both groups, when asked to rank values (Salminen 2006, p. 178).[5]

Since the turn of the 2000s, the communication structure of the central government has comprised information services, press releases and conferences, an internet site, public hearings, a centrally-managed online project register and a public diary for documents. The communication and public relations of bureaus have also become a subject of evaluation, for which strategies were outlined in 2005 (Valtioneuvoston kanslia 2005c). These activities were assessed in separate case studies (Valtioneuvoston kanslia 2005d), where five ministries were assessed against the three tasks of public sector communication defined in the Prime Minister's Office's recommendation for central government communication: to inform, provide advice, ensure opportunities for participation by the public (Valtioneuvoston kanslia 2002a, p. 12). A fourth assessment criteria was added in the case studies, namely public debate, the lack of which had also been criticized earlier by NGOs (Valtioneuvoston kanslia 2005d, p. 12; cf. Valtiovarainministeriö 2001, p. 14).

In the survey, 60 percent of Finnish citizens said that they had never used any means available for citizen participation provided by the central administration, while 59 percent of respondents had never had personal contact with a government ministry. Some 20 percent of the respondents had accessed government documents and 15 percent had contacted a ministry directly (Valtioneuvoston kanslia 2005d, pp. 76, 84–5). The citizens perceived their right to file complaints as the most effective means for civic engagement, while media, public hearings (and open doors events), access to information and online forums were regarded as the least influential means for citizen activism (ibid., p. 85). This shows a slight discrepancy between the new ideas of citizen participation, endorsing openness and active participation, and the views of citizens.

In 2000, a study on the use of market communication in the central administration saw the understanding between openness and marketing to have grown tighter in the public organizations studied (Valtioneuvoston kanslia 2000a). The use of market communication in the public service was justified with arguments such as democracy, organizational interest, enlightenment (of the citizens), appropriateness, national interest, and professionalism (ibid., pp. 31–3). There were no consistent observations on the impact of the media visibility of the organizations and the press releases were not systematically monitored (cf. Valtioneuvoston kanslia 2005d). Two studies published in 2003 and 2008, reported the media to be content with the communications work of central government, which was seen to have improved significantly. Despite some claims for limited openness, the overall system was evaluated positively in the survey of and interviews with journalists (Valtioneuvoston kanslia 2003; 2008).

Looking at the information services provided by the ministries (services on demand), there is an observable descending trend (see Figure 3.4). This most likely indicates the increased use of the internet and the availability of information online. In the early 2000s, the internet services provided by the ministries were still rather heterogeneous in quality (Tiihonen 2003), but this has changed over the years, as all ministries and most of the agencies now provide comprehensive information about themselves online. In 2006 and 2007, the largest number

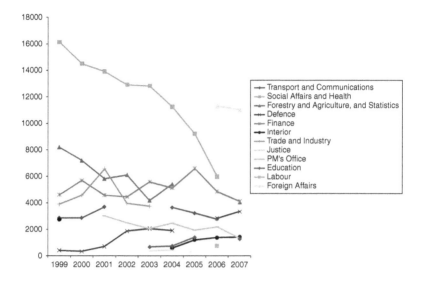

Figure 3.4   Information services reported by ministries, 1999–2007

of information services was reported by the Ministry for Foreign Affairs (see Chapter 5). The numbers in Figure 3.4 cover both services provided to the citizens and media, and services within the organization and between organizations. The ministries now also publish a large number of press releases and also hold press conferences, but figures for the whole central administration are not monitored. Chapter 5 provides some insight on this when it looks at the Ministry for Foreign Affairs.

The 1999 Act on the Publicity of Government Activities also requires all ministries to provide a public diary on their documents. Ideally, this would also allow for the public scrutiny of their work, providing citizens with a view about the issues (headings of documents) handled in a given ministry. It is, therefore, part of the communication structure of the ministries. The amount of new entries into the public diary of selected ministries is presented in Figure 3.5. Together with the publicly reported projects (see later) and the public diary of EU-documents (see Chapter 5), these comprise the core of issue management by the ministries. For each entry below, there was, in other words, a document that was either public or confidential (in full or in part) and at least the heading of the document should have been visible to the public. The diaries for secret documents were kept separately. The annual amount

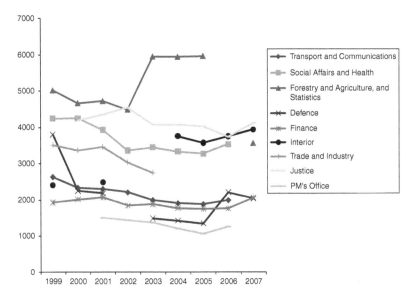

Figure 3.5   New entries to the public diary reported by ministries, 1999–2007

of new documents inserted into diaries is rather overwhelming: 25,645 entries in 2005 for nine ministries. Moreover, it is a moot point whether there is enough interest in these entries for someone to follow them or to ask to see the diary, as we shall see in Chapter 5.

Concerning public hearings, the ministries reported having different approaches. While the Ministry for Foreign Affairs reported annually holding thousands of public hearings and rounds of external commentaries, some ministries reported having just 10–20 (Holkeri 2007). The forms of hearings differed widely, ranging from case-specific meetings and hearings to telephone surveys and interactive radio programs. There were also joint hearings between ministries and a joint online discussion site for central government (Otakantaa 2010). As the public hearings and law drafting was entering the agenda of public administration reform, effectiveness and quality of governance, the government-society relations were both observed and evaluated and, also, guidelines for the inclusion of NGOs were made (Valtiovarainministeriö 2005a). This involved a joint declaration of principle for public hearings given out by the state secretaries of the ministries and the Association of Finnish Local and Regional Authorities (Valtiovarainministeriö 2005b).

But there was also a regretful reflexivity over the historical features of the Nordic model in Finland and the developments since the early 2000s, as the abolition of the state committee institution in 2003 was now seen problematic (Valtiovarainministeriö 2006b). The state committees dated back to fifteenth century Sweden and in Finland they represented features of Swedish government that had survived Russian rule (1809–1917) (Tuori 1976, pp. 15–17). They were used particularly in the 1970s, when the growth of the state and the drive for societal planning had increased in importance (Tuori 1976, pp. 8–10). Often providing a channel for civil society and interest group representation in state matters, including the drafting of laws, the committees had become a prime venue of inclusive policy-making and corporatist tradition that had developed in the 1960s (Tuori 1983, pp. 28–9).

The state committees have been credited for being able to provide detailed information for decision makers, contributing also to the flexibility and swiftness of policy making and coordination within the administration and between the state and private sector (Tuori 1983, p. 33). From the perspective of the democratic process and legitimacy, the state committee institution balanced the bureaucratic hierarchies, contributing to representation, interest mediation and conflict resolution (ibid., pp. 34–5). While these are all virtues of a deliberative democracy, also frequently mentioned in the programs for achieving open and inclusive governance, the tradition of state committees withered away in a time when public hearings became an explicit policy concern. The abolition of the state committee institution is not only problematic from the perspective of broad-based policy drafting. From the perspective of public scrutiny, the state committee provided a formalized institution that produced public memos and, moreover, named those who had been involved in the process of drafting new laws.

Figure 3.6 shows the development of committee reports from 1976 to 2008. While this also implies the number of actual committees that were active in this time frame, it tells more about the dissemination of information on the policy planning and drafting of laws that were accessible through the committee institution. Having reached their zenith in the 1970s, the committees were still widely used in the 1980s, but on entering the NPM in the late 1980s and the economic recession in the early 1990s, the number of committee reports (and the use of committees) dropped dramatically. Despite the explicit policy of public hearings and broad-based policy planning in the 2000s, this long lasting institution of inclusive policy-making produced just four reports in 2003. This has an impact on the accountability and external control of government activities.

Figure 3.6 Number of state committee reports, 1976–2008[6]

For instance, the debates on the legislation in accessing public information in Finland are traceable through its history largely due to committee reports. Since the early 2000s, there has been seemingly no policy work done in this domain. However, in the interviews, some legal experts noted that there were now ad hoc networks and working groups that draft guidelines for handling public information. Matters that concerned state security and commercial secrecy are often dealt with in this manner. Information on these gatherings was now only available through the actors involved, as there was not necessarily even a memo being written on the meetings. This effectively excludes actors outside the administration and related policy networks, since there is no way of knowing about such deliberations. Regarding the Nordic model, it is important to note that while Finland chose to abandon the institutional tradition of state committees, it is still widely used in Sweden.

To complement the loss, one new perception of openness has been the use of online registries on public projects initiated by the ministries. Also, Finnish legislation was now available online in a searchable form (Finlex 2010). The number of publicly reported projects between 2001

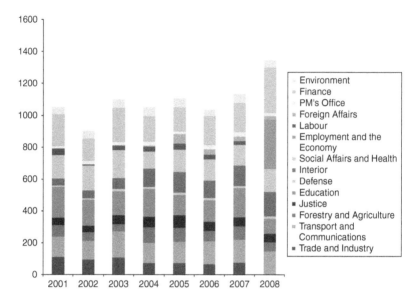

Figure 3.7   Publicly reported projects by ministries, 2001–2008[7]

and 2008 are presented in Figure 3.7. There is a genuine interest on the part of the administration in communicating its activities to the general public and other interest groups. Still, only seven ministries reported to have almost all of their projects registered online (PM's Office, Justice, Education, Environment, Finance, Transport and Communications, and Social Affairs and Health). The rest had either over half or less of their projects online (Labour, Defence, Trade and Industry). The Ministry for Foreign Affairs reported having only a limited number of its projects registered (Holkeri 2007). The ministries reported annually over 1,000 new projects in this public repository.

Despite the abundant information on the projects, a report on the future of the registry points out certain problems with regard to the openness of the present project register: the citizens have had problems in perceiving the contents of the registry, important projects are not easily separated from smaller ones, EU projects are not included in the online registries and the projects are described in administrative jargon (Valtiovarainministeriö 2008a, p. 9). Consequently, ministries are providing this type of information on their websites. The report concludes that the general information needs of citizens, based on their life situation, were not sufficiently served. The development of government projects – their history – was also difficult to follow.

The new state information strategy, stressing openness and transparency, has increased the range of information services provided by the central government. These serve well the information needs of the citizenry and media, adding to the low conflict reported by the judiciaries. However, while the central government pursued an active communication policy, the abolition of the state committee institution created a juncture in an institutional tradition, where different interest groups were included in preparing legislation. Despite the current emphasis on public hearings and the incentives to use them in preparing policies, it is difficult to get a systemic view of the inclusion of different actors in the process. Moreover, the ministries' use of public hearings differs significantly, as do their information services and use of project registers. Alas, while the use of active communication has meant that much information is published on the activities of the administration, and even if there is a push for using public hearings in policy drafting, it is difficult to make up for the loss of the state committee system, particularity in terms of participation and communication of the outcome of the deliberations, previously presented in committee reports. Moreover, the new information services are also increasingly being tied to the strategic ends of the ministries, including their performance management, signifying a shift from process accountability to accountability through results.

3.1.3 Performance management and budget transparency: citizens as shareholders

Through conversion, the institutions may, over time, start to serve new ends compared to during the initial context, thus leaving behind their functional origins (Thelen 2004, p. 36). Accordingly, the perception of access to government information may shift from the means of democratic control (publicity) to the active communication of government policies (openness) and further to performance management (transparency). The performance management reform that started in the early 1990s can be seen to have consisted of two phases. The first was centered on the notion of quality, viewing measures such as auditing, evaluation and benchmarking as its means for controlling the work of civil servants. The second phase introduced a more structured model, where the public bureaus were exposed to a more continuous scrutiny. This new model, resembling market or budget transparency, aims at creating fixed categories and items of measurement in the assessments of objectives and their fulfillment.

The shift, even if entailing an increase in political control over the public bureaus, still sees the ministries and their agencies as being responsible for outcomes and performance without taking into consideration the actual process through which these were achieved. The normative steering that was replaced with budgetary or managerialistic steering in the early 1990s (see Hautamäki and Mäkipeska 1994) was revived, even if in the form of information steering. The two different models are on a same continuum, having a same core in the private sector instruments of control. It perceives the responsibilities of public bureaus in business-like terms, making them responsible for pre-set and fixed details of their activities from the perspective of performance. Even though parliament gained a more central role in the process, its ability to control the ministries is, in effect, limited to their performance and policy outcomes.

Figure 3.8 shows the general outline of the performance management that has been introduced to the Finnish central government since 2004. The model consists of performance contracts negotiated between ministries and their subordinate agencies. This information is then forwarded to the Controller, a post established within the Ministry of Finance in 2004. The Controller collects all the information from the ministries and writes a summary that is then forwarded to the Parliament, which, since June 2007, also has a specific Audit Committee for strengthen-

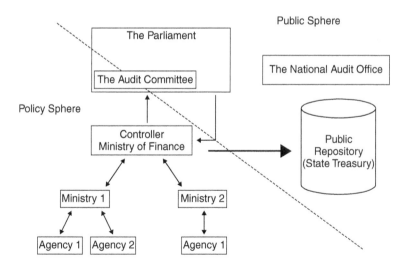

Figure 3.8   Performance management in the Finnish central government

ing parliamentary control over the budget process (Tarkastusvaliokunta 2007a, pp. 1–2). The Committee writes general reports on the information obtained, which are then approved by the Parliament. The results are further linked with the budgetary process, so that the results obtained are, ideally, used as basis for the decision on the budget for the organizations in question.

The dotted line in Figure 3.8 indicates the division between the policy sphere and the public sphere. The negotiations between the ministries and agencies are likely to be non-public, similar to the producing of the summary on the performance reports by the Controller. The parliamentary deliberations and the approved budgets are public. As mentioned, the numerical performance indicators of organizations are made public through the online repository. From the perspective of publicity, the process is linked to the public through a public repository, where all the performance contracts and performance reports are stored. They are easily accessible through a user interface that allows queries by organizations and, within their reports, by specific criteria of performance. The performance management system and online user interface primarily function on quantifiable information that the organizations observed are now expected to produce on their activities.

Other Nordic countries have also adopted performance management systems similar to that of the Finnish system. The autonomy that the public agencies had gained through the introduction of NPM was addressed differently in Nordic countries, with Sweden being by far the most occupied with controlling the agencies through performance management. Finland was assessed as falling somewhere in the middle together with Denmark, while Iceland and Norway exercised the least performative control over agencies, while also granting them the least autonomy. Another variation in performance management of Nordic countries is the level of involvement of the parliaments. The Finnish legislatures were the most engaged in evaluating and monitoring performance information (Peters 2008).

As noted by Peters, the current performance management systems provide few possibilities for citizen participation or any other type of external feedback (Peters 2008), the National Audit Office apart, which can perform inquiries on the organizations. Instead, to use a corporate governance analogy, the citizens are seen as stakeholders or shareholders, who only have access to standardized information on the performance of the ministries and agencies. The above system also provides few opportunities for feedback, so that anyone outside the system could make an initiative on what types of effects and outcomes should be measured. Though at present discussed as a tradition (see Chapter 2), the logic is fundamentally different to the principle of publicity, which makes potentially all the information resources of the organization subject to public scrutiny, not only those that are chosen in the performance negotiations between a ministry and an agency.

During the time that there has been a keen interest on increasing the government-citizen connections, other means for quality assessments and enhancement have also been used. In particular, evaluations are increasingly being produced on all aspects of public administration and their influence in the decision-making process has become formidable. However, this particular type of material is not necessarily accessible to the general public or media. This contradiction was also addressed in some of the interviews. The evaluation report on public (state) schools, for example, was not given to the press without a court procedure (Kemppainen 2005; Holkeri 2005).[8] Since evaluations have a significant role in steering the resourcing of the public sector, their methodology and results should be exposed to public scrutiny.

In the course of this study, the problem became apparent in the case of the registry management, where organizations in charge of critical registry data are primarily accountable for their economic performance through accrual charging. As the current system is fixed on this type of information, accessing information on other types of outcomes or effects of this activity can be difficult. Moreover, there is no ready-made channel for input, in other words a means for proposing new types of information to be collected, though there would be sensible and measurable indicators concerning democratic rights, such as privacy (see Chapter 4).

Overall, as the new ideas of performance are traversing the openness of public institutions, being embedded into the institutional practices, there is an observable shift in the perceptions of accountability. The essential added value, or contradictory term, that transparency has on the Finnish conceptualization of governance is the innovation that public acts of governance can indeed be economically efficient. While this is a very wide ranging idea, and often discussed under the general notion of openness, it is most apparent in the new attempts at providing standardized information on government, even to the extent that it can be expressed in numbers.

Therefore, in the institutional analysis to follow, I will mainly focus my practical observations on 'transparency' in the use of governance measurements, whether on a national level as in performance management or as in international governance indices and country rankings. Moreover, there is no single rationality to be observed in the different conceptualizations of institutional openness. Instead there are different aspirations that are potentially at odds with one another. On the level of general institutional developments these contradictions do not stand out. On the contrary, the general statistical data points to a low level of conflict in accessing public information in Finland. However, I will point out the rising contradictions with organizational cases. These are both linked to a conceptual shift.

With regard to the Nordic model, there are new uses and interpretations of the principle of publicity that are now forming within its institutional core, namely access to documents. The drive for openness as active communication and the budget transparency of performance management are institutional addendums that have no particular Nordic root. On the other hand, the abolition of the state committee institution has marked a juncture within a Nordic institutional tradition of inclusive policy-making.

3.2 Conclusions

The ideational changes induced by the international drive for transparency are apparent in the general institutions of public accountability. The new conceptualization of access to government information as a citizen right is apparent in the increased number of court appeals on denied access to public information, though this also indicates the public mediation of the existing legislation and institutional design around the matter. The new economic perceptions of budget transparency and performance management are apparent in the institutional developments that now see public reporting on activities as a means for accountability.

In the judiciary system, communication and information services, and performance management, the data and the previous studies presented here indicate that there are no major problems in accessing government information in Finland. On the contrary, despite the ideational shifts outlined in the previous chapter, general institutional practices seem robust and solid, having gained value as a citizen right and means of bureaucratic accountability. The pressure seems to be more a question of maintaining privacy, though no major concerns have been reported here, also. There is an apparent recalibration of citizen information rights owing also to their public mediation (Somers 1993; Thelen 2004). In this respect, the communicative discourse (Schmidt

2002) of openness has succeeded in explaining the legal and institutional design to the public.

But access to government information no longer solely belongs to the sphere of deliberation but also to performance – or rather these two now overlap. The civil service is expected to produce and publish information on its activities, including its ability to reach the goals it sets for itself. This poses a shift from accountability 'through process' to accountability 'through results'. In conceptual terms, the 'publicity' of government documents is now complemented by 'openness' as active and strategic communication and by budget 'transparency'. Because of the recasting of the policies on institutional openness, there is now a layering of old and new institutional practices (cf. Streeck and Thelen 2005, p. 31).

Comparing the historical narrative of openness to the above institutional changes, it seems that the policy discourse of Nordic openness has not only sparked interest in the issue but also bypassed certain developments that are at odds with the narrative. Most notably, the abolition of the state committee institution shows a clear departure from an administrative model that Finland had inherited from Sweden. Strategic communication and performance management are also external addendums to the Nordic tradition. Subsumed under a performance frame, democratic principles may start to serve new instrumental values. A closer institutional analysis of two cases provided next, highlights certain conceptual contradictions, contextual peculiarities, and respective institutional conversion: old institutions are redeployed for new purposes.

Chapter 4 discusses the reframing of government information into 'public sector information', a commodity, as budget transparency has introduced a new market logic into the activities of the bureaus. In terms of the state's information strategy, this is a surprising shift: the government is selling off its 'tools of government' (cf. Hood and Margetts 2007, pp. 3–5). Government information is elementary to the existence of a state. If the state's ability to govern and to seek sovereign power was originally based on its monopoly of information, and if access to information is central to representative democracy and citizen rights, then what is the condition of the state after NPM reforms with regard to information? And, what tensions can be observed in terms of democratic principles and public trust? I will try to answer this in Chapter 4, by discussing the institutional transformations of the Population Register Centre.

Chapter 5 explores the emergence of the concept of 'openness' in the Ministry for Foreign Affairs. As with the notions of openness and publicity, the new responsibilities of performance management are acknowledged in the ministry. This also points to the perceived normative binding of the performance management, now building a new hierarchy within the central government with a close interlinking of information services and new demands for effectiveness and budget transparency. Moreover, I will claim that the consensual integration function of the publicity of official documents is also drawn into the current debates on market transparency and effectiveness. I will elaborate on this in Chapter 5.

Part III
Organizational Developments

4
NPM, Budget Transparency and Census Information

4.1 Introduction

New Public Management (NPM) reforms implemented in the Western-European context during the last two decades have coincided with the digitalization of public information. Digitalization made public information reusable and thus a potential resource for the information economy. At the same time, market-based steering mechanisms, such as budget transparency (accrual charging), have created a system that charges a high price for public information. Due to the NPM and performance management, public information has become a market commodity, now sold by the agencies holding it. This has also created barriers for exchanging data within the public administration, as since the mid-1990s, public bureaus have charged each other for the use of data, regardless of whether it is needed for executing legally assigned tasks.

This poses a counter-finality for performance management in economic terms, as in Knowledge Economy policies, public information is perceived to have great economic potential for digital services, but the high pricing is seen to create barriers for the economic exploitation of public data. This European-wide 'problem' (cf. Bacchi, 1999) of public sector information (PSI), has led to attempts both by the European Commission and the OECD to draft policies for fixing the level of pricing in the name of economic competitiveness (European Commission 1998; see also FreeOurData 2011). These attempts at reverse engineering the NPM have proven difficult both ideologically and in practice. Moreover, they have coincided with a shift in accountability, making budget transparency and performance management even more prominent mechanisms for steering.

A lesser-debated problem caused by this development has been the negative effects it has had on access to public information, and potentially even privacy. In this chapter, I will examine the general European trend of privatizing public information, resulting from performance management concerns. In the Finnish context this development has come to challenge the 'principle of publicity', for example access to geographic information. Information resources fundamental for the functioning of the Nordic Welfare State model, such as the census data, are now seen as a commodity. I will further explore the influences of NPM and budget transparency on the Finnish tradition of maintaining census data, stressing the importance of ideational change and ideational embedding.

I will argue here that the case poses a paradox, as the high degree of trust in the census keeping of the central government allows for the privatization of this activity. In this particular context the discourse on Nordic openness now sees the vast registry infrastructure of a Nordic welfare state as a potential source of economic wealth in the knowledge economy (cf. Schmidt 2002). This has led to the economic exploitation of the registry data, following the rapid introduction of market-type mechanisms to the bureaus in charge of it. Hence, the sudden awareness of a long historical trajectory makes a surprising argument for its fundamental change.

The changes were initiated at the juncture of governance amid the economic recession in the early 1990s, but the ideas used to explain these changes were mostly derived from the European Union in the late 1990s. The Nordic welfare state depends on a broad collection of registry data, or rather the unconstrained combining of different registries, enabled by the high degree of public trust in these activities. Concerning census data, there has been a conversion (Streeck and Thelen 2005) in the activities of the Population Register Centre, which now sells its data primarily to the private sector. However, during the period that there has been an active attempt to make financial use of this feature of governance, there have been mounting problems in the area of interoperability and also increasing tensions in privacy. As a result, the reinvention of a Nordic tradition of registry keeping is at odds with its core elements, visible in the unintended consequences and trade-offs that are now emerging.

I will begin with an analysis on the invention of a market for public sector information, where accrual charging and budget transparency play a central role. I conclude with the view that the debate on public sector information has created a self-reinforcing political imaginary, where the problems originating from the use of market-type mechanisms can only be fixed according to market logic. This has ruled out other types of solutions to these problems and in part to other problems too, such as privacy concerns and limited public access to state information.

4.2 New perceptions of public information

Modern welfare states routinely collect and maintain massive information resources that form the functional base for public administration and the state. Registry data is used for various operations of governance – allocating goods and benefits, and producing statistics and governmental reports. Public information also has great value in the formation of public opinion and public debate: a vast majority of information on social issues originates from government institutions, even though it reaches the wider public through secondary sources (media, research institutions, private information services etc). The Nordic countries have one of the most comprehensive registry infrastructures in the world. Since the mid-1990s, this data has been used as a market commodity in Finland as public sector information.

In recent years, a technological transition has brought about the digitalization of administrative data and processes in most states. But the states still differ significantly with regard to their institutional trajectories in public information. Though the information society is often discussed as a revolution (Garson 2004; Forlano 2004; West 2005), public information does not just emerge from somewhere. Also, the general political climate as well as possible tensions between state and citizens differs between countries, making the application of information technology to public administration highly context specific (Dányi 2006).[1] Due to information society theorizing (Knorr Cetina 1999; Nonaka and Takeuchi 1995; Lash 2002, Castells 1996; Beck 1992), we have perhaps come to lose sight of the historical peculiarities of government information, such as registry data. Even though most countries have the means for (re)organizing their management of public data in a technologically uniform manner, there are great differences within data infrastructure and the cultural traditions in the way it is used. This is most apparent in the way countries differ in attitudes towards the use and gathering of personal data (Newman and Bach 2004). Public records of countries differ in their scope, coherence and integration.

In Europe, the liberalistic tradition divided Britain from other European countries during the birth of modern statistical bureaus, because the public opposed the state's attempts to acquire statistical information about them at the time statistical technologies were first developing (Désrosieres 1998). This is still seen to be behind Britain's and Ireland's reluctance to store personal data (Eymeri 2001, p. 10). Another dividing line in Europe is the experiences of the misuse of personal data in the Holocaust (Wietog 2001) and its political heritage to registry data in Europe, Germany and Austria in particular (Eymeri 2001, p. 10). Historical patterns are also evident in different approaches to privacy protection in Europe and the United States (Newman and Bach 2004).

The Nordic welfare states have collected comprehensive data resources on their citizenry for the general steering of the state. The historical traditions on the systematic collection of data go further back than in many countries. Swedish census data has an exceptionally long history. After first being collected by the clergy in the sixteenth century, the Swedish population statistics are continuous from 1749 until today (the Swedish statistical institution was officially formed in 1748), both in Sweden and Finland (Luther 1993, p. 21). According to Giddens, modern nation states could be called surveillance states as the public authorities' knowledge of their subjects of governance is highly detailed (Giddens 1985, p. 14). The Nordic welfare state has not only required in-depth information to be collected on the citizenry, but also on dwellings, real estate, communities and companies. This has led to the accumulation of a comprehensive registry infrastructure and use of unified identification numbers.

This 'transparency' of private life would encounter severe political opposition in many countries, if an attempt was made to impose it. For instance, the Finnish system of 'base registers' uses such unified identifiers as social security numbers, business identity codes and association register numbers, which allow for the combining of different registries (Karimaa 2001). This practice is wholly banned in several European countries due to the political sensitivity surrounding personal data. One can see this as an aspect of the open and uncovered means of governance; a trust-based Nordic institutional peculiarity (cf. Rothstein 2005). However, there is a global interest in registry-based census that has been used for some time in the Nordic countries (The Economist 2010b).

Due to the technological transition through digitalization in recent decades, new or at least growing interests and concerns are focused on public data resources. New economic interests emerged in the 1990s and, as a result, digital public data is increasingly seen as a commodity that should be better exploited for the benefit of digital service production and economic growth (Koski et al. 2002, pp. 99–109). Also, the improved ability to disseminate information has been seen to offer possibilities to enhance the public's access to information. There are new calls for rights in relation to the use of public information (Blakemore and Craglia 2006) and attempts at rethinking the constitutional frame of the digital state (Bovens and Loos 2002).

The same applies to public sector reform, which has had differing contextual applications. This is not to deny the changes that the digitalization of public information and the use of ICT have made possible. On the contrary, this technological change in the allocation mechanism has made it possible to perceive public information as a non-excludable good, which could be granted to everyone (cf. Lane 1993, p. 23). At present there are very few technical obstacles for disseminating public information. In principle, its use is possible within the frame of existing ethical standards and existing data resources.

But in order to understand the ideological and political underpinnings of accessing public data at present, the perspective of technological change is insufficient. Instead, a perspective combining history, technological insights and general understanding of prevailing administrative ideologies is needed. In Finland, the shift to NPM, coinciding with a grave economic recession in the early 1990s, marked an external shock to the standing traditions of governance. Furthermore, the digitalization of public information and the emerging ideas of the New Economy changed the way information was perceived and managed. The politics of this can be identified with an analysis on the policy problems and use of political concepts (Bacchi 1999; Skinner 2002a). Public information is now often perceived as 'goods' or a 'commodity' for which there is a 'market' (cf. Sirbu 1995). In Finland this debate has been somewhat removed from the general debate on openness. Instead, the debate has been conducted under the concept of 'public sector information' (PSI) by policy experts. The conceptualization of 'public sector information' has created a new domain of governance.

The diffusion, transfer and transformation of policy ideas have been important in this process of change (Simmons et al. 2006; Christensen and Lægreid 2007; Cheung 2005). The shifting concepts and political ideas of public information have been influenced by the EU's policies on the economic exploitation ('reuse') of public information. This has brought an addendum to Finnish perceptions of publicity. The new discourse is accommodated by a public narrative of openness as a central characteristic of Finnish governance (cf. Somers 2005; Somers and

Block 2005). Furthermore, the new discourses about the information society and national competitiveness (Castells and Himanen, 2002) have turned the historically accumulated information resources of the state, such as the base -registries and the core national geographic information, into policy concerns in the global economy.

4.3   The policy problem of 'Public Sector Information'

Policy problems have self-reinforcing qualities as they come to dominate policy agendas blocking other potential issues to become posed as problems (Bacchi 1999). Moreover, policies and policy problems often tend to revolve around shifting causal beliefs, such as the belief that there is or will be a market for public information. Since the mid-1990s, access to public information in terms of its reuse and joint use has been posited as a problem in Europe. This has led to lengthy debates that have dwelt on the pricing of public information. These debates, conducted among experts, have cemented the idea of public information as a market commodity.

I want to highlight the shifts in the accountability system in this process. In the early 1990s, NPM reforms brought about a general trend of making public bureaus responsible through performance. In Finland this meant imposing market-type mechanisms and performance management on these bureaus, such as new budgetary arrangements and accrual charges (Valtiovarainministeriö 1997) – early forms of budget transparency. The focus was on the performance of single organizations (cf. Hautamäki and Mäkipeska 1994, pp. 7–8), but since then there has been a general shift towards the paradigm of national competitiveness. In the context of registry keeping, these have been underlying aspects in the policies on base registries and national policies on geographic information (JUHTA 1997; Ministry of Agriculture and Forestry 2004).

4.3.1   Inventing markets for public information

The marketization of public information in Europe in the 1990s was, on the one hand, a result of the digitalization of registry-based data, and on the other of the NPM. Although the adoption of the NPM has not been a linear process with universal outcomes in Europe, there still seems to be a general trend of marketization in public information management. In order to understand the debates and problems of the present, we need a general view of the public information policies of the European Union and OECD, and national policies on accountability and budgeting (see Figure 4.1).

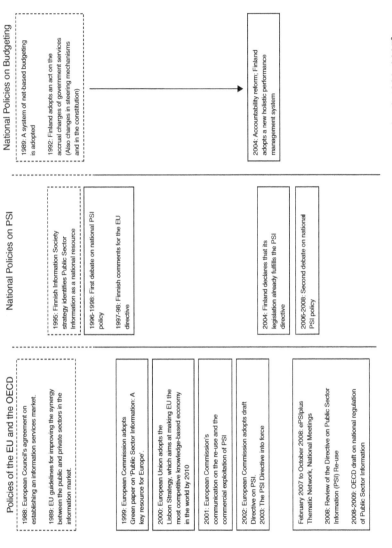

National Policies on Budgeting

1989: A system of net-based budgeting is adopted

1992: Finland adopts an act on the accrual charges of government services (Also changes in steering mechanisms and in the constitution)

2004: Accountability reform: Finland adopts a new holistic performance management system

National Policies on PSI

1995: Finnish Information Society strategy identifies Public Sector Information as a national resource

1996-1998: First debate on national PSI policy

1997-98: Finnish comments for the EU directive

2004: Finland declares that its legislation already fulfills the PSI directive

2006-2008: Second debate on national PSI policy

Policies of the EU and the OECD

1988: European Council's agreement on establishing an information services market.

1989: EU guidelines for improving the synergy between the public and private sectors in the information market.

1999: European Commission adopts Green paper on 'Public Sector Information: A key resource for Europe'.

2000: European Union adopts the Lisbon Strategy, which aims at making EU the most competitive knowledge-based economy in the world by 2010

2001: European Commission's communication on the re-use and the commercial exploitation of PSI

2002: European Commission adopts draft Directive on PSI.

2003: The PSI Directive into force

February 2007 to October 2008: ePSIplus Thematic Network, National Meetings

2008: Review of the Directive on Public Sector Information (PSI) Re-use

2008-2009: OECD draft on national regulation of Public Sector Information

Figure 4.1 Joint history of the PSI policies and performance management in Finland, 1998–2007[2]

Finnish policy on public sector information has existed in close evolution with the policy work of the European Union (cf. Kytömäki 1999). In 1998, the European Commission released a Green Paper on Public Sector Information, which portrayed public information as a market commodity. The Green Paper had its ideational roots in the New Economy theorizing and it was motivated by the perceived competitive advantage of the USA, where most of the public information was produced as the 'public domain', free of user charges, unlike in Europe (European Commission 1998).

According to the Finnish interviewees that were involved in the process of commenting on the draft of the 1998 Green Paper on Public Sector Information, this document was significant in bringing about ideational change regarding public data. The forthcoming EU regulation on the matter was also anticipated in the Finnish legislation. When drafting a general access law, the Act on the Publicity of Government Activities (1999), the notion of the 'reuse' of public sector information was adopted from the EU (cf. Chapter 2). Even though the NPM reforms had already set a new operational framework, the vocabulary upon which this would make sense or fit the norm came from the European Union: public sector information was portrayed as a market commodity. While the Finnish public administration was engaged in commenting on the Green Paper and the forthcoming directive on public sector information, the idea of a market for public information was introduced into the Finnish public sector jargon. Public information became conceptualized as 'goods', either 'public' or 'market-based'.

The digitalization of public information as well as the new economic interests led to a new reflexivity over the information resources maintained by the public authorities. In Finland, public information was viewed as a 'key resource' of production in the future informational economy largely due to its exhaustive scope and size (Valtiovarainministeriö 1995; SITRA 1998).[3] In terms of knowledge-based production, digital public information became a desired raw material of informational products and a trading-good of value-added digital services (Koski et al. 2002, pp. 99–109). In the 1990s, several committees and groups were created to plan for the best use of this newly found national resource. In particular, the Finnish base registry system – which is in its scope perhaps the most comprehensive in the world – was depicted as a national asset – (see JUHTA 1996a; JUHTA 1997; Kokkonen 2007). Similarly, geographic information became a national resource (JUHTA 1996b; JUHTA 1996c).

These references to national resources can be seen as the sign of a general trend in contemporary Finland, where responses to globalization and mounting economic competition among nations is making a strong political agenda of national competitiveness. Because of the reflexivity concerning Finland's historical peculiarity, a long historical tradition of registry keeping and, consequently, an exceptional registry infrastructure, are being reassessed. The references to 'national' resources indicate the level of abstraction where these goods, in effective and efficient use, were seen as serving the general good of society, public good or national interest (Kuronen 1998; cf. Ministry of Agriculture and Forestry 2004, p. 10).

The policies on the 'joint use' and 'reuse' of public information have been pronounced, for instance in the contexts of geographic information and base registers. The abundance of policy papers indicates the problems that ensued about the pricing of public information. Adopted in a commenting process (22 February–24 April 1999) of the European Commission's Green Paper on Public Sector Information (COM 1998, p. 585; Valtiovarainministeriö 1999), the concept of public sector information was a newcomer to the Finnish tradition, where the commercial exploitation of public information had not been seen as a priority. This is how the Commission's Green Paper, portrayed public information as a market item:

> The public sector, by nature of its size and scope of activities, represents the biggest single information content resource for the creation of value-added information content and services. Studies have shown that the bulk of commercial information services in the EU information market consists of services in areas where the public sector holds very important resources. [...] Public sector information is therefore a prime information content, essential to the information industry and a key enabler for electronic commerce applications. (European Commission 1998, p. 6)

Some interviewees described the Green Paper as 'strongly neo-liberal'. The contradicting terms were still acknowledged in the Finnish comments on the Green Paper in 1999.

> Perceiving public sector information as a market commodity can be problematic with regard to the [principle of publicity], which is related to control of government, public debate and democracy. (Finnish Government 1999)

The Green Paper was followed by a directive on the commercial reuse of public sector information (2003/98/EC). The promises of the reuse of public sector information in the name of economic competitiveness had been somewhat unfulfilled in Europe, largely due to the prevailing high pricing. While the European Commission took actions against the pricing of public information it did not name NPM as the source of problems let alone abandon the NPM paradigm. Instead of banning the bureaus from charging for their data, the directive aimed at setting some guidelines for pricing that were implemented in 2004. The Finnish government simply declared that existing access legislation already fulfilled the directive.

The European Commission's Green Paper shared the NPM reforms' presupposition of the applicability of market logic in public information management, preventing the actual fixing of the 'problem'. Consequently, the directive, at least in Finland, had only a modest influence on pricing. There is even an observable counter-productivity within the EU's public information policy. While the Finnish terminology and legislation replicate the discourse of 'public sector information' of the EU, legitimizing the experiential change, public information has remained an expensive commodity.

But as the issue of pricing remained unsolved and a topic of debate among the ranks of experts, it came to be encapsulated into a new economic discourse of 'public sector information', which has shaped the political imaginaries to an extent that the abstract idea of the market cannot be bypassed in seeking solutions to the problems. Though the EU directive seemingly had no influence on institutional developments, its drafting, in fact, gave a vocabulary and key ideational inspiration to the actors involved. In summary, the origin of the whole debate on the 'reuse' and 'joint use' of public sector information is in the NPM and budget transparency, but the ideational shift and embedding was a result of EU policies on public sector information.

Since the mid-1990s, when the first debate in Finland on PSI took place (Figure 4.1), national economic competition between countries has been perceived to have tightened. There are also more fine-grained analyses on the comparative advantages of nations, which now stress institutions (cf. Hall and Soskice 2001). In Finland, a national self-reflexivity on the particularly comprehensive base registry system has made it an issue of concern, seen as a key resource in the information economy. Having its historical roots in the state formation and early forms of institutionalized statistics of the eighteenth century, and later serving as a means of connecting different central agency bureaus, the registry system is now increasingly serving the needs of the private sector.

But while the market-based mechanisms were adopted in an attempt to make the public sector more effective, it has on a national level proven short-sighted in its emphasis on the performance of single actors and has failed to bring about its promises of efficiency to the whole public administration. Furthermore, at least in Finland, the NPM reforms have made the coordination of public information management difficult. The bureaus were given significant autonomy in managing their data resources and they now perceive ownership over the data they manage, and charge one another for its use. From the point of view of democracy, the fact that public bureaus are selling their information resources is also problematic. This has not, however, become a policy problem in Finland. Instead, the debate on the pricing of public information has been ongoing since the mid-1990s with two peaks, first in the mid-to-late 1990s and then in the mid-to-late 2000s. What this debate comes down to is that the 'marketization' of public information has had a negative influence on the coordination of public data management (joint use) and the 'markets' of public information (reuse).

4.3.2   NPM: flexibility or freeze framing?

The New Public Management was supposed to increase the flexibility in the way organizations conducted their activities. In terms of normative steering and hierarchical control, these reforms have undoubtedly increased the autonomy within the organizations responsible for data management in Finland. The agencies have, at present, a significant amount of flexibility in organizing their services. However, if the NPM helped to fix the perceived problem of rigid organizations, it created another iron cage (cf. Gregory 2007). The bureaus that already had information services at the time when accrual charging started in the early 1990s were, during the economic recession, drawn into the deep end, where they simply could not stop charging for their data anymore, unless major changes in the central coordination and budgeting were made.

Table 4.1 shows the general picture. The share of the accrual-based income coming from the conveyance of data varies from one organization to another. In the highly knowledge-intensive Population Register Centre it makes up 98 percent of all charged services. In the Finnish Vehicle Administration the amount is 10 percent. But in order to understand what is at stake for an individual organization here, we need to know how much income that particular organization is currently

Table 4.1 Accrual charges for digital conveyance in selected public agencies, year 2002

Public Authority	Customer (1,000 euro)			Total (1,000 euro)	Share of accrual charges (%)
	State	Community	Public enterprise, citizen		
Population Register Centre	2528	1223	4771	8522	98.0%
Finnish Meteorological Institute	4454	66	2127	6647	86,3%
Finnish Vehicle Administration	330	229	5017	5576	10.0%
National Land Survey	2728	236	1332	4296	9.0%
Tax Administration	757	151	87	995	27.0%
National Board of Patents and Registration	200	11	696	907	2.8%
Statistics Finland	365	43	22	430	5.0%
Legal Register Centre	0	0	254	254	76.0%
Finnish Forest Research Institute	6	0	231	237	23.0%
Environmental Administration	41	1	73	115	2.8%
Total (1,000 euros)	1 1409	1960	1 4610	2 7979	

Source: Valtiovarainministeriö, 2003b.[4]

expected to gather. For example, in 2007, the Population Register Centre had to cover 70 percent of its budgetary expenses by revenues from its own activities. The rest, 30 percent of expenses, came from the state budget. Should this organization decide to give away its data for free, roughly 70 percent of its budget would be gone. By comparison, the National Board of Patents and Registration is responsible for covering more or less 100 percent of its expenses through its own income. In other words, it funds its activities completely through accrual charges. While sales of data only make 2.8 percent of all charges, their absence would cause the same size loss in overall budget.

It would be too straightforward to conclude that the mere possibility of charging for services would automatically drive public organizations to do so. On the contrary, there are great differences in the Finnish situation on this issue. These differences are systematic: only those organizations that already had information services with user charges in the early 1990s rushed headlong to marketize these when the recession came. The recession was an external shock, which, combined with the NPM as an ideational impulse, altered these organizations somewhat permanently (cf. Marcussen 2007). The agencies where digital services were launched later had the chance to reconsider their position, which in some cases led to a totally different approach in pricing.

The Population Register Centre had an information service already in the early 1990s, when accrual charging combined with a perceived need for cuts and an acute need to attain income became pressing. It nowadays runs one of the most marketized information services. Another organization with a similar background is the Finnish Meteorological Institute, where meteorological information has become a major source of income. The institute charges for its information and has even been fined by the Finnish Competition Authority for its 'abuse of its dominant position' in the markets (Finnish Competition Authority 2002). It is worth noting that as the debate on public information is conducted in the sphere of markets, its limited access gets reduced to 'market disturbance'. The debate is thus removed from the sphere of democratic principles. The prevailing imaginary of market activity is limiting the range of solutions to the perceived problems.

Also the Finnish Road Administration maintains meteorological information collected from around the Finnish road network. The Finnish Road Administration, however, does not charge for the use of its data.[5] The Meteorological Institute marketized its activities early on, whereas the Digiroad initiative of the Finnish Road Administration was first launched in 2001 and completed in 2004, when problems related to high pricing were already known, thus allowing for reconsideration. The fact that the Finnish Road Administration and Finnish Meteorological Institute are both placed under the Ministry of Transport and Communications reveals the autonomy of the agencies, or rather their historical differences. The two organizations, which are in charge of similar data, are locked into two completely different approaches and ideologies in allocating it.

Finland's Environmental Administration has also chosen to avoid charging for its data (Ympäristöministeriö 2007). Although the decision was made in the calm of the post-recession period, it was largely ideological in character. The charging for data had created problems in accessing government data for external users and the civil service alike. The most vocal constituency in need of the data were those private companies that wanted to exploit it. The internal charging within the civil service had not been debated publicly, but there were concerns about this coordination problem, particularly as it now often required explicit regulation on legal terms (see later). In the interviews I conducted for this study, the above problems were seen as the unintended consequences of the new budgetary measures.

4.3.3 The persistence of the problem

The problems of coordination and particularly the problem of interorganizational charging were addressed most notably in 2003 by the Ministry of Finance (Valtiovarainministeriö 2003b). Previously, in the 1990s, there were similar committees working and memos written on the issue (see, for example, Valtiovarainministeriö 1997). Bearing in mind that the Ministry of Finance was also responsible for coordinating Information Society activities, the question arises about the understanding on which the decision on the marketization of public information was made in the early 1990s. Or if this even was a conscious act.

Here, the interviews with civil servants gave an insight into the bounded rationality based on which decisions were made. The reforms were launched without an inkling of the coming recession. The bureaus were given more budgetary flexibility on an ideological basis and the legislation on accrual charging was simply being reformed and unified, having before been scattered throughout legislation. At this point the recession was not in sight, but, a few years later, amid the economic crisis, the user charges were suddenly highly depended upon. The general outcome of their institutionalization was first seen in the late 1990s when the economy was getting back on track and the New Economy boom was coming to town:

> You had a question whether these problems were to be seen [in early 1990s]. [...My] understanding is that they were not seen. This is my understanding but nothing in the discussions that have ensued indicates this would have been seen. In the beginning of the 1990s, when the economic recession was on, money had to be found wherever possible. We had severe cuttings. The bureaus were given the message to charge for their services as much as possible to attain income. I think that in such an atmosphere no one thought what would result of this. (Civil Servant, Data Management, Ministry of Finance)

This was not only the case in Finland; a similar development had taken place elsewhere in Europe, where the NPM had been adopted (European Commission 1998, ch. 3). Consequently, the pricing of public information has become a policy issue in the EU and in the OECD, which reveals this to be a wider problem in advanced industrial societies. In the USA, public information is still being produced with 100 percent budget funding; a surprising argument often used to favor the American system of data management over European ones when discussing the economics of digital service provision. In Europe, this 'dysfunction' of NPM has received surprisingly little academic attention as it is usually discussed without proper administrative contextualization, which would explain why bureaus charge for their information to begin with (Craglia 1999; see, for example, Blakemore and Craglia 2006).

The inbuilt logic of accrual charges made the budgetary goals of a single state bureau a priority over the whole state apparatus, or 'state concern' as it was already then conceptualized (Valtiontalouden tarkastusvirasto 1997; Valtiovarainministeriö 1997). Although the New Public Management reforms mainly functioned on ideational change and diffusion with due institutional consequences, the conceptualization of what was at hand in this whole endeavor was also shifting and taking shape due to a mix of New Economy and New Public Management discourses. Public information was conceptualized as merchandise, the context for its use as a market and its ultimate owner, the state, as a concern, suspected for potential misuse of its 'monopoly' over some information resource that it, in certain cases, had maintained for some 400 years.

Since Finland's 2004 accountability reform, ministries and agencies have been accountable for the overall performance and effectiveness of their policies (Valtiovarainministeriö 2003a; Ministry of Finance 2006). While the previous practices of accrual charging also held performance as a mechanism of accountability (cf. Mulgan 2000) there is still a significant shift in focus, because the current performance management framework rests on the idea of transparency, combining index measurements and audit technologies in an assessment of effects and outcomes, over mere financial efficiency. The international country rankings also provide a site for comparisons and external scrutiny, spreading awareness of Finland's performance on an international level.

As the evolution within the budgetary system progresses, having started from accrual charging and organizational cost-efficiency before moving up to current holistic measurements of effectiveness of state policies, the historical problems within the NPM-based system are becoming increasingly apparent and explicitly pronounced. Nevertheless, the actors are still captivated by the adopted idea of public information as a market good, which is not only damaging for the integral use of the registries, but also problematic from the perspective of democratic principles. Moreover, as I will show, the New Performance Management schemes, building on budget transparency, are themselves deepening and further embedding the problem.

The case of the Population Register Centre provides some insight into how the organizational activities have changed in some data intensive agencies since the early 1990s. It also goes on to show two other important aspects in the debate. Even though the budgetary measures imposed on public agencies might in some cases later lead to the full marketization of these bureaus (cf. Savolainen 1996), this is not possible in the case of the organization in charge of census information. The marketization of these activities is hence prone to trade-offs and unintended consequences. In Finland, the change amidst the turmoil of the early 1990s was so rapid that the significant shift into marketizing census data received some attention from legal experts, but until now a general public debate has not been conducted on the ethical premises of this activity. This also signifies continuity: trust in registry keeping has been at the heart of the Nordic Welfare State model. Moreover, a historical narrative of openness now legitimates the conversion of activities.

4.4   Institutional conversion in Population Register Centre

The Finnish base register systems and the single register on citizens were created at the turn of the 1970s. The population register was designed to serve the central agency bureaus, and in the late 1980s the information services of the Population Register Centre were directed almost solely at public bureaus. The accrual charging and the economic recession in the early 1990s brought a conversion in the practices of this agency (Streeck and Thelen 2005), now serving the information needs of the private sector. Since 2004, the organization has been exposed to the increasing demands of performance management and budget transparency that have further cemented market-based practices.

4.4.1 Reorganizing activities

Accrual-based charges were imposed on the Population Register Centre before the recession in the 1990s. In charge of the census data and the management of the personal identification number of each Finnish citizen, in 2007 the bureau faced the task of covering 70 percent of its budget by itself. Today, its income mainly come from private businesses and individual citizens. Accrual charging has shifted the activities of the organization fundamentally. When we consider Figure 4.2 and Figure 4.3 it becomes apparent that if the organization in the mid-to-late 1980s still provided an information service primarily to the state, it is now increasingly serving the demands of the private sector.

Turning towards the end of 1980s, the information services' activities in the Population Register Centre had already started and some small amounts of data were already being sold to the private sector. In 1988, 2.7 million data units were conveyed to the pension institutions and

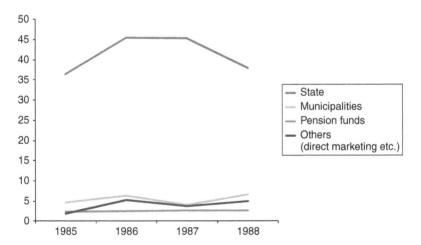

Figure 4.2 Conveyance of data units (in million units) 1985–1988 by customer[6]

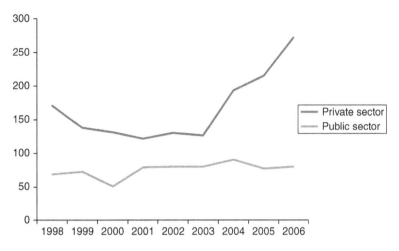

Figure 4.3   Conveyance of data units (in million units) 1998–2006 by sector

5 million data units given to other non-governmental actors, mainly to direct marketing. The figures for the state and communities in 1988 were, respectively, 38 and 6.6 million data units. We should note that the conveyance of data was allowed even before such activity was further commercialized. The accrual-based charging and the recession therefore simply pushed the emphasis towards this line of activity, while there was also an increasing commercial demand for such data.

As presented in Figure 4.2, the conveyance of data to the private sector still comprised a modest part of the total amount of data transferred in the late 1980s. Its share was less than 10 percent in 1988, comprising five million data units of the total of 52.3 million data units conveyed. Ten years later, in 1998, after NPM and the recession, the picture was completely different. The private sector's use of census information already made up 71 percent of the data units conveyed (see Figure 4.3), comprising 171 million data units of the total of 239.4 million data units. In 2006, the figure was 77 percent and rising: 272.2 million data units out of a total of 351.8 million.

The information services of the Population Register Centre have multiplied in the last 20 years. The total figure of data conveyance has increased sixfold since the 1980s (1988: 52.3 million units, 2006: 351.8 million units). And, as shown in Figure 4.3, the total amount of data conveyed has increased by some 150 million data units between 2003 and 2006 (from 206 million to 351.8 million). This growth comprised increased sales to the private sector, from 126.1 million units (2003) to 272.2 million units (2006). There had been changes in the use of private partners selling the data and also in the information systems themselves (in late 1999), which might have caused the reduction in the volume in 2000 and the sudden jump in 2003–2004 in the private sector figures.[7] The trend, however, remains clear.

This above shift in organizational activities, from serving the core functions of the state to running a profitable commercial activity, would as such be significant for any public organization. But the fact that the census information is at the heart of the state activities and the use of power makes this most interesting. In terms of the ethical and political tensions involved in census keeping, the practice is also unique internationally (cf. Curtis 2001; Kertzer and Arel 2002). Herein also lies the impossibility of marketization: even if the Finnish Population Register Centre already has 'marketized' its activities up to 70 percent of its budget, an activity like this cannot be privatized entirely.

According to interviewees who had worked at the Centre in the early 1990s, the changeover to marketization was not seen as an inescapable situation, but rather as a strategic reorientation of the organization: 'Why and for whom does the Population Register Centre exist?' Though the new market mechanisms, the entering into recession and active lobbying from the private sector to use the registry data were significant factors, the changeover was said to have resulted from an attempt to adapt to an altering environment. The founding analogy (see Douglas 1987, pp. 45–6) of the organization was that it became 'a reliable service centre for the information society.'

This also came about with a new appreciation of marketing, which was not previously held in such high regard but now was an 'appropriate' way of organizing activities, as one interviewee put it. This 'logic of appropriateness', or organizational compliance and adjustment to the norms and expectations of the outside world, is also an engine of institutional change (cf. March and Olsen 1989). From this perspective, the perception of strategic or voluntary change held by the interviewees can also be challenged. As March and Olsen point out, the logic of appropriateness in fact implies obligatory action (ibid., pp. 23–5).

The new analogy also suited the new governance models, where the division of public and private and market and bureaucracy was no longer evident nor regarded as important. The focus was now on the service of the whole of society. The marketization of information services was seen to have brought flexibility to the organization, allowing for a developing of products and services as well as enhancing the quality of data. During the time of tight normative steering and state-centric budgeting, information services were seen to have suffered from this because services sometimes ceased to be provided towards the end of the year as the budget had run out.

A twofold practice was used for the pricing of census data. For customers in the private sector, market-based pricing was applied, while for public sector organizations, a separate annually renewed statute was applied where the principle followed was stated.[8] The general principle over the years had been that the Population Register Centre only charged public sector organizations at cost price. The policy to sell at cost was also adopted in the general guidelines of pricing of data among public sector organizations (Valtiovarainministeriö 2003b). The current standard of pricing both for public sector and private sector had aroused criticism, which within the Population Register Centre was seen as a normal part of business, where 'a buyer is more likely to see the price as being high than the one selling.'

While the pricing for these groups differs, the total income to the Population Register Centre is almost equal from both of these customer groups, as presented below in Figure 4.4. The total sales income in 2005 was €10,200,470, of which sales for public activities comprised €4,738,351 and the sales for private sector use made €5,462,118. The main customer groups were the municipalities, organizations under the Ministry of Justice and the Ministry of Interior. Along with various private sector organizations, the publishing companies, credit companies and debt collectors, banks and direct marketing companies brought the majority of the revenue for their commercial use of the population registry.

The sale of data was not conducted by the Population Register Centre itself but through private partners on sales provision. In the interviews, the selling of data was also not seen to be an appropriate task for the civil service, which was rather to take care of the oversight of the quality and use of data, including on privacy issues. The use of private partners was seen as allowing civil servants to concentrate on such tasks.

Interviewees within and outside the Population Register Centre agreed that the information services the organization now provided were of high quality, thanks to the abundant funding and flexibility that the organization enjoyed. However, in terms of the general picture the perceptions differed. The scope of the problem in accessing information was seen as more relevant outside the organization than within. Interviewees in the Ministry of Finance also complained that limited information on the use and allocation of resources in the Population Register Centre was given out by the organization. This was done

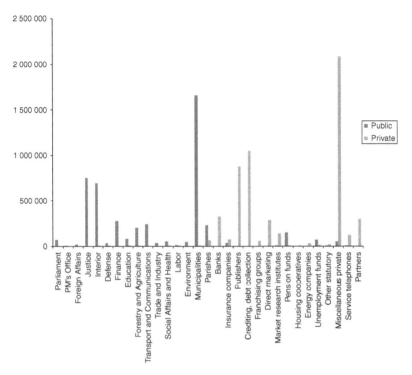

Figure 4.4 Sale revenues of census information per client groups (€), 2005

particularly in the case of electronic identity cards, a product developed by the Population Register Centre that it was supposedly selling at
market price, while it was apparent to everyone that their demand was
too low for this to be possible. It was acknowledged by the interviewees
that cross-subsidies from other sources of income were used to keep the
price of electronic ID cards affordable (see below).

The problems of coordination and case-specific contracts made
between the Centre and other bureaus were seen as unnecessary. One
respondent described the annual budgetary process as planning through
rear-view mirrors. Instead of really assessing the market for population
information, the assessments on where to set the price for each product
or service were made on the basis of the previous year. In general, the
fact that the data of the Population Register Centre was widely used
in society was seen positively. Interviewees mostly thought that this
made society function better, while still keeping the use of data under

control. Also, the coherence of personal data used in the country was seen to have remained high, since it was maintained centrally.

To summarize, there has been a conversion in the institutional practices of the Population Register Centre. Despite these somewhat fundamental changes, the interviewees still stressed continuity in their assessments of these practices. With respect to the low citizen interest and opposition towards the issue, in particular, openness was cited as an explanatory factor. Here history again stepped in as an explanation and a source of justification.

4.4.2 Perceptions of institutional history

The peculiarities of governing public data can be understood only through the analysis of institutional traditions, history and administrative culture. The general administrative context, including its reforms, is crucial in understanding how public information is perceived and administered. All in all, continuity has characterized the NPM reforms and the evolution of public administration in the Nordic countries (Marcussen and Ronit 2003; Pollitt and Bouckaert 2004). Contrary to these findings, the case at hand demonstrates that the marketization of public information has, at least in some countries, gone further in the Nordic context than elsewhere in the world. Somewhat paradoxically, this is a result of long trajectories of sound registry keeping, which have opened the way for more profound changes.

What divides the Nordic countries in this respect is not only the scope and coherence of data collected over time, but also the evolved institutional practices and ethical principles for allocating this data. The Nordic notion of the principle of publicity and the general connotations of openness, trust and social capital that are connected with the Nordic countries (cf. Rothstein 2005) are the most likely explanations for fundamental reforms in registry keeping. The trust-based ethical infrastructure that allows states to gather and use information has been more liberal in the Nordic countries than elsewhere. With regard to personal data, such as census data, this sphere of trust has now been broadened or borrowed from the civil service by the private sector in its use of the same data resources. In Finland, this was also tangled within a historical narrative of openness, reflecting the Nordic tradition.

Apart from Finland, only Sweden and Denmark have engaged in the practice where the state sells its census data. The scale of these activities differs. Denmark provides services where it updates the address databases of banks and insurance companies, but does not give data for direct marketing. For this purpose data is only sold in single units (per person) and not en masse. In Sweden, the state's allocation of its census data comes closest to that of Finland, as the name and address information is extracted and placed on a separate register, from which one private company is allowed to sell the data.[9] In Finland, the census register as such was being used for sales activities. The selling was not done by the Population Register Centre but by private partners.

Openness was referred to in two ways in the interviews conducted at the Population Register Centre and the supervising ministry. Openness as a general feature of society explained public trust towards the civil service. But openness was also a metaphor for the wide interoperability and use of the base registries. The Nordic roots of these activities were referred to in the interviews. Yet, Finland was still seen to stand out with regard to its exceptional openness that allowed for wider economic use of the registries than in Sweden.

Norway and Denmark were seen to have even more different systems. Even though there are enough similarities to speak of a Nordic model in terms of registry infrastructure and privacy (cf. Blume 2001), Norway and Denmark have been more reluctant in handing out their data for private sector use. Here, a historical explanation might in fact apply. Sweden and Finland have a long, common administrative history, as do Denmark and Norway. The European practices of privacy and managing census data are generally also shaped by the experiences of the Second World War (Eymeri 2001; Newman and Bach 2004). During the war both Denmark and Norway were occupied countries, which might partially explain their guardedness in using personal registries. Nevertheless, the interviewees defined the core of the Nordic model in terms of serving the Welfare State and its central agencies, remaining solid until the 1970s. This was now seen to have somewhat dissolved.

According to the interviewees, when the so-called base register infrastructure was formed in Finland in the 1970s, its activities were said to have functioned mostly on the pragmatic principles of central government. Since then, privacy and data protection have become more pressing and have started to spread internationally – Finland adopted its Personal Data Act in 1987. Finnish legislation was influenced foremost by the Swedish Datalagen of 1974. All in all, the relevant international contacts that the Finnish census keepers had were in the sphere of the Nordic countries.[10] The systems elsewhere were simply too different. There had also been an official exchange of data between the census keepers since 1969, with regard to the possibility to move and work freely in another Nordic country.

In Finland, the legal and ethical aspects of the marketization of census information were discussed among legal experts in the 1990s, but this had not sparked a general debate (see also Korhonen 1997; 2003). Even though privacy issues were seen to have been addressed adequately, there was still discomfort about how the marketization of personal data had been adopted without debate in the 1990s. In the interviews, the civil servants acknowledged the anomaly of the lack of an important ethical debate and made elaborate assessments of this with regard to their responsibilities.

In explaining the Finns' immense trust in registry keepers, the long unbroken tradition of some 450 years of firm registry keeping was seen as the main reason for the relaxed attitude towards the use of registry data. Also, the tradition of low antagonism between the state and civil society was referred to, linking also to the general idea of the open Nordic society. Another census data expert also estimated that the citizens' high trust in the Population Register Centre was a results of the openness of its activities, meaning that the address source (Population Register Centre) is tagged and traceable. Moreover, refusals for the use of personal information may be filed with the organization, ensuring that these citizens' information was not to be given out.

By contrast, one legal expert interviewed for this study expressed the personal opinion that the low interest of the Finns towards the use of personal data signified not only their high degree of trust but also their lack of knowledge of these activities. When asked whether the politicians were concerned, the legal expert noted that 'there isn't a single politician who would dare to oppose openness.'

The interviewees thought that the sporadic and minor public debate on the issue was a potential problem. But instead of taking up the initiative of starting to debate the issue, civil society organizations were called to the fore. The office of the Data Protection Ombudsman was also seen as a plausible initiator of debate, even if already at present overworked. Increased public relations activities were also seen as an option. There had been attempts by the agency to provide information about its activities, but these had been met with a low level of public interest. There is an annual day of 'open registers', meaning that the various registry keepers make a joint appearance in downtown Helsinki to discuss with members of the public on the matter and allow them to request information on the public register of their choice. This event has drawn crowds over the past ten years. There is also an abundance of information available online. Nevertheless, the citizens' rather unquestionable trust in the civil service was perceived as having had a negative effect on public debate.

History, thus, had a double role in accommodating change. First of all, the long continuity of the practices of registry keeping makes for an explanation as such, having remained cohesive and void of controversy over time, and having started well before the transnational communication of standards in privacy protection in the 1970s (Bennett 1997). Second, this long tradition, even if a plausible explanation for the Finns' general trust and low level of interest in the issue, also made for an ideational reference point for the decision-makers at present, in isolation from the new moral concerns (cf. Neustadt and May 1986). The ethical justification of activities largely rested on the non-action of citizens. The low controversy over the commercial activities of the Centre was seen as a form of silent approval by the public. Moreover, the public had a right to prohibit the use of their data.

To summarize, the narrative on Nordic openness in the context of census keeping, highlighted public confidence in the state and civil service. Openness was a metaphor for the wide registry infrastructure that was integrated through single identifying numbers (social security numbers, business identity codes and association register numbers) stored in the different registries, allowing for their integrated use. Openness also referred to the sharing of personal information with the private sector, which, to an extent, also partially separated Finland from the other Nordic countries. Nevertheless, by naming this activity 'openness' it acquired positive connotations. The high level of trust in civil servants was seen as a potential problem in terms of limited public debate and the political appeal of openness was also criticized, but these were minority views.

4.4.3   Tensions with privacy and the role of civil service

At present, the legal framework for using census data consists of the Act on Personal Data, the Act on Census Data, and the Act on the Publicity of Government Activities.[11] Based on these, categorical codes of conduct were made within the Population Register Centre. A separate code of conduct for data conveyance to the public and private sectors were made, but there were also specific codes of conduct on cases where other restrictions applied (see Väestörekisterikeskus 2004a; 2004b).[12] These terms of use are liberal in an international perspective, but as the interviewees stressed, they were strict and effective tools in controlling the use of data.

Altogether, the shift in activities had significantly increased the discretionary power of civil servants in the Population Register Centre and in the office of the Data Protection Ombudsman. Instead of having a categorical approach to all requests on the use of personal data, the civil servants now also had to pass a judgment case by case, sometimes including negotiations with a representative of the Data Protection Ombudsman's office. This was seen to have worked rather well, though certain cases had caused complaints. The Population Register Centre assessed such cases individually and at times changes to certain campaigns could be proposed by its part. Some requests for data were also refused.

The new role of the agency was also received with sarcasm. Referring to the change of affairs in the activities of the Population Register Centre and its double role as a seller and regulator, some interviewees said that the office was now facing a task of 'selling the private information of Finnish citizens in order to sustain data protection in Finland'. This was in fact a retelling of a saying about Alko, the Finnish state alcohol monopoly, which also has a dual role as seller and regulator: selling alcohol to keep the Finns sober.

As for the regulative framework and mechanisms of accountability, the general argument of diminishing normative steering was seen to apply only partially to the case of the Population Register Centre. Even if flexibility within the organization was significant, the legislative framework around the issue of data protection had grown remarkably at the same time. Thus the idea of governance and the NPM meaning an automatic end to normative steering does not fully apply.

But even in this context the issue of pricing loomed up, obscuring other potential policy problems. A new law on census data was produced in 2008. Though the legislative framework in the making concerned foremost the legal principles upon which the personal information of the citizens should be handled, the policy work again got stuck on the issue of the pricing of census data. Instead of just assessing the ethical framework for using the data, a committee report on the reform of census act contains wide elaborations on the organization and financing of census keeping including, also, proposals for collaborative models in using the data – there are 73 references to user charges (see Sisäasiainministeriö 2006).[13]

In terms of privacy protection, a survey of 2006 showed that the public still trusted the government to safeguard their privacy (Muttilainen 2006). Moreover, the majority of the conflicts over privacy concerned private companies, judging by the cases of the Data Protection Ombudsman. One category that constantly drew complaints from citizens was direct marketing. In 2004, this was the third biggest category in the issues brought to the attention of the Data Protection Ombudsman

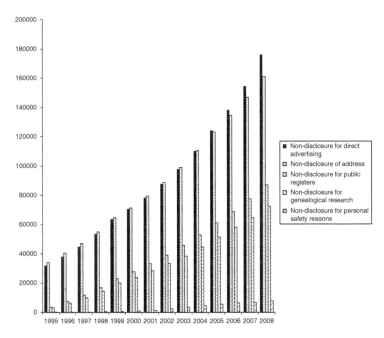

Figure 4.5   Restrictions on disclosure of personal information, 1995–2008

(Muttilainen 2006, p. 52). However, direct marketing is largely dependent on information provided by the Population Register Centre, as we have seen. In this sense, there is a link between the activities of the agency and the rising complaints and inquiries to the Data Protection Ombudsman (see Chapter 3).

According to the law, citizens can also restrict the use of their personal data. These requests are filed directly with the Population Register Centre, by phone or by filling in a form. There are five different types of restrictions: disclosure for direct advertising, disclosure of address information, disclosure for public registers (such as the listings of former students at an institute of education), disclosure for genealogical research, and restrictions for safety reasons. Figure 4.5 depicts the development of restrictions in the above categories between 1995 and 2008. The figures have been constantly rising, and the restrictions for direct marketing, for example, have increased almost sixfold in this time frame (being 32,025 in 1995 and 188,033 in 2008). There is an apparent tension between the current allocation of personal information and the private sphere of the citizens, evident in the multiplication of restrictions.

History accommodated the change in the activities of the Population Register Centre. The long continuity of practices in exhaustive registry keeping in Finland had created a generally trusting atmosphere for this activity. And, when the agency outlived a fundamental transformation in its responsibilities and, duly, in its activities, this sparked no public debate, let alone an outcry. The long history of registry keeping also created an ideational reference point for the decision-makers, becoming their moral backbone in assessing the new ethical questions they now were facing. When asked whether the current practice would have been possible had the public been asked for permission for the use of their data when the information services were started, an interviewee at the Ministry of Finance estimated that the outcome would have been 'quite different' – there most likely would be no product to sell.

Over the years, the Supreme Administrative Court had dealt with cases concerning census data. Figure 4.6 shows the number of cases between 2000 and 2008. There are annual fluctuations but we can still identify a rising trend over time. The overall number is low, being the highest in 2008 with 10 cases. This is not many, but still comprised 4.9

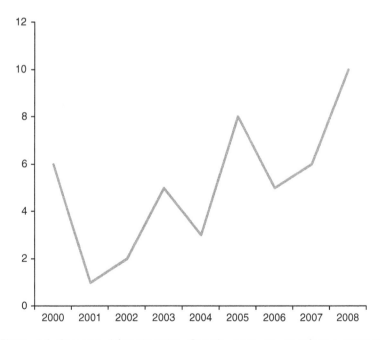

Figure 4.6 Supreme Administrative Court's cases on population register, 2000–2008

percent of all cases on general administrative law (on which there were total of 203 cases in 2008). One interviewee at the Ministry of Finance noted that there might have been more cases than those appearing in the statistics of the Supreme Administrative Court because some cases were difficult to link with the register. Judged on the basis of the officially classified cases (Figure 4.6), there have been continuous legal conflicts over the population register in the 2000s. The number of cases has been rising slightly, but it is still modest.

The relatively low level of legal conflict points to the strong continuation of trust in census keeping, though practices have changed significantly. The weak public mediation of the changes in the practices of the Population Register Centre had undoubtedly also made the shift less painful. Moreover, the new open self-image of Finns was likely to normalize the process of change. Because there was no public debate on the topic, it was only debated by policy experts.

At the time of conducting the interviews, criticism of the Population Register Centre was mounting within the ranks of civil servants, with regard to pricing and expenditure.

4.4.4   Problems of interoperability

If the selling of census data might cause tensions on matters of privacy, it has also rearranged the interoperability of different registries – the core idea of the Nordic model for registry keeping. Within the sphere of internal affairs a long lasting dispute ensued concerning the Police Administration paying the Population Register Centre for the use of census information.[14] The problem had been known and debated within the administration since the 1990s but without resolution (cf. Sisäasiainministeriö 2006). The logic was that 'someone always pays for the data', if not the police then the Population Register Centre. The logic that the data always has a price was also frequently used in the debates on geographic information.

The interoperability between different registries with common identifiers can, as such, be seen as highly efficient. However, there are at present new transaction costs in the use of registry data, namely juridical agreements on the uses of the system (Williamson 1981). The Act on the establishment of the new Emergency Centre Network, which was established in the early 2000s, specifically stipulates that the Emergency Centers are to receive information at a cost of its removal and not at the significantly higher cost price.[15]

This imbalance in treating organizations under the same ministry differently led, in 2006, to a formulation of a yet another committee position on applying removal costs within the same sector of administration, but in vain (see Sisäasiainministeriö 2006, p. 31). As the Population Register Centre relies heavily on its accrual charges, the rules for handing data to peer organizations have at present to be dealt with case by case. The pricing disputes between the police and the Population Register Centre show how far away census keeping has drifted from its historical roots in controlling the country's population.

With the approach of 2008 there were again attempts at reforming the system of data management. Information society initiatives and Finnish IT management had been criticized for not providing online citizen services and efficiency gains at the rate anticipated. A lack of coordination was seen to have caused this lapse, which was keenly monitored against the performance of other countries with the help of the governance indices.

The coordination of data between local and central administration had proven especially difficult. New emphases on national competitiveness were also more prominently on the agenda. This had shifted the perspective of accountability, now stressing effectiveness over efficiency and productivity over performance. The perception of the NPM had changed and the self-interest of actors was seen as its problematic feature.

Looking at the big picture of the public information services in Finland and e-government or online services to citizens, the promises of the basic registry systems and other high quality data resources had gone somewhat unfulfilled in this respect. A much publicized UN e-government survey published in early 2008 ranked Finland 15th globally in online public services (United Nations 2008).[16] Finland's Nordic peers, that is Sweden, Denmark and Norway were ranked first, second and third, with the USA fourth.

In the 2005 rankings, Finland had held 9th position. Unlike other Nordic countries, including Estonia, which ranked 13th in 2008, the relative online service quality in Finland had been in decline. The participatory aspects of e-government in Finland were particularly poor, making Finland (ranked 45th in 'e-participation') second to many developing countries. The model used for the benchmarking assessed 'connected governance', stressing joint forms of governance and cooperation between the different government agencies (United Nations 2008, pp. xiv–xv). The UN report directly cites the NPM as a source of dispersed agency-driven e-government models that now should be reversed to adopt centralized models (United Nations 2008, p. 73).

Even before the poor results were announced, the state of e-government in Finland was reflected in the interviews for this study and in the media (Helsingin Sanomat 2008a; 2008b). The results were viewed as dire in recent years, lacking in any big picture and even the interviewees at the Ministry of Finance blamed this on performance management. One expert on IT management at the Ministry of Finance named the Netherlands as the model to follow, because of its firm legal infrastructure on the information society. Overall, more normative (legal) steering was called for and the role of the central government was seen as being too weak. The same critique is also to be read in the strategies of the government's Ubiquitous Information Society Action Programme (2008–2010) and there are also new initiatives for widening the public use of government data (Arjen tietoyhteiskunnan neuvottelukunta 2008, pp. 11–12).

Performance and economic competitiveness comprised the normative yardsticks against which the poor interoperability between the registries was assessed in the interviews. When I asked one interviewee at the Ministry of Finance why it was so important for Finland to fare well in these rankings, the respondent said that this was necessary because 'it helps attract international companies and investment.' The Ubiquitous Information Society Action Programme also contains a specific appendix for 'Finland in Information Society rankings' (Arjen tietoyhteiskunnan neuvottelukunta 2009, p. 26).

The weakening position of Finland in the rankings was also reflected in the agencies. For instance, when negotiating the performance goals for the Population Register Centre in January 2008, the head of the agency assured their counterparts in the negotiations (now the Ministry of Finance) that 'Finland still has the chance to reclaim the top position as an information society.' The Population Register Centre perceived itself as a potential motor for the development of the information society, calling for more support from the Ministry of Finance (Valtiovarainministeriö 2008b, p. 2).

Elsewhere, certain activities by the Population Register Centre were met with explicit criticism. A National Audit Office's report on the use and development of electronic identification in the public service criticized the agency harshly and declared its attempts at developing an electronic identification card a failure and called it to stop this and concentrate on its civil service tasks (Valtiontalouden tarkastusvirasto 2008, pp. 163–6). Though this might seem a sidetrack in understanding the allocation of census data, it is relevant in terms of the use of the revenues attained. The costs of the development of the electronic personal identification card, together with its low sales, had led to the practice where the agency subsidized the development of a practically non-used electronic identification card out of the sales revenues. This was heavily criticized by one respondent in the Ministry of Finance, who declared that the activities of the agency were not 'transparent'.

4.4.5   The promise of performance management

Altogether, the problems of coordination in data management were mounting in early 2008 (Valtiontalouden tarkastusvirasto 2008). In the interviews conducted in 2007 and early 2008, the Ministry of Finance was seen to be in a key position as the ministry responsible for solving the coordination problems and, in particular, the issue of pricing.[17] There was evident fatigue regarding the policy work done on the topic over the years. As one respondent remarked sarcastically this was a 'patient diagnosed to death.'

Another interviewee at the Ministry of Finance bounced the ball back, claiming that there was no recession anymore and so the bureaus should change their ways, and even move towards a 'Rechtstaat' model, meaning central coordination and tighter normative steering. On the other hand, many interviewees remarked on having already suggested in the 1990s that legislation should be made to fix the problems, but that some officials from the Ministry of Finance had firmly opposed the suggestion.[18] Ideas of the potential new agendas were apparently on the table, but the interviewees hesitated to say that change was on the way, let alone how it would happen. Mostly the issue was seen as best dealt with by budgetary means, so that the bureaus depending on user charges would be compensated for their loss.

There were proposals for other solutions, however. A consultant's report of 2007 saw the further institutionalization of pricing as one plausible strategy, so that all bureaus would charge for their data (Valtiovarainministeriö 2007a). This would mean the economic burden distributed to those using the data and not to those maintaining it. Furthermore, the new means of performance management, the 'performance prism', was seen as a solution too (see Chapter 2). Having evolved from the budgetary system focused on finances, the new system made several other activities of offices to be measured and assessed in the annual performance contracts (see Ministry of Finance 2006). In the case of data management, making the bureaus responsible for the amount of data conveyed, and not (only) for economic performance, was seen as an alternative (Valtiovarainministeriö 2007a, p. 17).

This would have supposedly also allowed for more central steering, as the sector ministries and the Ministry of Finance above them would have been more keenly involved in the setting of performance goals and their key indicators. In terms of historical perspective, it is worth noting that the novel solution of the performance prism has its roots in the budgetary procedures that had caused the policy problem of pricing to begin with. In the interviews, the new emphasis on holistic performance management was seen as keeping bureaus charging for their data now and in the future. In the Population Registry Centre, for instance, the performance goals for 2008 contained clear objectives for sales revenues: 10.6 million euros (Valtiovarainministeriö 2008b).

There is an important observation to be made regarding privacy and accessing information on the outcomes of the Population Registry Centre. The performance contract of the organization does not monitor the level of privacy. In concentrating on the sales revenues and the work atmosphere of the organization it does not thoroughly assess the outcomes from the perspective of the public. For instance, the restrictions on the use of their information filed by the citizens would be a sensible subject to follow (Figure 4.5), yet this is not done. From time to time there have also been court cases on the use or access of census information. Reporting these would also be an obvious assessment of the outcomes and effects of the activities of the organization. For this study, the above information had to be requested from the Population Register Centre and the Supreme Administrative Court.

This example demonstrates the shift from accountability through process to accountability through performance, and its likely problems. As the organizations are now perceived to be responsible for their economic performance, information on the legal side of their activities might be difficult to access. Moreover, as the agencies together with their ministry now themselves judge what counts as a result, they are placed in a position where they legitimately get to decide what information is produced on the organization. Altogether, the whole performance management scheme provides no feedback mechanism or means for citizen involvement (cf. Peters 2008). Only those involved in the process of drafting the performance contracts can influence the agenda, but filing an initiative on a new aspect to assess, as the ones outlined above, is not possible. At first glance one gets to know how much revenues the organization made in a year, but the effects that this had on the basic rights of the citizens is not tracked.

In short, there has been a significant conversion in the practices of the Population Register Centre (cf. Streeck and Thelen 2005, p. 31). Instead of providing information for the central agencies, it now provides data for wider societal use, primarily for the private sector. Though there are little reported problems on this activity in terms of privacy, there is a tension between the selling of data and privacy. Moreover, the lack of central steering has led to unintended consequences. One can critically argue that Finland had a highly functional registry system well before the NPM and that the introduction of market logic has in fact caused tensions in the cooperation of agencies, causing unnecessary transaction costs. Yet, an even more critical assessment can be made with regard to the emphasis of efficiency over rights and democratic principles when formulating the policy problem of 'public sector information'. Also, the legal framework compromises between these two (Korhonen 1997; 2003).

The economic mindset has created a policy problem of pricing, which occupied the actors to the extent that other policy problems, such as the ethical concerns, hardly made the agenda. On the other hand, there is a strikingly relaxed attitude among Finns with regard to the use of their personal data that leaves the civil servants isolated by the problems that ensued with introducing the NPM and performance management into census keeping. In the policy sphere, the market logic according to which the state registry data was now allocated proved difficult to bypass. Before I conclude, I will briefly look at the captivating nature of the idea of markets in the debate on alternatives.

4.5 Embedded ideas and the difficulty of reverse engineering

After 15 years of NPM in data management, there was a sea change to be seen in Finland. This was taking form in new attempts at enhancing the central coordination of the state's IT management, a central theme in the Information Society strategies since Matti Vanhanen's first government. This also led to reorganizations in the responsible ministries. The new strategies now also explicitly named the pricing of public information as a problem. When discussing the policy problem of public sector information on a general level, the interviewees gave explanations stressing markets both as a root and a solution for the problems.

4.5.1 The difficulty of reverse engineering

Since 2006, there was perceivable turmoil in the field, as certain agencies and even policy sectors had pursued individual strategies opposed to the market logic, producing memos critical of the pricing of public information. For instance, the Finnish Environmental Administration published a general policy objective, which stated that sustaining the natural environment in Finland would be achieved better if everyone had access to environmental information and could use it free of charge (Ympäristöministeriö 2007, p. 3). In the new policy of the Environmental Administration of 2007, the information was given out free of charge for research and collaboration, to public and private organizations alike (ibid., p. 17). The focus of the activities, protecting the environment, was seen as a priority.

Historical antecedents were being addressed but now in a twofold manner, as a structure of opportunities but also as a 'prison'. Performance management was under criticism for failing to see the big picture, and hindering the bureaus in promoting their policies proper. Moreover, a new emphasis on national competitiveness and productivity had cast previous ideas of efficiency in a new light, making them appear inefficient and rigid. In the late 2000s, the fact that the practice of user charging was institutionalized in some organizations was criticized retrospectively.

Assessing the developments some 10–15 years later, civil servants saw that the reforms brought about unanticipated outcomes that had impeded the steering of state tasks. The shift to accountability through performance created incentives for bureaus to compete and trade with one another, but not cooperate. Charging for public data led to an exchange of money between agencies, and entirely within the state budget.

Instead of introducing a new flexibility to the practices of all bureaus and agencies, the practices of accrual charging have freeze-framed the historical situation in which the agencies were living at the time of the recession when the practice of accrual charging and result-based budgeting was introduced to the government. This has locked agencies into different approaches or patterns within the model. These patterns are economical, so that the organization simply cannot bear the 'alternative cost' it would face if no charges were levied (cf. Pierson 2000a). But these changes are also cultural, in the ways that the organizations now see how their duties and ideational fit in the existing reality (March and Olson 1989; Mahoney 2000). This can lead to them adopting two roles, that is as a regulator and seller of the same information.

In this second debate on the national PSI policy (see Figure 4.1), Finland's exceptional information infrastructure was still cherished, but now the captivating aspects of the NPM were coming to the fore (Valtiovarainministeriö 2007a, p. 2; 2007b, p. 12). The debate on the pricing of public data was now said to have a history of its own, referring to the variations in approaches to charging and particularly some bureaus being locked into their never-ending recession. In the interviews, the difficulties of reclaiming the promises of exceptional data resources were openly addressed. Also, the scattered coordination of information management, often bearing institutional divisions, was seen as a work of 'history', spiced up by organizations' self-interest bred by performance management.

Interviewees made quite straightforward claims about the vices of performance management leading to the poor coordination of the information infrastructure and IT management, as well as the (perceived) low number of connected online citizen services. The coordination of public information management, until 2008 residing under the Ministry of Interior and the Ministry of Finance, was particularly seen to have suffered from the stark division between state and municipalities. Starting in 2008, the coordination work was transferred to the Ministry of Finance. The large number of different national councils for public information management was also seen as adding up to a scattered picture, which also involved some protectionism over information resources resulting from current practices of performance management. Some of these councils also ceased to exist in 2008.

One reason for the persistence of the problems of accrual charging was said to be the insignificantly small amount of money that the state gained from its selling of data compared to the whole volume of other user-based charges collected by the state. But if the economic gains from the perspective of the state were meager in the healthy economic situation of early 2008, why not turn back and give the data producers proper budgetary shares for covering their expenses? Three arguments for abstaining from this were given. First, to provide a budgetary compensation for each of the data producers would be too difficult. It would consist of defining the numerous bureaus that should be compensated and, moreover, defining the right sums of compensation. In some cases this would be easy and straightforward, but for the smaller bureaus (big in number) it would be a matter of throwing in some extra ten thousand Euros, making it in most cases an oversized exercise compared to the resulting gains.

The second argument was ideological. Despite the potential gains in efficiency, in cooperation among bureaus, and promises of positive overall economic developments, the idea of supplementing market-based practices with traditional budgeting was seen as a step back that would not be in line with the current trend of performance management. It simply would not fit the current mentality of governance. Thus, for the time being, abolishing the practice of user charges was seen to be somewhat unrealistic or at least difficult to realize. Here the interviewees referred to the state of evolution of the reform (cf. Thelen 2004).

> I could add that as we have practiced the net based budgeting for 10 years, it evolves to such a point that a significant share of income comes from own activities, which makes abandoning it mentally hard. I have always said that I want to see the finance manager who is willing to do this. If you meet one, let me know. The same goes for the managers of agencies. This leads to self interest of organizations. (Civil Servant, Data Management, Ministry of Finance)

The third argument generally used was that the problems at present were minor and in the absence of knowledge about the scope of the potential market, it was not sensible to change the current policies. The notion of markets also reflected the Lisbon strategy of the European Union, which initially was to make Europe the most successful knowledge-based economy by 2010:[19]

> The Lisbon strategy is on much higher level [of abstraction]. We have also had the same [problem]. Because there is no way to show what kind of market would result [from making information available for free], nothing is being done. Regarding the act on the accrual charging, I have sensed that the Ministry of Finance sees it to function reasonably well. It would be an awful political struggle if some bureau that now makes half of its budget by selling data [would lose its income]. Where would we get the budgetary funds for the transition period? Don't fix it if it's not broken. (Senior Civil Servant. expert on PSI policies)

In this interview extract, the logic goes that the actual markets for the public sector information are very difficult to estimate. The interpretation then is that there is no guarantee of increased tax revenues from the resulting economic activities, should the accrual charging be banned. This embedding of the idea of the market has a catch-22 character: one would first need a comprehensive market analysis to abandon the market principles.

Furthermore, the problems in accessing public information, whether for commercial or noncommercial use had not been studied nor consistently communicated to the Ministry of Finance.[20] Therefore, nothing is being done. In ten years it had become the norm to perceive public information as the subject of trade. Though the incentive for commercializing public information was created by the NPM and the digitalization of public information, the change was normalized to institutional practices through an ideational shift that public institutions are actors in information markets.

Broken or not, the policy problem of pricing has not gone away. Even though the interviews pointed to the general understanding prevailing at the Ministry of Finance that the pricing of public information would not pose a big enough problem for something to be done, certain organizations maintaining data were of a different opinion. Some organizations became active in producing policy papers on abolishing or reforming the prevailing practice of user charging (see Ympäristöministeriö 2007).

Within the sphere of geographic information management a study to define the potential markets of cartographic information was made in 2007 (Hermans and Hermans 2007). In the search for markets, the study simulated the possible outcome of producing data for general public use free of charge. The argumentative basis of the document is 'national competitiveness'. Though the policy reports on base registers and national core geographic data in the 1990s had made reference to the national importance of these data resources, attention was still focused on the organizational level: how and under what conditions can different users make use of this information? The paradigm of the 2000s seemed to be that of national competitiveness, where the organizational aspects are given less attention (Hermans and Hermans 2007, pp. 33–4).

This new perspective of economic performance, even if still building on market logic, is more pronounced in its criticism of the perceptions of efficiency brought about through the NPM doctrine. A same shift is visible within the system of budgeting, which has also matured for some 15 years. Having started from general budgeting, such as accrual charging, it has now developed into a general tool for performance management, measuring not only financial performance but also policy outcomes. The new framework of budget transparency ('performance prism', presented in Chapter 2), attempts to collect performance information not on an organizational but a national level. The shift in perspective thus follows a general shift within the system of budgeting (cf. Figure 4.1).

There was also mounting international pressure to solve the issue. In 2008, the European Commission planned a follow-up to its directive (2003/98/EC). Also, a new ISPIRE directive on establishing a European Geographic Data Infrastructure (2007/2/EC) was given in 2007, containing regulations for the pricing of spatial data. In 2008, assessments of the implications of the directive for Finland's data management were being made, which also looked at the implications for pricing (Maa- ja metsätalousministeriö 2008, p. 9). Moreover, the OECD became interested in the topic in 2007. A draft on the policies of the pricing of public information was circulated for comment to the OECD member states.

This not only points to the persistence of the problem but to its scope. After the marketization of certain government activity in most OECD countries, a joint policy is being sought to find a rule of thumb for the correct pricing, as a repair. The institutional isomorphism not only covers public sector reform, but also the resulting problems and incapability or reluctance at addressing them in a straightforward manner. If no one knew how big a market potential there really was for PSI, then why did everyone introduce the market-based mechanism into this activity to begin with?

The discussion of the very existence of the 'market' is in fact quite typical for NPM. NPM often functions on the assumption of its existence and, moreover, has the tendency to create quasi-markets. This emulation of market conditions makes the public bureaus and organizations outside them acquire new roles as producers and purchasers, even if in reality there would be no competition (Gregory 2007, p. 228). In information management, information resources, such as cartographic information, are simply too costly to produce to make it worthwhile competing in this activity.

Even though the market-based mechanisms and concepts had become the organizational logic on which the Finnish data management was functioning, there was common understanding among the civil servants that there actually were no proper market conditions for public information. Yet even the criticism followed the market logic, as interviewees acknowledged that the current system had several 'monopolies', thus leading to inefficiency. And in the case of marketizing census information there is no room for real life competition, due to the ethical sensitivity of census registers.

1.5.2 Unintended consequences and trade-offs

Because the issue had been consistently tackled as a market problem, other plausible viewpoints could no longer fit the political imaginary, let alone the policy agenda (cf. Bacchi 1999). The most obvious alternative viewpoint would have been democratic principles such as the principle of publicity according to which everyone in need of government information should have had unrestricted access to it. High pricing, in contexts where this occurs, could be seen as violating the principle. Also, the concerns of privacy were partially subsumed under the debate on pricing. But because this debate is conducted in economic terms and not in the name of democratic principles, everyone wanting to engage on the topic of public sector information first has to get acquainted with the standing legislation on pricing and the ongoing reforms around it, including the finer details of past PSI debates. A shift from democratic principles as the basis of argumentation is obvious.

There are unintended consequences in the current system, building on performance management and budget transparency. The above account on the interoperability between bureaus points to a conflict with inter-organizational openness and budget transparency, as the agencies now charge each other. Even if in their performance contracts the bureaus were made responsible for cooperation, it would still keep up an instrumental rationality in the way the bureaus operated and perceived the information they held. In terms of publicity and privacy, the current practice also poses problems. In many cases, the public service no longer hands out its digital data without receiving payment for it. This has influenced not only the companies, highlighted in the PSI policies, but also noncommercial activity, for instance academic institutions in need of geographic data.

As for privacy, the accrual charging and net-based budgeting has led to organizations such as the Population Register Centre increasingly selling their data, which poses a potential conflict with its double role as a keeper of privacy in the country. Moreover, the organization at present is primarily responsible for presenting information on its economic performance, which is rather symptomatic of the political imaginary of market activity. The perception of citizens' or basic rights was not a central part of the new performance management paradigm.

The actors themselves consider that the core of the Nordic model of registry keeping comprises the broad collection of registry data, the rather unconstrained combining of different registries, and the high degree of public trust in this. Paradoxically, during the time that there has been an active attempt to make financial use of this feature of governance, there have been mounting problems in the area of interoperability and increasing tensions concerning privacy. Therefore the reframing of a Nordic tradition of governance, and its related policies and new institutional practices, are at odds with the tradition itself.

In terms of the Nordic model of registry keeping, the problems of interoperability suggest the compromised ability to use the registries for the purpose that they were initially collected, namely governance itself. This diminished efficiency of activity is a counter-finality of the efficiency-seeking NPM reforms that have disregarded holistic perspectives. There is also an apparent trade-off in the shifting responsibilities of the Population Register Centre that is now selling personal data to maintain privacy in Finland. This has already had implications concerning public trust, evident in the increasing restrictions on the disclosure of personal information.

To some extent, even the EU legislation seems to have had unintended consequences, posing a counter-finality in outcome (cf. Baert 1991; cf. Borowiak 2004).[21] While trying to create a regulation under which pricing could be controlled and the economic exploitation of public sector information could be enhanced, it came to further conceptualize public information as a commodity, which indeed can and should be seen in economic terms and not in terms of democratic principles. The directive thus paved the way to the more institutionalized or legitimate practice of commercializing public information on the part of the civil service, as their practice now 'fulfilled the EU directive'.

In looking at the past 10–15 years, a couple of interviewees referred to the period optimistically as a passing phase. Most of the elements for the functioning of the base register system, such as the high social trust and social integration and close collaboration between public organizations, are the result of long societal developments. Yet the captivating aspects of this model both in economic and ideational terms seem far from solved. As the ideas and practices of budget transparency become established and embedded in the current system, it is difficult to even perceive a world beyond them. What was left to do was the fine-tuning of regulations that set the limits for the department's economic gains. The policy problem remained.

The inter-organizational setting that had evolved from the conversion of the institutional practices of agencies was described as a 'dysfunction' of the NPM. With a decade of NPM in data management, the political reality was changing, acknowledging at least some of the problems. But at the same time, a renewed emphasis on budget transparency made it even more difficult to recall the decisions made earlier. As the above analysis shows, there is no single rationality to institutional openness and transparency, but many conflicting rationalities. These are also at play in the institutional practices. Looked at closely, the unintended consequences are in fact the results of conflicting intentions of policies pursued.

4.6   Conclusions

The introduction of the NPM has had an unintended consequence for the publicity of government data, now regarded as a commodity. This privatization of public information is further embedded with the means of budget transparency, introduced to the civil service as an element of performance management. The drive for transparency and account-ability through performance has, therefore, had a negative impact on the access to government information, posing a problem for democratic control through publicity. At the same time, there are also tensions in the sphere of privacy, as public agencies perceive the personal infor-mation of the citizens as a good to sell. In terms of efficiency, there now seems to be a broad consensus that the performance management reforms are likely to have had a negative general effect on the economy, signified by the policy work on public sector information by the EU, OECD and UN.

In understanding the full effects of New Public Management and budget transparency on Finnish registry data, an understanding of the historical peculiarities and the general reform agendas is needed. Even if the policy problems on a European scale are shared, there are still differing national trajectories. This can provide somewhat paradoxical outcomes, as long-held institutional traditions and high citizen trust are able to pave the way to larger transformations. In Finland, the NPM has significantly changed the way single agencies function. In the case of the Population Register Centre, the NPM has reversed its activities altogether, making the private sector the most important client. In the institutional history of census keeping this is a most significant turn as the information previously used for the purpose of coordinating state activities is now primarily seen as a commodity.

Furthermore, the reflexivity over history and traditions is accommo-dating these changes. The discourse of Nordic openness legitimized the above conversion in census keeping (cf. Schmidt 2002), framing the registry infrastructure of a Nordic welfare state as a potential source of economic wealth for the knowledge economy. The actual ideational input for the economic exploitation of public data was adopted in the process of drafting an EU directive on public sector information.

The actors themselves defined the Nordic model in registry keeping by the broad collection of registry data, the government's ability to com-bine the different registries, and the high degree of public trust in these activities. The economic exploitation of registry data marks an insti-tutional conversion (see Streeck and Thelen 2005), resulting from the rapid introduction of market-type mechanisms that have since evolved into budget transparency and performance management. Concerning the perceptions of a Nordic model, the long historical trajectory in central government registry keeping makes a surprising argument for the marketization of these institutional practices. There are apparent trade-offs and unintended consequences involved, that also have implications for accountability.

Regarding interoperability, of the 450 years of registry keeping, the last 15 years stand out as the most intense period of producing policy documents on the use of registry data. To the extent that this is to do with previously unseen human concerns, such as privacy issues, this is understandable. But the policy texts produced on the mere execution of administrative tasks among agencies is a different matter. The perseverance of this question points to a real and somewhat profound problem in coordination. Even if discussed within the paradigm of efficiency, the current system, built on the efficiency-seeking NPM doctrine and performance management, is seen a major obstacle to productivity in current debates – a sub-optimality for the practices of budget transparency that they both build upon.

As for ethics and democratic principles, the excessive debate on information markets runs the risk of removing 'public sector information' from this domain. In the search for alternatives, on national and transnational level alike, the current political imaginary of markets appears still dominant. On an agency level, the Population Register Centre is now expected to have revenues from the sale of census data, and there is an apparent tension in its role as the regulator of the same information, marking a trade-off between privacy and economic exploitation of the personal data. The increase in the restrictions on the disclosure of census data points to declining public trust in the new activities, albeit a gradual decline. In short, in the context of Finnish registry keeping, the economic reframing of the Nordic model seems to be at odds with the very core elements of this perceived tradition.

5
New Domains of Openness and Transparency: Performing Foreign Affairs

5.1 Introduction

In the 1990s, data management in Europe was being, at least partly, subordinated to new market principles (see Chapter 4). The information of government agencies was framed as a market commodity, public sector information. The burst of the New Economy at the turn of the 2000s made this development seem like an encapsulated event that went by its own rationality. However, there is a similar instrumentalization of knowledge to be observed in organizations of a more general kind. The Finnish Ministry for Foreign Affairs serves as a case for exploring these ideational and institutional shifts. I will begin with a brief account on the code of secrecy in foreign affairs that had prevailed up until the 1990s, pointing to a change in ideas and practices towards the turn of the 2000s.

This, I suggest, was a result of the ideational change concerning access to government information and a reassessment of the role of the Foreign Services in contemporary governance, both sparked by the juncture in governance in the 1990s (cf. Marcussen 2000; Peters et al. 2005). I will portray the shift that took place in the concepts legitimizing the activities of the ministry: while 'public interest' was previously coupled with 'secrecy', towards the turn of the 2000s it was suddenly best served through 'openness' (cf. Skinner 1989). I explore the changing mentalities in the ministry through accounts given by the interviewees both within and outside the organization. I draw on selected strategy documents, instructive material and time series data.

The main findings underline the new strategic value of openness in an image-conscious and performance-driven time (Klagge 1997; cf. Yiannis

2005). I conclude that openness became a cause to promote in the Ministry for Foreign Affairs in order to keep up its functions and resources. As the new practices of performance management and budget transparency have entered the organization, the information services have become one of the few activities in foreign services that can be quantified. There are also more general mechanisms of market transparency that have created pressure for accessing foreign political information.

The institutional conversion (Streeck and Thelen 2005) concerning access to information was discussed in the Finnish context as Nordic openness. This policy discourse helped to communicate the new ideas of openness and transparency within the state organization (cf. Schmidt 2002), whether in citizen access, public appearances by civil servants, information services, the use of public hearings or public monitoring of performance. However, the new emphasis on openness in the ministry has not necessarily brought an end to the secrecy of foreign political material. Rather, the concurring structural changes in governance have shifted this material into new domains.

The new pressures of performance management and transparency have made information a central resource for the ministry. The allocation of information is now seen as a prime task of the Foreign Service, partially because its more general functions cannot be quantified. The new perception of global competitiveness and transparency has also prompted the organization to share confidential information with strategic partners in Finland. This non-public activity was somewhat paradoxically termed as 'openness', which is now seen as a Nordic institutional peculiarity.

5.2 Archiving foreign affairs

The internationalization of governance is often perceived as a single grand transformational trend of contemporary governance (Pierre and Peters 2000, pp. 77–91; Marcussen and Ronit 2003). The organizational analysis, then, often tends to focus on those organizations that are getting more internationalized or gaining importance. What have perhaps received less attention are the influences on the organizations that before were responsible for the contacts with the international sphere but are now losing their privileged position in this area. There are at present major institutional changes in the Foreign Services in all developed countries (Hill 2002).

On the domestic level, this development brings the issues of international policy-making and coordination to the national agenda, changing the roles of ministries in Finland. For instance, the Ministry of Forestry and Agriculture now conducts its activities in a larger EU framework. Moreover, all ministries now conduct international relations and transnational policy agendas are more tightly knit than before. But the shifts have also transformed the field in which the Foreign Services operate. Looking at the Ministry for Foreign Affairs, the structural changes in the Finnish governance during the 1990s resulted in a search for new justifications for its role as well as for a functional logic. The issue of 'openness' taps into this.

The metaphor of archiving fits the current activities of the Ministry for Foreign Affairs in two respects. Foreign Services are mainly responsible for collecting and disseminating information on world events. They function as an 'archive' and organizational memory for foreign affairs (cf. Hill 2002; cf. European Commission 2005). I argue that this conservative function is currently changing due to the fluctuating environment and activities of foreign services, which ultimately calls for a reorientation in the information strategies of these bureaus. Also, the attempts at cutting the budget of these bureaus has brought pressures for providing value for money, namely providing reportable and calculable results, a type of transparency. Consequently, as stressed by interviewees at the Finnish ministry, the traditional practice of the Foreign Service is itself becoming archaic.

It is not my aim to write a history of foreign affairs or of the ministry, on which there are several books (see Susiluoto 2002; Mansala and Suomi 2003; Soikkanen 2003; Soikkanen 2008). What I explore are the ideational shifts that can be seen to be taking place generally in the public administration, processes that bind ministries together, not separates them. The viewpoint therefore concerns the history of the administrative reforms and ideational changes that are of relevance in information management. Moreover, as many of the interviewees stressed, the domain of foreign politics had become a part of everyday life, and the ministry was just 'one ministry among others'. Still, the organizational context in the Ministry for Foreign Affairs offers a unique setting for analysis in many senses. The work in the Ministry for Foreign Affairs is highly knowledge intensive. Unlike other ministries, the Finnish Ministry for Foreign Affairs does not engage in preparing legislation. Altogether, Foreign Services are a model example of public bureaus, where the outcomes and effects of activities are difficult to observe (Wilson 1989; Pollitt et al. 2004).

The Finnish Ministry for Foreign Affairs was, for a long time, perceived as one of the most secretive public bureaus in Finland. Its policy agenda was dominated by the agenda of Finnish–Soviet relations, which was a specific characteristic of Finland. This was due to the pressure of the Cold War and the strong semi-presidential tradition prevailing in the country. The ministry was seen as the 'President's ministry', through which all international affairs were channeled (for the term see Soikkanen 2003). The secretive image of foreign affairs comes from the traditional idea of diplomacy, which stresses maintaining trusting relations between countries, but also from the premises of the Cold War that in Finland were more acute than in many other Western European countries. After the end of the Cold War in Europe, the practice of openness had significantly changed in the ministry. The Finnish ministry now resembled its counterparts in Europe, sharing their problems.

Following the collapse of the Soviet Union, the ministry faced a new working environment. The notion of openness came into the picture during this phase in which the ministry was redefining its role in a new governance environment that favored efficiency and cooperation, and where the work of practically all ministries had become 'international'. There have been similar transformations in all European countries.[1] Consequently, Foreign Services are also forced to adjust their service operations. Furthermore, these developments have led to active comparisons with other countries and to attempts to learn from them.

Though the grand changes in the environment of the foreign ministry undoubtedly triggered the process of change, the shifts in the accountability system in which the ministry worked, and moreover the insider perceptions of these shifts, were the mechanism of change within the ministry. These changes were thus partially imposed upon the organization. But they were not a result of civil society pressure. Rather the organization adopted new ideational models to follow. The motives and strategies for adopting new ideas were crafted to serve the purposes of the ministry. Moving towards the present, ideational change has progressed further, making openness the key element in the service and a customer-oriented paradigm. This has intensified with the attempts at measuring the performance of the ministry, within the practice of budget transparency that I have outlined in Chapter 2.

Also, the notion of national competitiveness has come onto the agenda, making transparency and the allocation of information part of Finland's competitive edge in the globalizing economy. This economic perception of the issue also links to the agenda of the ministry itself. Becoming public was part of a strategy to secure its status and operational level. There were central actors within the organization that had promoted these policies and the organization as such was seen to benefit from the process. In the interviews this was often described in terms of appropriateness, adhering to the general norms of the society outside (compare March and Olsen, 1989).

It was candidly acknowledged that the organization and its key officials were deliberately pursuing a new information strategy to make the work of the ministry more observable and measurable to outsiders, particularly to the Ministry of Finance and to financial auditors. Since the early 2000s, there had been demands voiced for producing calculable information on the activities of the ministry made, for instance, by the Parliament's Finance Committee, the National Audit Office, and the Parliament's Audit Committee (Valtiovarainvaliokunta 2001, p. 7; Valtiontalouden tarkastusvirasto 2006, p. 1; Tarkastusvaliokunta 2007b, pp. 6–7). This was the major policy 'problem' (cf. Bacchi 1999) that led to the adoption of new 'open' measures of governance. In order to justify and maintain the level of its activities and budget, the ministry had felt the need to produce information about itself. This communication now also counted as a measurable activity.

Notions of 'openness' and 'public diplomacy' were introduced into the vocabulary of the ministry and gradually also new ideas of media strategies and service. This started in the early 2000s. The new policy discourse of openness was also communicated to organizational domains that had previously sought their legitimation from (diplomatic) secrecy. At the heart of the above changes are the new ideas of accountability, particularly financial ones, that the ministry was exposed to. While referring to the general coordinative discourse of openness (Schmidt 2002; see Chapter 2), the ministry still had its own interests to pursue.

5.3   New conceptualizations of foreign political information

The perceptions of information resources in the ministry can be roughly divided into two categories. Firstly, foreign political information was perceived as historical and secretive material, subject, at present, to 25 years of secrecy. The secret-public dichotomy appeared when handling requests for documents made by journalists, researchers and occasionally by citizens. The second perception framed information as a strategic resource with which the ministry could pursue its chosen goals, but only if this resource was made available to others. There was a new strategic communication by the ministry, now sharing its information with its strategic partners in society, a point I will return to in detail. Moreover, the abstract notion of openness also appeared in the comparisons with other countries, as a characteristic of Finland or the Nordic countries.

In the early 2000s, the ministry published a report on the challenges facing Foreign Services in the twenty-first century (Ulkoasiainministeriö 2001a). Within the ministry the report went by the name of 'Mother-report' (*'Äiti-selvitys'*), pointing also to an advent of something new. The report was by and large centered on a new orientation of the ministry, describing changes in the international system and in the field of duties of the ministry. Though the main motivation of the document was for securing sufficient funding for the ministry, it listed many changes in the environment of the ministry.[2] The most obvious of these was the end of the Cold War, which was also raised in the interviews conducted in the organizations. The other megatrend referred to was globalization, consisting of new forums of politics, channels of information, and networks of trade and tourism.

The report on the challenges facing the Foreign Services was presented to the parliamentary Foreign Affairs Committee, which forwarded it to the Finance Committee for comment. The former stressed that the current level of operation was to be maintained (Ulkoasiainvaliokunta, 2001), whereas the latter stated that the allocation of resources should be reassessed and the institutional tasks of the ministry should be re-evaluated in the new globalizing environment, calling for enhanced efficiency, effectiveness and productivity (Valtiovarainvaliokunta 2001, p. 7).

Somewhat surprisingly, the internationalization of governance had put the Ministry for Foreign Affairs in a position where it had to rethink and re-establish its functions, and legitimize its existence and scope of activities in the evolving institutional setting. The above document on the challenges facing the Foreign Service also acknowledges that the traditional tasks of the ministry had kept it distant from the public but that this was now changing. Foreign policy and foreign affairs were becoming a topic of 'normal debate' in civil society and the media, which also called for an 'open and efficient' communications policy (Ulkoasiainministeriö 2001a, p. 6).

All in all, the turn of the 2000s marked a shift in the policy of the ministry, making the issue of 'openness' and public relations topical. There is a strong link between the demands for better efficiency and effectiveness within the ministry. The maintaining of the Foreign Service's level of work was also directly tied with the notion of national competitiveness, which now rested on Finland's internationally acclaimed good public institutions. The reference point already in 2001 was the international comparisons and country rankings on national competitiveness (cf. Porter 1990):

> No research that seriously deals with [economic] competitiveness will ignore the role of public power. What is the role in all this of the Ministry for Foreign Affairs and our embassies abroad? This is a good moment to speak about this, not because we would have an answer to everything, but because the question of the challenges and resources of the Finnish Foreign Service have been made more visible than at any time before. [...]We are of one mind – and without disputes about territory – that important task of the foreign missions, embassies and consulates – almost a hundred Finnish antennas – is communications and the promotion of the internationalization of businesses and opening the doors for Finnish enterprises. (Undersecretary of State, Pertti Torstila, speech to the conference on competitiveness, Haaga Institute 14.11.2001; Torstila 2001)

Before, until the 1990s, the ministry was a closed organization and the ethical basis of diplomatic secrecy was almost unquestioned in Finland. The term of secrecy shifted between 40 to 50 years (see Table 5.1). In fact, the ministry was largely able to set its own standards of secrecy and, to some extent, act as a censor (Favorin 2003). When the first law on accessing government documents came out in 1951, the ministry was taken by surprise as it was treated like any other government agency. This led to a response to change the legislation and a 50-year rule of secrecy for all material relating to foreign affairs was enacted. Given that the ministry was founded in 1918 and the Finnish state gained its independence in 1917, all foreign political material, despite its age, was unavailable to the public.

Public pressure from the academic community in need of research material led to revising the secrecy rule to 40 years in 1966.[3] But, in 1984, the 50-year rule was imposed again for fear of documents from the immediate post-Second World War period reaching the public domain (Favorin 2003). Over the years, foreign examples had been used to justify the lengthy secrecy term. Since all European countries had long terms of secrecy for foreign political information, this was a successful strategy. Hence, the development of the term of secrecy in Finland closely reflects international developments particularly to do with the Cold War.

However, the Cold War also set a specific agenda for Finland as Finnish–Soviet relations were a key concern of Finnish foreign policy.

Table 5.1 Development of the term of secrecy at the Ministry for Foreign Affairs 1952–2001[5]

Year	Term of secrecy	Description
9.2.1951 [into force 1.1.1952]	The first law on the public access to government documents. The general term of closure for secret material was set at 25 years.	At first, the law on public access to government documents did not differentiate between foreign political material from other types of government documents.
5.6.1952	The term of secrecy for foreign political material was extended to 50 years.	The general term of closure for secret material remained 25 years, but the term of secrecy for foreign political material was set at 50 years.
10.2.1967	The term of secrecy was adjusted to 40 years	Academics, backed by political influence, criticized the 50-year term of secrecy, which did not allow access to primary sources. The criticism of the lack of research material led to the adjustment in the term of secrecy.
7.9.1984	The term of secrecy was extended back to 50 years.	In the order to maintain the secrecy of the material of the immediate post-Second World War period, the Ministry for Foreign Affairs together with the military drove the extension back to 50 years. Also, international models were referred to, since secrecy was a prevailing standard.
10.12.1992	The term of secrecy was altered to 40 years.	In practice, research permits had already been issued for material less than 50 years old. Many other European countries had already adopted a 30-year term of secrecy.
8.2.2001	The previous particular exemptions for foreign political material were removed. The new Act on the Publicity of Government Activities (1999) now applied, setting the term of secrecy to 25 years.	The new law set the same standards of secrecy for all government documents, including foreign political material. Particular conditions for secrecy for foreign political material were seen to be unnecessary. International standards were further changing too.

This led to particularly sensitive attitudes towards Finnish foreign political material, which, when it was leaked to public, threw the administration into turmoil.[4] Censorship also concerned information on major issues, such as the failing health of President Kekkonen, which was partially withheld from the public (see also Paastela 1995). Even movie censorship was influenced by Finnish–Soviet relations (Helsingin Sanomat 2006). There was also a keen element of self-censorship on the part of the media (Helsingin Sanomat 1991).

A background memo for the 1984 proposal to the Council of State seeks to justify the extension of the term of secrecy by referring to 'public interest' (Ulkoasiainministeriö 1984). Arguably, the release of these documents could lead to their misuse and consequently cause harm to Finnish relations with foreign countries and damage to the individuals involved. Therefore, the ministry should have a longer term of oversight for these documents. Moreover, the ministry states that prolonging the term of secrecy would not hinder the scientific research and other activities 'acceptable for public interest' (Ulkoasiainministeriö 1984).

Referring to public interest and its legal right of discretion for the conditional use and publication of the material prevailing at that time, the thus ministry perceived itself in a position of a censor. The extension was passed in September 1984. This proved to be a rather ill-timed adjustment, as Mikhail Gorbachev shortly after becoming the General Secretary of the Communist Party of the Soviet Union initiated the 1987 perestroika reforms favoring 'glasnost' – a notion related to openness and freedom of speech.

In later accounts, the ministry saw the actual practiced term of secrecy to have been significantly shorter. Research permissions to more recent archives were said to have already been given to several researchers at the time. Also, in practical terms, the term of secrecy was said to have been moved back to the previous 40 years (Ulkoasiainministeriö 2001b; Favorin 2003). When the new law on the openness of government activities was drafted, the possibility of a 30-year secrecy term for foreign political material was discussed in the ministry. The idea was abandoned. According to one interviewee, the decision was based on the fact that this would have made the ministry look bad, especially since the actual amount of secret material was declining. Again, international examples were investigated.

But by the end of the 1990s most European countries had readjusted their terms of secrecy, often significantly. After the Cold War, the standards for secrecy in the sphere of Foreign Affairs were seen to lack foundation. When the ministry itself proposed doing away with the 40-year secrecy of documents concerning Foreign Affairs, it based its judgment on the standard of 30 years prevailing elsewhere in the European Union (Ulkoasiainministeriö 2001b). The press release on the reduction of the term of secrecy to 25 years declares that the Finnish access regulation to Foreign Political material was now 'one the most open in the world if not the most open' (Ulkoasiainministeriö 2001c).[6]

Finland's current 25-year term of secrecy is slightly more liberal than in most European Union member states that have a 30-year term. Denmark has a 20-year term of secrecy for foreign political information. Some countries favor mixed models due to their national history. For example, Hungary declared that records created prior to 2 May 1990 were subject to 15 years of secrecy counting from their date of creation. The records created after 1 May 1990 are available to the public 30 years after their creation.

In 2001, the adoption of the 25-year term was an adherence to a new norm now prevailing internationally, though the standard term in Europe tends to be five years longer. Sweden opts for a maximum of 40 years of secrecy in some cases. The term is assessed every time information is requested, and can be judged significantly shorter. The same assessment also applies to the foreign political material in Finland, which is judged upon request. However, when the material is assessed as secret, it does not appear in the public diary, making it most difficult to identify in a request. (For terms of secrecy see European Commission 2005.)

Over the years, different international models were used in the assessments for the term of secrecy in Finland. Other national models were studied for finding a justification for secrecy, but towards the 2000s there was a shift in logic. The references to other countries were now made in order to demonstrate to the outside world that the standard of 'openness' in the Ministry for Foreign Affairs was in fact higher than elsewhere. This also marked a shift in the vocabulary of the ministry as the public interest was no longer connected with keeping things secret but, on the contrary, demanded their publicity. Furthermore, the concept of openness replaced secrecy as the term used when referring to the responsible use of the information resources held by the ministry (see, for example, Lähteenkorva and Pekkarinen 2005).

In Finland, the openness of foreign political material and the activities of the ministry were also related to mounting pressures for reform within the ministry. When referring to the reforms of the 1990s at the Ministry for Foreign Affairs, one senior civil servant used the German word *'Stau'* in reference to the rush or block of reforms due to the recession, laborious EU negotiations and the number of ministers with concurrent mandates in foreign affairs, at most five, all of them from different parties.

Though the collapse of the Soviet Union had dramatically changed the environment where the ministry operated, it was not before 2000 that the change led to deliberate attempts at reforming the ministry. The notion of 'openness' became a new rhetoric of institutional legitimization (cf. Skinner 1989), and the allocation of information a subject of reform. Secrecy, as a counter-concept of openness, is elementary in understanding how foreign political material has been perceived in the organization and why the problematization of 'openness' matters (Bacchi 1999). Even if 'secrecy' might not have been seen only in positive terms, its ethical basis was seen as being solid. While the term 'secret' does not appear in the current strategy documents that the ministry was producing on itself, the concepts of 'secrecy', 'confidentiality', 'openness', 'publicity' and in some cases 'transparency' were used in the interviews. The terms were part of the narrative describing change within the organization, shifting from old secretive forms of governance to a new open mode of operating.

Transparency or administrative openness is usually perceived as following as a result of mounting pressure by civil society, or due to general calls for democratization. But the change can also start from an organizational adaptation to the outside world, legitimizing its existence, which is a more appropriate description in the case of the Ministry for Foreign Affairs. Moreover, the narratives, analogies, norms, and concepts of governance change at a general juncture of governance. They also carry the potential for institutional change. In the context of the Ministry for Foreign Affairs, this meant an institutional reorientation after the Cold War and amid the internationalization of governance, in which openness became a new norm and a legitimizing concept for the organization.

In the interviews, three strategic policy documents were highlighted as having communicated the change to outsiders, but also to those within the organization: the policy assessment of challenges facing the Ministry of Foreign Affairs at the beginning of the twenty-first century (Ulkoasiainministeriö 2001a), the strategy of the ministry in 2005 (Ulkoasiainministeriö 2005), and the future assessment of the ministry in 2006 (Ulkoasiainministeriö 2006). These documents were frequently referred to in the interviews and also placed on a logical continuum in the press releases of the ministry (Formin 2006). They therefore contributed to the new communicative discourse of openness. Furthermore, they introduced the idea of openness to the vocabulary of the ministry's personnel and gave a signal to those observing the organization from outside that things had changed, becoming a coordinative discourse among the policy actors (Schmidt 2002). These documents for the first time framed Foreign Affairs as an open activity.

Here, the concepts of openness, transparency, efficiency and expertise function as classifications or analogies for organizations. They have pejorative counter-concepts (secret, closed, rigid, elitist, inefficient) that are non-desirable (Koselleck 2004). Thus, commending concepts and conceptual change also brings about clear mechanisms of change in the institutional sphere (cf. Skinner 1969; Skinner 1989; cf. Koselleck 2004, p. 155). In the Ministry for Foreign Affairs, the matter of openness was largely related to the process of rethinking the role and fit of the organization in the changing institutional design. What were the responsibilities of the ministry? What was it supposed to do, for whom and how? I will elaborate on this in the following.

5.4   New practices of information management

A fundamental change that was raised in the interviews was the relative decline in the status of the ministry (cf. Kauppi 1997, pp. 61–62). Many other organizations were now responsible for foreign political information and, also, the information content of documents had changed. Moreover, the ministry was now faced with demands for presenting outcomes for its activities and assessments on its performance on these activities.

5.4.1   Changing information content

Unlike in the past, all ministries were now able to make international treaties and they handled their own connections to the outside world. EU-related issues were also reorganized in 2000, changing the balance between the ministries.[7] The Government Secretariat for EU Affairs functioning under the Prime Minister's Office was now responsible for coordinating EU-related tasks in all ministries (see Finnish Government 2010b). Also, other coordination tasks of increasing significance were now conducted elsewhere. In the case of OECD cooperation, on administrative reform for instance, the *locus* was the Ministry of Finance. At the same time, the importance of the international institutions of economic development and finance such as the OECD and World Bank had increased.

The interviewees saw the above shifts to have altered the role and importance of the ministry significantly. The changes also ultimately led to a diminishing number of secret documents, a perception shared by the interviewees.[8] In legal terms, foreign political information was treated like any other government information concerning the terms of disclosure.[9] To sum up, the interviewees perceived that the amount of secret material had diminished significantly since the Cold War period. This was largely caused by the changes in the operational environment of the organization, and the redefinition of its tasks influenced the information resources in its possession.

Information was now also in digital format, making it harder to control (cf. Drezner and Farrell 2004; Fung et al. 2008). Furthermore, the fact that new modes of governance involved more international actors and non-governmental organizations made the controlling of documents, not to speak of general information, a troublesome task. Many interviewees noted that the EU documents and information on meetings of EU bodies tended to 'leak out'.[10] In many cases the information had already reached the interested parties by the time the Finnish representative in the meeting finished his or her memo on it. Also the tightening networks of policy ideas and expertise carried information that used to be collected through the embassies. The internationalizing media and tightening country comparisons had made the collection of certain country-specific information unnecessary.

The focus of the activities within the ministry was also shifting, because of the increased mobility of Finnish citizens. Finns were travelling around the globe as tourists and for work in unprecedented numbers. This led to an increase in citizen contacts with the ministry. As a result, there was also more and more personal information ending up in the possession of the ministry. This was referred to in the organization as a completely new type of non-public information that was growing rapidly (see also Favorin 2003).

One further shift in the tasks of the ministry related to trade. With Finnish companies increasingly engaging in activities abroad, the ministry was seen as a helping hand. This general shift also influenced the allocation of information. In fact, the citizen interest in the information material of the ministry was more limited compared to that of private companies. Though bigger companies had undoubtedly already comprised an interest group before, they were now even more so, and small- and medium-sized enterprises were also becoming a customer group. This was reflected in the demands for information, which were increasingly coming from companies rather than from the media, NGOs or the public.

When the ministry was formed in 1918, it first consisted of three departments: the Political, Trade and Archives Departments. Since 1923, the Archives Unit was joined and subordinated to the Administrative Unit. Looking at the brief descriptions of the histories of data management and archiving of the Foreign Ministries in the EU, it becomes apparent that the practice of archiving has been fundamental for these organizations, even pivotal to their activities (European Commission 2005). At present, there is a separate Unit for Information and Documentation subordinated to the Department of Administrative affairs. At the time the interviews were conducted, the rules of procedure stated that the decisions on access to the information were decided by the Head of the Information Service. This signaled the perception of the importance of organizational memory, as the level of decision at present was very much based on actors. However, the fact that the decisions were made internally signified the shift in the perceived importance of the decision. During the Cold War, the Council of State made the decisions on exemptions to secrecy of material that was less than 50 years old.[11]

Inquiries on information concerning ongoing administrative work, on the other hand, were channeled to civil servants in charge of that given issue.[12] Actual requests for information usually came from interest groups other than citizens. Journalists, researchers, other ministries and, increasingly, private companies operating in an international environment now made up the bulk of the clientele. Citizens were also seen as 'customers'. The new shift towards service orientation also brought a new sensitivity to issues of image:

Q: You referred to the attitude and there has been a long tradition, in which 10–15 years is a short time. How were practices maintained? Were they discussed?
A: I don't think that they were discussed. Always when there was the case of a leakage of documents it was discussed. There are no experiences from other bodies. The basic idea here has been cleverly understood that certain documents are confidential. The idea that openness is a good thing is a newer notion. But yes, here the majority understands that confidentiality and openness are not opposites. Both are justified. The attitude is good. Now and then there's the view that the media's and citizens' information interests are of no concern, that it's none of their business that we are in charge of this. But these are fleeting. It's not politically correct to say that you don't care about your clients. (Expert in Information Services, Ministry for Foreign Affairs)

The interviewees saw the citizen interest to be sporadic and considered the work of the ministry to be too technical and uninteresting for citizens to be engaged. Citizens were seen to have an interest in crises such as the Asian tsunami, when their involvement was seen as a necessity, though also in terms of the image of the ministry (see also Valtioneuvoston kanslia 2005e). This was coupled with the fears of diminishing resources: to maintain operations the citizens had to be served. The same views were present in the media strategies.

Regarding the number of requests of information, the picture was somewhat unclear.[13] No exact figure was made available but the annual numbers of decisions were in the dozens rather than hundreds. The use of legislation, with actual reference to it when requesting information, was seen as somewhat limited, if it was used at all. Citizens were seen as lacking in knowledge about legislation, and journalists were seen as prepared to settle for less than actually might have been available according to the law. Regarding the control function of the law, the interviewees often saw that the actual in-house issues were of little relevance to the general public and that the journalists tended to be after stories on ill-spent resources. The subject matter proper was very seldom accessed by requests for documents.

Following the Act on the Publicity of Government Activities, the ministries were also made responsible to provide public and secret diaries on their documents. The public diary contained the heading of the document, which itself could have been classified as confidential, either partially or in full. Should there be a public interest in the public diary of the ministry, the headings of the documents would be visible to those outside the organization. As a consequence, civil servants were instructed not to take too much 'artistic licence' with the titles of their documents and not to give out too detailed information in the headings.

Yet, the external interest in the public diary of the ministry was small. Only the main Finnish newspaper, Helsingin Sanomat, regularly requested the public diary. There were also others who requested it just after the 1999 act came into force, but as time passed no-one else bothered to ask for this information. Only big media cases such as leaks of confidential foreign political information and crises such as the Asian tsunami or the case of Finnish tourists taken as hostages in the Philippines had been the subject of greater public interest, bringing sudden media exposure to the ministry. Altogether, in 'normal times', the publicity shed on the activities of the ministry through the right to access its documents was perceived as being very small, and the control function of access to information was considered to be limited. The issues dealt with in the ministry required expertise that was possessed by only a few, and even fewer knew what to ask and how when requesting information.

General figures were also made available on the shift towards the openness of foreign political material. At the time when the follow-up studies of the new Act on the Publicity of Government Activities were underway in the early 2000s, the ministry collected some figures on the amount of secret documents. The figures concerned secret messages sent within the organization, which amounted to the single biggest type of secret documents – these are presented in Figure 5.1. During the Cold War there had been some 5,000 such secret messages a year, but the figure reduced in five years to almost half that amount. Finnish accession to the European Union again caused a peak, indicating tough negotiations over membership. In 1994, there were a little more than 2,500 incoming secret messages to the ministry and some 500 secret messages leaving. The figures remained static and even increased slightly until 1997, after which they started to decline. The Finnish EU Presidency in 1999 again caused a slight peak (some 2,400 incoming secret messages, and about 900 outgoing) (Ulkoasiainministeriö 2003).

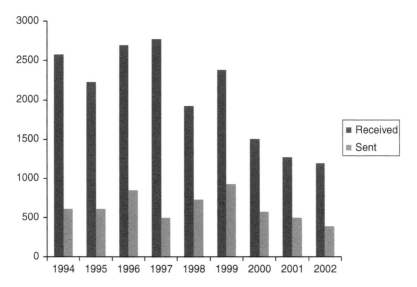

Figure 5.1   Secret messages received and sent by the Ministry for Foreign Affairs in 1994–2002

Source: Ulkoasiainministeriö 2003.[14]

Since the issue of openness became topical and was re-enforced by law in December 1999, the number of secret messages was reported to have dropped in the Ministry for Foreign Affairs.[15] An internal document of the ministry dating from 2003 mentions that world events such as the 11 September 2001 attacks in the US, international campaigns against terrorism or the conflicts in Afghanistan and Iraq had not increased the numbers of secret messages (Ulkoasiainministeriö 2003). The general understanding in the interviews also was that there were very few secret documents at present.

Figure 5.2 presents the overall number of secret documents between 2002 and 2008, with a categorical classification for the years 2004–2008 (source: secret diary of the Ministry for Foreign Affairs). The annual number of secret documents varies between 1,507 (2002) and 2,168 (2006) and is by no means declining. Statistics prior to 2002 are not available because the information system for secret documents was brought into use in that year. This transition may still be visible in the lower figure of 2002, as Figure 5.1 would indicate that alone the (total) number of secret messages was over 1,500 (Ulkoasiainministeriö 2003).

Figure 5.2 includes all secret documents in the record of secret documents of the Ministry for Foreign Affairs. The total number of secret documents has increased slightly, with a peak in 2006, presumably caused by the Finnish EU presidency (cf. Ulkoasiainministeriö 2003).

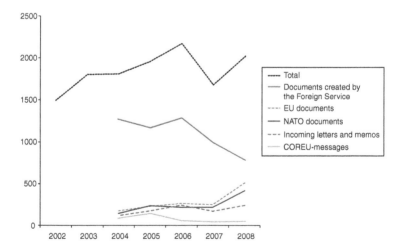

Figure 5.2 Number of secret documents in the Ministry for Foreign Affairs 2002–2008[16]

It shows a rather stable level of secret documents. The largest group of secret documents was that created by the Foreign Service, that is the ministry and the embassies, which has been on the decline since 2004. At the same time, there has been an increase in such groups as secret EU documents, NATO documents and incoming letters and memos. The smallest group of secret documents, the so-called COREU messages, had been on the decline since 2005, remaining at some 50 messages a year.

The overall number of documents processed annually in the ministry was said to be roughly 100,000. Some 60,000–70,000 documents are being generated within the organization and about 20,000–30,000 are received from elsewhere (for instance from international organizations and from interest groups and private companies). The secret documents thus made up 1.5–2 percent of all documents. The figure was reckoned to be low by the interviewees and they saw the secretive image of the ministry to be unfounded at present. Nevertheless, secrecy as a concept was firmly in everyone's vocabulary and the perception about access to the material was often realized through the ministry's archives.

Figure 5.3 shows the number of documents created in the Foreign Service that were stored in the public records, meaning that their heading was visible to anyone wishing to access the public diary. They are mostly public, but some are confidential. The current information system used by the ministry does not enable making statistics on the different classifications, such as public and confidential. Hence, only an estimate could be given on the number of confidential documents: the figure was estimated as somewhat small. In 2002, some 20 percent of all non-secret documents produced in the ministry were classified as confidential when they were created (Ulkoasiainministeriö 2003). However, the content of a document was always checked when it was given for non-governmental use, and so the classification is reassessed every time a request is made for a particular document. The grounds for confidentiality may no longer apply after a certain period of time. The classification therefore implies the perceived status of the document at the time of its creation.

Along with the new access law there were new instructions to civil servants in the foreign ministry. As a general rule, information concerning third parties – often other countries – was perceived as secret, providing that access to such 'documents could damage or compromise Finland's international relations or its ability to participate in international co-operation.'[17] These concerned particularly the handling of documents coming from outside the ministry, from EU bodies or other international organizations. Also, the country reports written by diplomats containing assessments on their country of stay might be

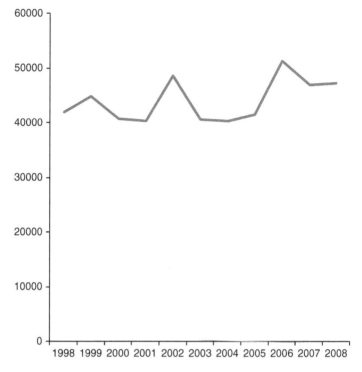

Figure 5.3 Non-secret documents created in the Finnish Foreign Service

categorized as such, particularly if the assessments were negative. There was also an 'originator control' applied in some cases. This applied to NATO documents (and WEU documents). These documents were not handled according to national legislation but according to NATO's internal security rules. EU documents with security classifications were handled similarly (Ulkoasiainministeriö 2001d).

The close collaboration within the EU and other international actors was not seen to have led to the increasing number of secret documents in the ministry. As already stated in the interviews, the number of secret and non-public documents was, in fact, seen to be in decline. This is most likely the case in comparison to the Cold War years. However, the above figures show only a decline in the number of secret messages and in the secret documents created in the Finnish Foreign Services, while the over-all number of classified documents has been on a slight increase since 2002 (compare Figures 5.1 and 5.2). In recent years, the gradual increase has come from secret EU and NATO documents and from other incoming letters and memos. To summarize, there are now fewer secret documents created inside the ministry but more coming in from outside.

In the interviews, the secrecy of military and political activity was said to be on the decline. There is also more of an exchange of trade-related information, and one senior executive expressed as a personal view that 'most of the secrets in the contemporary world are commercial secrets.' The ethical core of the foreign political or diplomatic secrecy was perceived to be in protecting the negotiation positions of other countries from becoming public without their consent. In the EU context, for instance, the stands of other countries engaging in negotiations were considered as information that could compromise Finland's international relations if made public. Furthermore, documents that contained information on negotiations between the EU and third parties were also not to be disclosed. This, arguably, would reveal strategic information on how far the EU might afford to negotiate. I discuss this further in the next sub-chapter.

5.4.2   New domains of foreign political information

The above account, including the statistical information on the secret material, points to a change of activities within the Ministry for Foreign Affairs. Many interviewees stressed the role of Finland's EU membership in redefining the role of the ministry. But this also applied to other ministries. Because of Finland's EU membership and the growing competencies of the European Union, several policy fields that were previously domestic matters are now subject to EU regulation. Documents from EU bodies are likely to contain the negotiating positions of other countries, which are not public information according to internationally adopted diplomatic practice.

Moreover, in trade policy in particular, political conflicts within the member states were seen as internal weaknesses that were to be withheld from the negotiation partners of the Union:

> I've never seen a top secret document. There are secret ones circulating every week. There are a lot of confidential ones and this is due to the fact that when you start negotiations your positions should be kept secret from the other side, and that if and when there is a dispute within the EU on some matter of detail, we can't tell the media that Italy or France is the stupid country that brought down the project. In other words, internal EU disputes should be dealt with internally within the EU, otherwise this other side may benefit from

the EU's weak spots. In the function of negotiations and in internal negotiations there are occasions in which [information] should be kept confidential. This means that the typical stuff that is written here, the memorandum of the meeting, has to be classified as confidential, because individual countries express delicate positions that must not be communicated outside the EU system. (Civil Servant, Ministry for Foreign Affairs)

When referring to new domains of foreign political material, the civil servants in the ministry often mentioned agricultural policy as an example of a potential domain where new practices were adopted. Referring to negotiations where the cultivation of sugar beet was at stake in Finland, the question was made whether Finnish farmers had the access to the information concerning their trade:

I don't know. I think that this old idea, that the positions of other countries are not to be revealed, maybe increased the amount of secrecy. If, before, Finland decided how to deal with its sugar beet it was public information. If it is now decided in a meeting in Brussels, in which each country gives its point of view, these meeting reports are not publicized, just the decision that a Finnish sugar beet factory will be closed. Perhaps it would show up better in the Ministry of Agriculture and Forestry, as to how these things have changed from the days when they were considered wholly matters of domestic policy. (Expert in Information Services, Ministry for Foreign Affairs)

As a matter of convention the stands and positions of other countries in negotiations were not to be disclosed. Moreover, negotiations were seen as a strategic procedure where one should not express one's negotiating leeway. There is thus a tension between the logic of diplomatic decision-making and national publicity. In general, the positions of other countries were seen as posing a dilemma as civil servants in Finland would have had to follow the international media to judge whether some information was public or not. Had the information been discussed in the national media in, say, Spain or Germany, it would have been possible to tell this to the Finnish audience too. But without the position definitively being public, one was not to do so in Finland either.[18]

In assessing the potential influence of the increasing amount of EU documents and EU-related issues, the interviewees acknowledged that these had increased immensely in recent years. Whereas before there were few specific bodies handling such tasks, the Ministry of Forestry and Agriculture alone had dozens of active working groups on EU matters. The number of people involved in handling EU documents had also grown respectively. Moreover, it was increasingly difficult to judge what was and was not an EU matter. Was the Swedish potential membership in the European Single Currency an EU or a domestic matter? And in the case of the Russian government's taxation on the Finnish imports of raw wood, where Finland later opted for the EU's help in 2008, the definition is also unclear – at what point did it become an EU matter?

Concerning EU documents, the number of non-public foreign political documents was in fact potentially seen to have increased, a view held in the Ministry of Justice and the Ministry for Foreign Affairs. The Prime Minister's Office was more hesitant, saying that non-public material might not be univocally increasing and at least this should be assessed in more detail. Placed under the Prime Minister's Office, the coordination of EU tasks also involved a separate information system, where the documents on EU tasks were stored. This allows a separate assessment of their number.

Figure 5.4 shows all EU documents created or received in Finland from 2002–2008. A single data point for 1995 was also made available

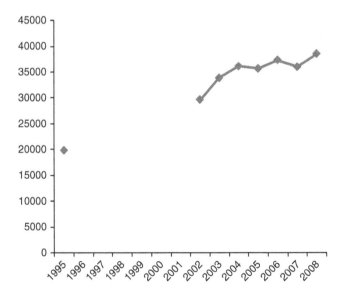

Figure 5.4 Number of EU documents in the Finnish central government, 1995, 2002–2008[19]

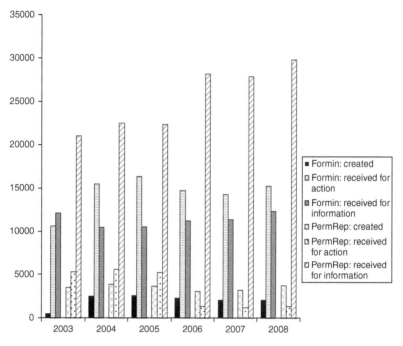

Figure 5.5 EU documents created and received at the Ministry for Foreign Affairs and by Finland's Permanent Representation to the EU, 2003–2008[20]

from the year of Finland's EU accession, which is inserted as a reference. Due to a change in information systems, there is no comprehensive data available for the whole of Finland's EU membership. In 2008, there were 38,498 EU documents in the Finnish central government, and in 1995 the figure was 19,810 (see Figure 5.4), marking a significant rise in the documents. Altogether, the central government's repository for EU documents (EUTORI) contained some 629,897 documents, with all attachments and language versions included.

The following section presents a detailed view of the division of EU documents in the Ministry for Foreign Affairs and Finland's Permanent Representation, Prime Minister's Office and in the Ministry of Agriculture in 2003–2008. The volumes of EU documents in the Ministry for Foreign Affairs were on the rise since 2003 (see Figure 5.5). The Ministry for Foreign Affairs and Finland's Permanent Representation to the EU still handled the majority of EU documents, either creating them or receiving them for action or for being informed. The overall anatomy

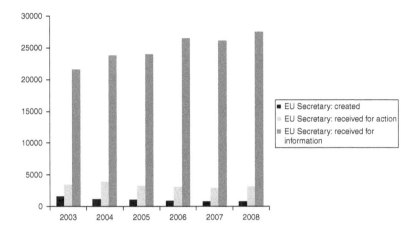

Figure 5.6   EU documents created and received in the EU secretary of Prime Minister's Office, 2003–8

of EU documents consisted of documents created in Finland and documents that were received from EU institutions. The figures on received documents comprise documents originating from EU institutions and other Finnish ministries.

The EU secretary of the Prime Minister's Office also handled a large amount of EU documents, mainly receiving them so as to be informed on activities (see Figure 5.6). The number of documents created in the organization was quite small, but the secretary, like the Finnish Permanent Representation, received a lot of documents notifying about activities.

Figure 5.7 shows the respective numbers for the Ministry of Forestry and Agriculture, and here one sees the influence of EU documents on the ministry's information management. As noted by the interviewees, this particular ministry had abundant EU activities due to the primary competences of the Union in the agricultural policy. Also, here the number of received documents was significantly larger than those created in the ministry. The overall trend, as in other organizations, is increasing.

The above anatomy of the EU documents in the three domains of EU-related tasks shows that the majority of EU documents are still handled by the Foreign Service and the Prime Minister's Office, but that there are also other ministries now in possession of substantial amounts of EU documents, such as the Ministry of Agriculture and Forestry, as

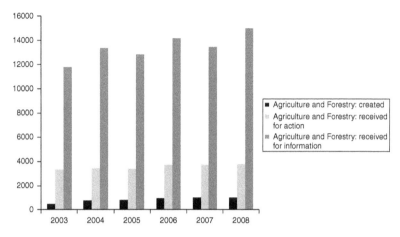

Figure 5.7   EU documents created and received at the Ministry of Agriculture and Forestry, 2003–2008

estimated in the interviews. It is altogether another matter how this has influenced access to information. Perhaps some assessments could be made on the classifications of the documents. However, the figures on the publicity of the documents were not available for each organization, but only for the administration as a whole.

Figure 5.8 shows the EU documents created in Finland according to the classification of public–non-public. Non-public documents made up by far the biggest category and the number of documents classified as public was minimal. We should be cautious with the figures though, as the label non-public might not apply at the time the document was requested. The classification only indicates the perceived status at the time the document was created and stored in the system.[21] A third category included, 'assessed later', referred to documents that had no label regarding publicity classification. The Prime Minister's Office explained the large number of documents in this category with the fast pace of reporting following EU meetings. The reports have to be written within 24 hours after the meeting, which left the civil servants very little time to consider the publicity of their report. The non-labeling was therefore to be interpreted as postponing the assessment until later, should someone ask for the document. The Prime Minister's Office held the view that these documents were most likely perceived as non-public, rather than public.

The majority of the EU documents created in Finland were perceived as non-public information. As we have seen, the figures

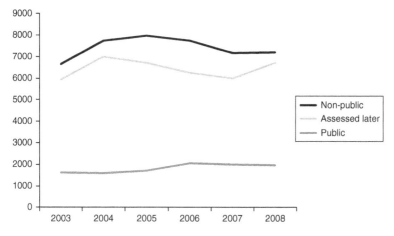

Figure 5.8 EU documents created in Finland by publicity classification, 2003–2008

presented here refer to the assessment when the document was written. In the interviews, the perception of an open administrative culture prevailing in Northern Europe was also based on the classification of documents, which was seen to be more liberal in the Nordic countries.

However, when we compare them to the EU documents received by Finland's central government from EU institutions (see Figure 5.9), one is faced with the somewhat surprising situation that despite the secretive image of EU bureaucracy, public documents up make the biggest group of such material. Even though non-public and non-classified documents (limited, confidential, restraint, and non-classified) are by far greater in number also here, the share of documents classified clearly as public is significantly bigger with respect to the documents received from EU institutions than in those created in Finland. Of the documents originating from EU institutions 36 percent were classified as public in 2008, whereas this was the case for only four percent of the documents created in Finland.

Even if one assumed that the non-classified documents were all public but was not indicated as such, the share of public documents for EU institutions would still stand at 49 percent and the Finnish administration at 48 percent (in 2008). In other words, Finland more often classified its documents as non-public than other member states and EU institutions.

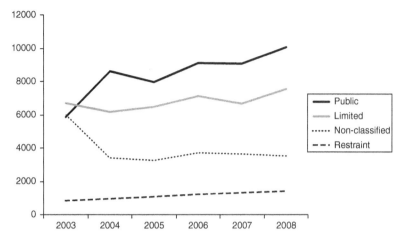

Figure 5.9 EU documents received from EU institutions by publicity classification, 2003–2008

Because we do not precisely know the content of the documents, there might be a structural bias influencing the numbers that one should take into account: Finnish civil servants might not have been categorically more secretive, but perhaps doing a different type of reporting. EU documents created in Finland are mostly reports on the meetings of various EU bodies, concerning the policy process, which is perceived to be non-public before decisions are made and later concerning the positions of countries. The documents received from EU institutions might be more diverse in content, explaining their relative publicity. Nevertheless, the interviewees' view that Finnish civil servants would classify the documents more liberally than the representatives of other EU countries or institutions is not supported by the above statistics.

In principle, the Ministry for Foreign Affairs was not allowed to give its non-public documents to national interest groups let alone the general public, even if these documents concerned the public interest. However, apart from the worries of the EU's negative influence on Finland's administrative practices expressed by the parliamentarians in 1998 when debating the Act on the Publicity of Government Activities (see Chapter 2), this had not become a policy issue. The interviewees in the ministry were assured that all policy actors got the information they needed, even if it was classified as confidential. This activity of circulating confidential information was in the interviews named as 'openness'.

Moreover, openness now also comprised strategic communication. I will explore these practices and their motives in the following section.

5.5 Openness and transparency

The practices regarding citizen or media access to the documents of the ministry were discussed as publicity, as opposed to secrecy. But the strategic communication of the organization was discussed under the label 'openness'. This comprised several new institutional practices, such as public appearances by experts, public hearings, and information services. But it also referred to circulating confidential documents to strategic partners. Those new activities that took place in the public sphere can be linked to the demands of reportable outcomes of activities due to performance management. The circulation of confidential information, a non-public activity, was also mainly a response to the perceived pressures of economic globalization.

1.5.1 From diplomats to experts

The role of civil servants became rethought in the process of change at play in the Ministry for Foreign Affairs. They were no longer to be seen as diplomats but as experts in their field. This was tightly connected to the new perception within the ministry that it was suddenly competing with other organizations. Interviewees both in and outside the organization drew attention to the fact that in the early 2000s civil servants at the Ministry for Foreign Affairs were actively encouraged to make public appearances. This policy aimed at promoting the use of the foreign political expertise of the organization.

In June 2002, an instruction on public appearances and use of expertise was given to the ministry personnel (Ulkoministeriö 2002). It stated that the Foreign Ministry and its embassies still possessed the most significant expertise on Finnish foreign relations and international politics, but that there was 'healthy competition' posed by organizations in different fields of administration and research institutes:

> The Foreign Service continues to concentrate on Finland's foreign relations and the importance of expertise in international politics in our country. This should more effectively be at the disposal of society, through among other things media and conference presentations and such like. The Foreign Ministry is itself in a robust competitive situation in which many other actors, such as other administrative sectors and research institutes are able to provide expertise to the

media on international questions. (Ulkoministeriö 2002 [Foreign Ministry, 2002])

The instruction also highlights the dichotomy between the roles of an 'expert' and a 'bureaucrat' that should be taken into account: whether one is expressing a personal opinion or a position coming from Finland or the EU. Also, the interviewees identified heightened competition among different public organizations as the primary motivation for the ministry's active policy of communication.

The competition was also a result of the new tasks and competencies of other ministries, and research organizations too were now seen as being in competition with the ministry. The perceived competitors of the ministry included military experts at the National Defence University, who were seen to have publicly commented on issues that belonged to the sphere of Foreign Affairs and the ministry. A senior civil servant expressed this as below:

> One reason was that the world had changed. If we take 11 September 2001, you couldn't from the viewpoint of our ministry think that on current affairs programmes, where expertise is needed, that there would be colonels and lieutenant-colonels appearing night after night. And the expertise of our ministry wasn't used at all. (Senior Executive, Ministry for Foreign Affairs)

Competition caused jealousy over certain of the ministry's information resources. In particular, the country reports that the embassies were producing had found a commercial use, which annoyed certain civil servants. The ministry did not publish the country reports since they included classified information. But at least the non-classified part was given out to other users, such as Finpro, an association providing Finnish companies with internationalization services, which sold this information to its customers. The ministry, as the producer of the information, was planning to make it public in order to claim credit for it. Concerning the selling of information, the possibility for accrual charging was also referred to, yet this is not seen as a plausible strategy to pursue (cf. Chapter 4).

It is also worth noting that the public information produced by the ministry was one of the few activities that the ministry was able to present in numerical form. Like other ministries, the Ministry for Foreign Affairs was increasingly responsible for its performance. As its activities were judged by productivity and outcome according to the new performance management criteria – budget transparency imposed by the 'performance prism' (see Chapter 2) – it was of great importance to have quantitative results.

5.5.2   Measuring foreign affairs

From 2004, a new accountability reform had made all the state bureaus subject to reporting the effectiveness of their activities. The working order of the Ministry for Foreign Affairs states explicitly that 'true and fair information' will be produced on its activities.[22] But measuring performance in foreign affairs had proved difficult. The abstract task of the ministry and the complex field where it was operating made the effects of its activities almost impossible to measure. The Foreign Services are in fact a classic example of an agency model that produces neither observable outputs nor effects (Wilson 1989; cf. Pollitt et al. 2004). But if you cannot measure it, does it count?

The new demands to produce numerical information on the activities of the organization were met with frustration and irony in the interviews. Many also pointed to the absurdity of reporting only those aspects of the activities of the ministry that were quantifiable:

> But how do you measure foreign policy? [...] A part of our activity is very easily quantifiable. For instance, last year we issued half a million visas. It's easy to determine. But what about effectiveness? (Senior Executive, Ministry for Foreign Affairs)

From a broad perspective, the general goals of the organization were the same as the Millennial Goals of the United Nations. As some sarcastically noted, it would be impossible to quantify the effect that Finland, or indeed the ministry, had had on fighting absolute poverty in the world. Such abstract macro-level issues were difficult to measure to begin with and the impact of a single actor was no longer possible, nor sensible, to establish.

Though there was some understanding outside the organization that the Ministry for Foreign Affairs was facing a particularly difficult task in trying to quantify its results, the demands for this were nevertheless mounting up (Valtiontalouden tarkastusvirasto 2006, pp. 1–2). Within the organization, the demands for the quantification of activities was met with bewilderment as the civil servants were trying to think of ways to measure their activities. A thorough quantification of activities was seen as problematic, but the demand for numbers was becoming more accepted as a way to proceed; even if with 'qualitative measures'. The analogies were sought even from disciplinary measures of psychology.

> It is hard for us to depict our result objectives in a functional way, and its measurability. I don't personally see measuring as a problem but rather the impossibility of measuring as an optical illusion, because it can be done in so many ways. [The National Audit Office] has developed purely qualitative multiple scales, which are then based on yes-no estimations, less-moderately-a lot. There are gradual divisions, which are always subjective, but which can be made in a reasonably uncontentious way [...] I remember hearing on the radio last summer a psychiatrist explaining how schizophrenia is diagnosed. There are about 20 things that a trained psychiatrist goes over with the patient, all of them qualitative assessments. Then comes the index, in which there are tolerance limits [...]. To my understanding it works. Established practice, indexed figures bring differences of degree. Not absolute ones, but if the score is high, you can draw conclusions. If it is low or medium, you can draw other conclusions. I think that there are the preconditions to measure our activity and its effectiveness. We have to be able to determine our objectives and that is the difficulty. (Senior Executive, Ministry for Foreign Affairs)

In 2007, the organization was in the process of assessing its objectives for which instructions were given in 2001 (Ulkoasiainministeriö 2007a). The embassies were requested to give proposals for performance contracts. The model performance contract states that the objectives should be derived from the government programmes and the strategy of the ministry. Moreover, an analysis of the context of activities, assessment of the operative logic of the bureau – why the embassy exists (compare Douglas, 1987) – and an output analysis were required (Ulkoasiainministeriö 2007b). The different units of the ministry were again seen as being difficult to assess in terms of performance: they lacked direct hierarchical relations and their goals were the same as those of the ministry as a whole. The Administrative Unit was seen as the only unit to have enough identifiable and traceable activities to consider it a subject of performance management.

The embassies were given a scorecard that they were supposed to use in planning their proposal for a performance contract concerning the budget proposal (Ulkoasiainministeriö 2007c). As a starting point for the identification of the objectives of the organization, five performance goals were identified: 1) an influential Finland in the international community, 2) security creating for the international community, 3) a just world, 4) a successful Finland, and 5) an open and serving Ministry for Foreign Affairs (Ulkoasiainministeriö 2007d). The first three were macro-level goals that involved grand policy processes comprising, for instance, Finnish input to EU policies, transatlantic relations, crises management, reforming the global finances, and the fulfillment of the UN Millennial Goals.

These are, to put it mildly, bold ambitions for a single ministry. This was acknowledged by the organization, but as the pressure for measurable outcomes was mounting, they had to be named. In practice, these three goals were so abstract that they were not to be translated into the objective of a unit or an embassy (see Ulkoasiainministeriö 2007c). The only defined objective was reporting the economic development in a country and solving 'barriers of trade'. The indicators to measure this were 'the amount and quality of reporting', the amount of solved cases of trade barriers, and customer response (from the companies).

The latter two goals – a successful Finland, and the open and serving Ministry – were more concrete: concentrating on helping Finnish companies in their international activities, promoting Finland internationally, and exporting Finnish culture; and presenting Finland abroad, responding to customer needs, and exploring the new possibilities of online media. In 2007, the goals of 'a successful Finland' and 'an open and serving Ministry' were practically the only domains where the Ministry for Foreign Affairs had been able to define clear objectives that were measurable: the quality and quantity of various types of reporting, solved customer cases, customer response, responsiveness in an emergency abroad, the processing of filed applications to enter the country, tracking the amount of users on the ministry's internet site.

The difficulty of quantifying the activities and the resulting strategic shifts bear an element of mismeasure, the inability of a numeric objectification to solve a problem that it seeks to tackle (Hummel 2006). Even if influence in the international community, international security concerns, or development goals such as a 'just world' could not be measured easily, these are still perhaps the most important goals for the Foreign Service of a country. Should this be agreed upon, one might also accept that the outcomes that the organization was now setting for itself were emphasizing alternative goals, pointing to a slight counter-finality (Baert 1991), the unintended consequence of this activity. Already earlier, the openness of the activities of the organization had been necessary for its strategic aim of maintaining its budget, but due to the performance management and the mandate to quantify activities this now counted even more than before.

5.5.3 Meeting the public at home

The information service of the ministry had already become a priority in the early 2000s. As a motivation for this, the revised Act on the Publicity of Government Activities was named. Also, the Communication Recommendation for Central Government, released in 2002, was seen to have an ideational impact on what should be done in this domain (Valtioneuvoston kanslia 2002a). The media services of the ministry were said to have developed rapidly, particularly in the late 1990s and early 2000s. The information strategy of the Finnish EU presidency in 1999 put forward the process of utilizing the internet for foreign political information services and led to the launching of the ministry's own website in 2000. Intranet solutions had already been used for far longer and a Virtual Finland site had also been running for a long time. Technology was not an obstacle but rather the model for operating was seen to have shifted in the early 2000s, now keen to address the media. Other previous experiences were gained from Finland's EU accession, which involved citizen information services. This practice was later institutionalized and the Europe Information Service of the ministry now provided 20 sites for EU-related information all over the country (Eurooppatiedotus 2010). There were also a lot of publication activities in this domain.

The Ministry of Finance conducted a survey in 2007 asking the ministries about their use of public hearings. The Ministry for Foreign Affairs stood out as the ministry to conduct by far the most public hearings annually, thousands with commentary rounds included. Even single embassies conducted public hearings (Holkeri 2007). This was seen as a strategic activity of the organization that the units were organizing independently, according to their contacts. In 2001 and 2002, the ministry undertook a road show to cities in Finland to improve its profile among the public. There were some 20 visits to different Finnish towns and cities, where the ministry presented itself to the public, attracting large audiences. The Ministry of Finance acknowledged this in its 2005 memo on public hearings as an example. (Valtiovarainministeriö 2005a, p. 29)

During a normal Helsinki day in June 2002, the Ministry for Foreign Affairs' offices in Helsinki were opened to the public and over 1,000 people visited the premises. In 2003, the ministry assessed the same event to have brought 2,000 people to visit it in a single day. After these experiences, the annual meetings of the heads of embassies were also made partially public to the press. In 2007, on visitor's day, the ministry faced the public in a tent put up next to the ministry, with the doors still open to groups wishing to enter the main building (Formin 2007). The general interest towards the work of the ministry, at least its physical premises and personnel, shows that there was a certain amount of curiosity towards foreign affairs or the ministry itself. But the above elements of spectatorship do not entail any active attempt at uncovering or influencing the current policy issues of the ministry, but rather aim at clarifying its routines and tasks.

Openness, understood as opening the physical premises of the ministry and letting the public meet their representatives abroad, might have helped to explain the work of the ministry to the general public. But the ministry was faced with a more critical audience at the Ministry of Finance. In the interviews and public speeches, the developments were part of the reorientation of the ministry and thus also of strategic value to the process of ensuring resources (Formin, 2002). In other words, when the Ministry of Finance acknowledged the work on the public hearings done in the Ministry for Foreign Affairs, a goal had been reached.

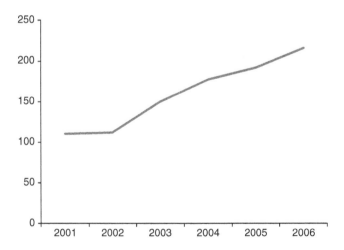

Figure 5.10 Annual number of online news items, 2001–2006

The provision of online news increased during the 2000s (see Figure 5.10) and there was also a large amount of press releases issued by the organization. For the general public, who were now increasingly travelling abroad, the organization published travel notices on country conditions throughout the world. These were also types of information services that one could count. But even if the new policy of openness was seen as a means for making reportable and measurable results, there was also criticism of its logic. The Ministry for Foreign Affairs was, among other things, responsible for making Finland known internationally. In addition, it was the only organization to follow its progress through the press screening by its embassies, and has published an annual report on this since 2000 (Ulkoasiainministeriö 2009; Formin 2010). But it could not take credit for most of the visibility that Finland was getting abroad. As one civil servant noted, there was very little credit that the ministry could take for the sudden media publicity resulting from the Finnish victory in the Eurovision Song Contest in 2006.

Measurability was thus a problem also in terms of the communication of the organization, but less so than with several other types of activities. Regarding the new communication policy's influence on the public debate, some interviewees held the view that there in fact was now more foreign political debate in the country and connected this with the activities of the ministry. We may ask, though, whether this was rather a result of the passing sensitivity of foreign politics in Finland, and, if so, how much credit the ministry could take for it as it also had acted as a censor until the end of the Cold War.

The interest in public appearances shows that there is keen interest in the ministry and its organization. But the interest towards the actual policies the ministry performs is another matter. As already indicated, the actual amount of information queries made by citizens formed a minor share of all those addressed to the ministry. The actual policies were seen as being too abstract or uninteresting to the public. Instead, the actual right of accessing information was utilized by those directly concerned: companies, other public bodies, press and academics.

In terms of accessing information, the role of the citizen was that of a customer or spectator rather than that of a participant. Though the issues with which the ministry dealt were increasingly concerning individual citizens, the idea of citizens accessing the foreign political documents proper was not seen to bring much added value. Instead, the ministry provided information services. In 2006 and 2007, the information services provided by the Ministry for Foreign Affairs were by far the most voluminous in the Finnish central government. The figures for

2006 and 2007 were 11,294 and 11,034 respectively, while the second highest number of services was 5,982 provided by the Ministry of Social Affairs and Health in 2006 (see Chapter 3).

In general, the volume of information services has been on the decline in Finnish ministries during the 2000s, most likely due to the influence of the internet. While this has also resulted in a relatively large difference in the volumes of services of ministries, it is also remarkable that the Ministry for Foreign Affairs first started to report the volumes of its information services in 2006, coinciding with the pressures for measurable outcomes. Even though information services were seen as serving the public interest on foreign political information, this did not mean that there were no documents leaving the organization. On the contrary, there was now an increasing emphasis on getting the information to trusted contacts. This practice was also discussed as 'openness', but opposed to 'publicity'.

5.5.4 The grey area of openness

When discussing the circulation of foreign political information in society, the interviewees stressed that this changed significantly. Whereas the information collected by the ministry in the 1970s and 1980s still was distributed to a very limited group of actors, the ministry was now sharing its information with others, mainly with organizations of interest mediation, NGOs and, most notably, with the private sector:

> Often a message is given outside the ministry [...] that some issue is being prepared, the information on which is not yet public, but will be tomorrow, or next month it is already made public. I don't see any alternative to this in the current working environment. You should assume this of individual civil servants. Coming to the service principle and effectiveness, you should know which sorts of partners are important to us in this matter that they should receive this information. It is in most cases easy, because those concerned are in daily contact with the interest groups. But sometimes the person who has drawn up a report has to consider who would be interested in it. It depends on networking. This too demands that there is a new way of thinking, concerning what information to distribute without stressing its confidentiality, but that both sides understand that it is not beneficial if it is found in tomorrow's [newspaper]. This is a big grey area in which we can move fairly smoothly. But is requires that civil servants are up to their tasks. (Senior Executive, Ministry for Foreign Affairs)

This shift was said to be necessary to serve society and provide it with value for money by sharing the information held by the ministry. Yet, there seemed to be two parallel histories in the narratives of the civil servants. When referring to the practices of the past years in the organization, the interviewees often concluded that the information resources were tightly kept within the small circle of foreign political elite led by the president. But when they discussed the new measures of allocating information to wider circles in society, the interviewees referred to another historical Nordic tradition, that of consensual decision-making where actors trust each other and work together.

> I would think that the Nordic countries, Finland, Sweden, Norway, Denmark – I don't see any massive differences between them. Although there are many individual differences, this kind of general attitude is very similar. It's the sort of climate of trust that prevails. Information is distributed and it is presumed that there is this grey area – that it is not to be dealt with publicly but everyone knows. Should the information come out to public [...], there is no crying over spilled milk. Extensive openness, which comes from our principle of publicity and trust in the activity of the authorities, [meaning] that we have to serve different interests. This is a different way of thinking than in some larger EU member countries of continental Europe. (Senior Executive, Ministry for Foreign Affairs)

Openness became a third term in the public-secret dichotomy allowing for the reframing of the previous democratic principle attached to the access law. Instead of implying that the information leaving the organization would be 'public', 'openness' was now described as a 'grey area', where information could be circulated without it becoming public. This perception was tied to the tradition of governance and the 'principle of publicity'. This again was contrasted with other countries. The collective positioning was also extended to the perceived economic competition between countries, where the high level of trust in Nordic societies was now their strength.

> I think that it reflects their societal strengths – they are these not necessarily consensus societies – I'm not saying that – but these societies that rest on a high degree of trust, in which the authorities work pretty well together and also well with non-governmental actors. This is the main strength of society. Through it you get trust.

It is in the interests of all actors that it continues this way. (Senior Executive, Ministry for Foreign Affairs)

The narrative of the consensual tradition effectively allowed the interviewees to bypass the secretive history of their organization and the troubled history of Finnish–Soviet relations. Perceiving foreign affairs as a secret activity was said to be a misunderstanding prevailing in the outside world. But when the issue was discussed in terms of the legal culture, the foreign political information was again perceived as secretive and the point of reference was the term of secrecy.

Regarding leaks of information, the ministry stressed that all major cases had come out in the press. In minor cases, the possible leaks of information were said to be handled by informing those giving information to outsiders in an inappropriate manner that their activity had been spotted. The interviewees in the ministry framed this in a non-dramatic way. But two external interviewees (a journalist and an NGO representative) saw this to be an acute threat for those involved in the circulation of classified documents. A leak of information to outsiders or premature publicity on an issue that was still not made public was said to lead to a rather ill-spirited phone call from the ministry. Moreover, the person breaking the circle of trust would be left out of the loop, receiving no more documents.

The interviewees outside the organization representing trade policy, EU policy and development policy, all confirmed that there were documents circulating rather freely, even if these were not public. In government-opposition terms, some interviewees in the ministry said that opposition leaders were also broadly informed about foreign political issues.[23] Describing the context of political journalism concerning Finnish–EU relations, the journalist interviewed referred to an institution of trust. The circulation of information was seen as a means for conducting journalistic work. In reflecting the sharing of confidential information described above, the interviewee saw it to entail an element of control for the journalist profession. Journalists were given information that was still confidential and it was up to them to decide what to write about it. This discretion assured access to information but further amalgamated the journalists to a joint mission with the administration.[24]

Paradoxically, the somewhat broad circulation of information can have a negative influence for publicity. As central actors and even members of the media were included in the distribution of documents they potentially grew dependent on them, yet they were not able to write about them. This entails self-censorship through a dependency on the information provided. The consensual practices of decision-making now evolving in the context of the Foreign Service also entailed a power relationship between the ministry and those it chose to inform.

Some interviewees could term the practice of circulating information among different policy actors as efficient. For instance, a civil servant referred to circulating confidential memos of EU committee meetings to various interest groups as an 'efficient' way to keep 'everyone' informed of what was being planned and what the Finnish interests were. The response of interviewees at the Ministry of Agriculture and Forestry was similar to those at the Ministry for Foreign Affairs concerning this – the organizations concerned about a coming EU regulation were well-informed about what was to come and were also provided with sufficient documentation on it.

The classified documents were also processed in Parliament, but the ministries did not emphasize their confidential nature since the parliamentarians disliked being reminded of it and the chances of such detailed information as a position of some country becoming public were, in any case, seen as minimal. In 2005, an assessment of the practices of handling EU matters in Parliament was made: the document does not mention the confidentiality of material as a problem (Eduskunta 2005). Nevertheless, the documents now circulating among an extended group of actors in Finland contained non-public information that they all agreed to keep to themselves.

This could be deemed as a contextual particularity, which should be taken into consideration when assessing the practices of openness in a small consensually governed state. It has potential implications for the relatively low number of complaints made to the judiciary, as there is no need to fight over documents (see Chapter 3). But a general observation can be made on the unintended consequences of trust-based sharing of information; surprisingly such forms of collaborative governance may have a potentially negative influence on the publicity of policy information and perhaps even on public debate. Because there is an incentive not to publicize the information obtained, it is likely to be deliberated among a group of experts. In terms of accountability, the circulation rather strengthens the processes of peer review but it does not necessarily amount to 'public' scrutiny.

Apparently, there was no numerical data available for the above described practice because it was now handled by individual civil servants. Also the participants in the ministry's networks were not disclosed in detail. There were few permanent lists of circulation maintained, but the activity was said to exist outside these also. Interviewees outside this particular organizational case – for instance the legal experts and experts of financial management – also stressed the broad circulation of information as a common practice in the country. This is evident in such contexts as labor market negotiations, but several other contexts were also named.

Moreover, the deliberative aspects of governance and the circulation of information were now seen as part of the new performance paradigm, making it a means for achieving strategic goals. This is where the deliberation and budget transparency again meet, making the former an instrument of the latter. In the perceptions of civil servants, 'openness' was seen as a central remedy to ensure Finnish success in the globalizing economy. In terms of collective memory, the existence of this already broad-based sharing of information elsewhere in the country made the Ministry for Foreign Affairs party to a national institutional tradition that in its present scale was a novelty in this particular context.

5.5.5 New public diplomacy

In the interviews, some sources of new ideas of openness and transparency were referred to. There was no single forum where the governance of foreign services would be discussed, but cooperation was nevertheless developing among countries. The Finnish Embassy in Brussels was mentioned as a key site for adopting a new media policy, which was later taken up by the rest of the Foreign Service. The international media and individual actors played a role in this. The international media exposure of the Brussels office in the early years of the Finnish EU membership and during the 1999 presidency had brought in new ideas of how to serve the domestic media, too. The executives of the Brussels bureau were mainly named as the instigators of this policy.

But as mentioned, all foreign services at present are facing similar demands for focusing their activities and cutting costs. In the early 2000s, when 'openness' became an issue of concern in the ministry, the British Embassy in Helsinki was also consulted about the matter and an Anglo-American model of '(New) Public Diplomacy' was taken into consideration. At the time of the interviews, the model, or its Finnish version, was discussed and debated in the organization. In this respect also, individual actors became important as carriers of knowledge. In particular, one high-ranking interviewee named a British diplomat as an important source of ideas.

Though there was no general forum for exchanging ideas on how to organize foreign services, there were some conferences organized on the matter. Also, new constructs, such as the EU Foreign Policy and the European External Action Service were likely venues for an exchange of practices. The EU had already provided a perspective on the work of other foreign services, the matter of addressing audiences, whether domestic or foreign, was also addressed elsewhere. Concerning the information services, the internet now provided a site for learning about the practices of other countries. Again, the Anglo-American models were mentioned, such as those of the UK and Canada. The websites of the above foreign services served as a model or a *locus* of comparison for the Finnish practices that the interviewees referred to.

The internet had made the practices of 'others' easier to assess. The cost of acquiring information on the practices of other countries had fallen significantly. Compared for instance to the Cold War era, when the comparisons of the foreign political terms of secrecy in different countries were still conducted through diplomatic channels, this sort of information was now accessible online.

Some foreign services, Sweden's for instance, had invested in its web presence by setting up a site in the Second Life portal. The Finnish site, Virtual Finland, a country-specific information portal, comes perhaps closest to that. Together with the dissemination of information, both of these are sites for country branding. Also, the country-specific internet sites of Finnish Embassies, such as a game site of Moomin characters for Japan, was created (Embassy of Finland in Tokyo 2010). For the Finnish presidency of the OSCE in 2008, an internet game of Tetris was published, symbolizing, arguably, attempts at 'removing small arms from conflict areas' (OSCE 2010). The current model of Public Diplomacy does not bear an apparent idea of making the actors accountable (cf. Patomäki 2004). The new Anglo-American model of Public Diplomacy operates on a different logic, which aims at getting a strategic message out and entailing no apparent mechanism for public scrutiny.

A collective positioning over nationalistic boundaries of 'us-them' appeared in the interviews when discussing the future of diplomacy, including reflections on patriotism and experiences gained abroad (cf. White 2009). As one interviewee noted: 'the longer you live abroad the more patriotic you become.' When reflecting on national customs and administrative cultures, the changing nature of diplomatic work came to the fore. Those interviewees that had been stationed in foreign countries had had the opportunity to make such assessments during their expatriate shifts. This also provided a perspective on the new notions of market 'transparency', which, coupled with the Asian financial crisis of the 1990s, was experienced in the field. This was seen to have inevitable consequences for diplomacy:

> One of the factors of globalization, which was discussed, was that the electronic environment made possible the movement of money, which shocked economies and led to currency speculation. I was [in Asia] in 1997 and 1998 and the economies started to crash. A main reason was short-term off-shore capital. This wouldn't have been possible or likely in the old world, but the trend towards it was driven by this sort of online global economy. Whatever, this presents many new challenges in conducting foreign policy in this new operational environment. Accomplishing such aims in this environment, which was possible with traditional diplomacy, is, as a rule, no longer possible. (Senior Executive, Ministry for Foreign Affairs)

In short, there was an increasing awareness that the measures for effective foreign policy and diplomacy were changing. Compared to other policy fields the foreign services relied more on peer contacts and assessments made by the ministry. There was not an apparent policy feed on organizing governance as perhaps in other policy fields, drawing influences from the OECD and the EU. Despite, or because of, the long lasting standing contacts with the outside world and diplomatic traditions, the efforts to tackle the perceived new challenges were not as tightly coupled as in other policy fields.

The most coherent policy feed was the model of Public Diplomacy, the content of which was being defined during the time of the interviews. More precisely, the actual content of the notion of Public Diplomacy was debated. Some saw it rather as a means for pursuing diplomatic strategies abroad, whereas some linked it more with issues such as country branding. Some perceived it as a means for conducting diplomacy altogether. In other accounts it was seen more as a means for cultural exporting or country branding (Opetusministeriö 2007).

Finlandization, a pejorative expression from the 1970s that referred to the close Finnish–Soviet relations and Finnish leaning towards the east (cf. Vihavainen 1991), was also raised when describing Public Diplomacy. During the Cold War, Finnish diplomats had to explain to their international counterparts that Finland was not slipping to the east and they tried to describe their country in more positive terms. As one interviewee active in the drafting of the Public Diplomacy concept noted, some people in the organization rather saw the new methods to be mostly the same that had been already used back then.

But the message had changed. In particular, the international country comparisons now provided new facts about Finland that were well-received internationally (on numbers as social facts see Desrosières 1998, p. 9). Finland was no longer the borderland or gateway between east and west; instead, it was a low-corruption country (according to Transparency International), with an excellent school system (rated by the OECD), ranking among the best in economic competitiveness (for instance in the World Economic Forum's rankings). According to one interviewee, in getting a favorable message out to the world, one only needed to rely on facts. The new governance indices and rankings had created new social 'facts' that the Finnish civil servants were now echoing. This new reference system provided them with a social scientific basis for argument, when pursuing the interests of their country.

The Finnish success in the country rankings was seen as an opportunity for having an influence on global governance. The 'model of statehood' was seen as essential for the future. In this scheme, openness becomes a factor of national competitiveness:

A: I would say that if we want to succeed in the world, we as Finland – or in general we can say the prevailing Nordic or EU concept of what is a good state, and what it does, then you have to play by the rules and act in such a way that it brings about the good that it claims to be its product. When we look ahead at economic or societal developments, I see these kinds of developments. Openness, transparency will increase and new economic forms – not just private sector ones, but new types of business activity.

Q: In other words, openness is a factor in competitiveness?

A: Particularly. To a great extent that's it. (Senior Executive, Ministry for Foreign Affairs)

When asked whether this was a whole new conceptualization of the publicity of government information, the above interviewee acknowledged that the new perception of transparency no longer stemmed from democracy. Yet it was 'no significant change':

I don't know whether it is a question of great changes when we speak of matters that somewhat coexist. True, the law on publicity relates to the public control [of government] and democratic principles, but in this we're talking about rather different things. It's hard to draw the line with it.

From the perspective of accountability, this is a most significant change. As the principle of publicity is increasingly being reframed with economic connotations, it is moving from its ideational roots of democratic control. Now seen as an element of national competitiveness, it is slowly being redeployed for different purposes than initially intended (see Streeck and Thelen 2005, p. 31). Moreover, there is an observable misunderstanding in the above accounts of transparency. While the interviewees saw transparency to be best served through circulating information to Finnish strategic partners, the idea of market transparency means that all actors have access to the same information (Stiglitz 1998). The interviewees were in fact legitimizing a protectionist strategy with a market-liberal rhetoric.

Currently, there is an increasing tendency of making countries attractive to Foreign Direct Investment and potential emigrant workforce. Internationally, there are numerous, often government-lead, PR campaigns for this (for example, Invest in France 2010; Invest in Georgia 2010). One civil servant with expertise in public diplomacy saw this to be mostly a waste of resources noting that 'you cannot buy reputation.' Concerning the reputation of a country, the country rankings were seen to have become important. The idea of attracting an educated workforce on the basis of comparatively low corruption, good education, a healthy natural environment and economic competitiveness was stressed in some of the interviews – the thinking being that the small well-performing countries would benefit from this in terms of inward mobility.[25] This is also echoed in the livability rankings of global cities (Financial Times 2011).

The above examples show how countries' attempts to claim prestige have entered the sphere of governance indices (Weber 1978, p. 910). These social scientific instruments of policy coordination have now become an essential part of Finland's diplomatic toolkit, giving it unforeseen visibility internationally. From the perspective of a small well-to-do country, this provided a possibility to have a real international influence. But what was in fact measured, for what purposes, by whom and how, seemed to be a lesser question. The new activity of governance assessment was not reflected critically by the interviewees, if at all. The prestige that was at stake in the numbers also had a nationalistic side to it, as openness and transparency were now becoming internationally acknowledged qualities of Finnish governance.

Even if the new image concerns of the country were becoming more explicit, now termed openness by the ministry, the interviewees were slightly reserved towards country branding through PR campaigns.

Since the interviews, however, and after a change of Foreign Minister, the PR aspects of country branding also moved forward as Finland launched a working group on country branding (Formin 2009). Headed by the former CEO of Nokia, the country brand working group aimed at securing Finland's visibility, since other countries had already launched similar projects. The governance indices were referred to in the process, echoing the perception of a competition between countries that called for such a measure as country branding.

To sum up, since 2000 there have been efforts by the Ministry of Foreign Affairs to increase the public visibility of the organization and provide information on its activities. Somewhat surprisingly, this development can be linked with the increasing demands for performance and transparency as reported outcomes. Facing the difficult task of identifying its objectives and measuring the results, the ministry had to put more efforts into its communication policies, not only towards the citizenry but also increasingly towards other stakeholders such as private companies. There is an apparent tension between different conceptualizations of the 'public' to be observed. Publicity, understood as public access to documents, was complemented by strategic communication and by a trust-based practice of 'openness', meaning broad circulation of confidential information. As discussed above, this is not likely to culminate in the increased publicity of the same information. Moreover, despite the ideational shift from secrecy to openness as the official operative logic, the ministry was still in a position to mostly define the information that was given outside. This activity was now legitimized with the perception of global economic competition, where the Nordic openness was seen as an institutional advantage.

5.6   Conclusions

Historically, Foreign Services have enjoyed long terms of secrecy for their activities. This has changed in the last two decades, as has the whole practice of the Foreign Service. The end of the Cold War and the new trends of global or transnational governance are making some of the previous functions of these organizations less important. At the same time, the Foreign Services as organizations are under scrutiny for their performance, thus making their activities transparent. In Finland, the above reasons led to the redefining of the information strategy of the Ministry for Foreign Affairs. The policy discourse of openness carries a new operational logic (cf. Schmidt 2002), legitimizing also the activities of the ministry.

The history of information management in the Ministry for Foreign Affairs is characterized by secrecy up to the turn of the 2000s. The coordinative discourse of Nordic openness has been appealing in this context, since it fits the present values and norms of the society. In terms of statistics, the overall development of foreign political confidentiality is difficult to assess. There was a strong argument for diminishing the volume of secret information in the ministry and the estimates given for confidential documents were also modest. But considering that foreign political material now exists in various fields of administration it is difficult to assess whether there has been a decrease or increase in the amount of non-public information in total. It is to this that the organizational perspective of this study is confined. Moreover, contrary to the self-perception of the Finnish interviewees, the EU documents created in Finland were more often classified as non-public than those attained from EU institutions. On closer inspection, while the Finns have been promoting openness in the European Union (Chapter 2), Finland's accession to the European Union was one of the main factors and ideational sources behind the emergence of openness in the Ministry for Foreign Affairs. Finally, the citizen and media interest in the documents was perceived as low and the control function of the principle of publicity seen as limited.

There has been a rather remarkable emergence of public communication by the ministry since the early 2000s. The public appearances of the civil servants, numerous public hearings, and news and information services make the Ministry for Foreign Affairs perhaps the most visible ministry in the Finnish media. As has been argued, the policy problem that triggered this development was the diminished status of the ministry, pressures for cutting its budget and, most importantly, the drive for transparency to produce measurable results on the outcome of activities. The attempts at introducing performance management into the sphere of foreign affairs have proven difficult, which is no surprise for an organization of this type. As these activities are generally non-quantifiable, the information services are an exception to the rule.

Nevertheless, there is now a strong political imaginary of competition that traverses the activities of the Foreign Service. This competition not only takes place in the domestic institutional context for resources, but also increasingly in the sphere of the global economy. What are significant in this imaginary of competition are the new attempts to make the effects of the work in the ministry measurable, entailing budget transparency, and on the other hand the new country comparisons that make the national institutional traditions transparent to external scrutiny. The emergence of active communication policies in the organization, both domestically and abroad, can be linked with the demand for observable results. The ministry has improved its public presence significantly, particularly in the domestic context.

Based on this analysis, the strategic aims of the organization seem to be, to some extent, directed to measurable goals. The broad objectives, such as being influential in the international community, maintaining peace and security, and striving for a just world were a sidetrack in the performance management scheme. The above goals are difficult to measure, which has made them less appealing or at least brought new extrinsic strategic aims, posing a potential unintended consequence – a counter-finality – for such measurements. These are the traditional tasks of foreign services and, in many respects, the obligations of a country. That the ministry serves its customers the best it can is only welcome, but priorities should not be set through what can be measured.

Perhaps the most surprising finding is the conceptualization of openness as a non-public 'grey' area, leading to the reportedly wide practice of sharing confidential information with strategic and trusted partners. The concept of publicity appeared in the organization as a legal term, but the notion of openness allows its re-description in a way that could even come to limit publicity. This integration function of sharing information in collaborative governance can be perceived as a form of representation, but it may also entail the potential for self-censorship. The above examples of the somewhat paradoxical effects of openness and transparency might also apply in other contexts, suggesting more complex dynamics of information access laws and trust-based consensual decision-making than are readily apparent. The interviewees stressed the contemporary drive for transparency as a justification for the above non-public activity, but providing favors for domestic private companies only is ideationally quite opposed to the international codifications of market transparency.

As the principle of publicity is being reframed within economic connotations, it is moving away from its ideational roots of democratic control. This is the most significant change from the perspective of accountability. Now seen as an element of national competitiveness, it is slowly being redeployed for purposes that are different from those initially intended, marking an institutional conversion (Streeck and Thelen 2005). Public Diplomacy or country branding does not offer any means for making the actors accountable. The same applies to openness as a strategic communication, which highlights performance through calculable results but does not necessarily provide a mechanism for holding the actors accountable for their actions in the sense of bureaucratic accountability.

Conclusions

Throughout this study, I have explored how the new economic and performance rationalities have reframed the publicity of state information during the last decade and what institutional transformations we can detect. The understanding in this analysis is that the essential innovation that transparency brings to the conceptualization of governance is that public acts of governing can indeed be economically efficient. Though a very broad idea, this is most apparent in new attempts at providing standardized information on government, even to the extent that it can be expressed in figures.

Current transnational governance is making the differences between national models visible. It involves the construction of policy problems, bringing about new political concepts or the rediscovery of old concepts. The paradigm shifts in public governance and institutional economics are increasingly communicated through the networks of professionals engaged in international policy assessments. This communication of ideas is either direct through policy networks or indirect, for example through reflexivity over governance indices.

Before, the institutional practices had been crafted for the most part nationally or by comparison with peer countries. While previous institutional analyses have stressed specific networks of expertise in policy diffusion, there are now overlapping sites for the ideational transfer and diffusion of policies. The increasing numbers of country rankings and comparisons provide a new arena of policy diffusion, with up-to-date information on how a particular civil service stands in comparison with other countries. Country comparisons and the use of the internet have massively cut the cost of acquiring information on the policies of other countries.

On an ideational level, it is plausible to argue for a policy convergence within concepts of transparency. At a time of political turmoil, institutions are prone to be renegotiated. But the new ideas adopted and used in these debates are absorbed by existing institutional design and path dependencies, which calls for contextual analysis. Moreover, within a particular discourse there may be a number of contradictory ideas that open up several political horizons, not just one. Therefore, actual institutional developments are often paradoxical and characterized by trade-offs and unintended consequences. The most obvious paradox is that increased transparency might not always lead to increased democratic accountability.

During the last two decades there has been a shift in the understanding of access to government information, driven by the global policy discourse of transparency, an addendum in the vocabulary of government. Before, the emphasis was almost solely on the democratic control of government through publicity. But amid the pressures of globalization and new forms of governance, the issues of trust and efficiency have become increasingly pressing. As a result there are now calls for openness in citizen–government relations that aim for trust-based and consensual forms of participatory governance, which is also deemed effective. Moreover, there are calls for market and budget transparency, thus raising awareness of enhanced market efficiency through access to information and use of performance indicators.

As we saw in the empirical part of this book, there is a distinctive trajectory in the governing of state information and, in particular, the openness of public institutions in the Nordic countries. However, during the last two decades these practices have changed significantly. This has come about due to an ideational change following an apparent juncture in the conduct of governance in the 1990s, where coping with the demands of efficiency and competitiveness have become mandatory and more pronounced. As we see with the case of Finland, long-lasting institutional practices, such as access to government information, have been reframed in economic terms. Alongside previous control and integration functions, there is now a new economic function for the access to state information. Consequently, there are institutional transformations that also have paradoxical qualities and are hindered by unintended consequences and trade-offs. Because they are discussed within a policy discourse of Nordic openness that fits the current values and public narratives of the Finns as an open and progressive nation, these changes tend to go unnoticed.

The talk of Nordic openness exemplifies the current emphasis on trust-based efficiency, be it in the exploitation of registry information or the sharing of foreign political information. Consensus and

collaboration have become mandatory amid the pressures of globalization. Though there are contextual peculiarities in the Finnish case, the
general trend is nevertheless shared by other countries, which are now
assessed from afar for their competitiveness. The discourse on Nordic
openness is therefore a variant of the international policy discourse
on transparency, highlighting its modalities in conceptual nuances,
whether related to control (publicity), trust and collaboration (openness) or efficiency (transparency).

Moreover, the perspective of a long institutional history in Nordic
countries renders the general ideational changes visible, as access to
government information is actively reframed from a previous democratic understanding of publicity to trust-based openness and economic transparency. Though access to government information is
a multifaceted institution involving many functions, there can be
changes of emphasis between them, indicated by the conceptual shift
from publicity to openness and transparency. Also, the paradoxes
and unintended consequences of transparency presented in this
book are potentially general problems of contemporary governance,
though their intensity and frequency might vary from one country
to another.

In summarizing the empirical observations in the Finnish case, I
detect ideational and institutional changes in the steering mechanisms and in the organizational cases regarding the state's information
strategy. Though the changes in selected administrative contexts took
a slightly varied shape, they are still bound together by the juncture
of governance of the 1990s, comprising a shift from government to
governance following an economic crisis, the digitalization of public
information and the introduction of the NPM and performance management. The transnational context of governance is also important,
involving collaboration in the OECD and EU contexts, and exposure to
global governance indices and country rankings.

While there are endogenous and exogenous pressures for change, this
was not the result of pressure from civil society, which is often seen to
be the driver for developments in the public sphere. The new ideas that
are propelling the change have their root in the economic understanding of transparency and in each context the access to state information
has been reframed within market and performance terms. These are by
no means the only changes, as there has been a recalibration of citizen information rights too. But alongside the previously defined control
and integration functions there is now an economic function of the
access to government information.

The concept of openness emerged in the mid-1990s in political steering as a reference to the Finnish accession to the EU but also to the global (open) economy (Chapter 2). The conceptualizations of openness and (later) transparency carried connotations of open market, as opposed to 'public' or 'state' regulated. These normative and cognitive aspects have since merged in the new nationalistic discourse of Nordic openness. This discourse marks a reframing of the Nordic principle of publicity, which is shifting semantically, being increasingly reframed within market and performance ideas. The communicative discourse of openness, aimed at the general public, emphasizes the normative aspects of openness and depicts Finland as a particularly open and progressive nation.

The new coordinative discourse of Nordic openness shared by the policy actors has communicated the new governance ideas of openness and transparency in normative and financial steering. In the context of normative steering, an outdated law of 1951 was revised after unresolved efforts. While political tensions prevented the revision of the law in the 1970s, largely similar initiatives were adopted in the late 1990s as a response to vast structural changes that the Finnish governance model was experiencing. Crucially, the political tensions around the issue had dissipated. The civil service was required to provide information services, later interpreted as strategic and effective communication. This new communication strategy is termed (in the law) 'openness', which complements the previous legal term 'publicity'. At present, openness is often also termed as being 'efficient'. New economic interests towards public information also surfaced in the 1999 law. Public sector information is now perceived as being an economic asset due to the digitalization of data resources. The ideational input for the legislation came from the European Union, though the source of the policy problem was the marketization of public information due to the NPM-driven accrual charging, budget transparency, that has since become part of the new performance management scheme.

In the sphere of financial steering, openness also became a policy issue under other themes. Public hearings and citizen participation now involve macroeconomic ideas: the long historical trajectory of an access law and open administrative culture is seen as important for economic performance. OECD meetings served as a venue for the exchange of ideas on this. The policy work done on administrative ethics, conducted in cooperation with the OECD, made administrative openness a further issue of concern, now as a counter-balance to the NPM reforms though still stressing performance. Lastly, transparency based on indicators is now part of the new perceptions of accountability, brought to the agenda by a performance management reform. Though performance management had already developed domestically, the OECD provided an ideational input through a peer review.

In general, the legislative framework in Finland is working well and the legal conflicts in accessing information are minor (Chapter 3). The institutional statistics speak for a firm democratic institutional core. There is a low level of conflict over access to information, judging by the judiciary system, and the pressure seems to be more on privacy issues. However, the reframing of access to state information in market and performance terms is a new addendum to the previous principle of publicity. There is an observable layering of new institutional ideas and practices on the edges of the institution.

Moving to the organizational cases explored, there is a conversion in the information strategies where the old institutional practices are redeployed to new purposes. As we saw in Chapter 4, a policy problem of pricing public information evolved in the context of data management. The digitalization of public data resources coinciding with the NPM reforms made public data a commodity to be sold. Public sector information became conceptualized as market goods in EU-wide policies, now also sold by the public bureaus in charge of it. The shifts in the budgetary system and the drive for budget transparency led to coordination problems in the allocation of the data. The concept of public sector information has removed the debate from the previous democratic conceptualizations of publicity. The state's information strategies on public sector information now view the historically formed registry infrastructure as a source of economic wealth. Even census information is subject to trading, which is a contextual peculiarity. Paradoxically, the long unbroken history of high standards of census keeping allows the practice to be marketized without public debate. There is a strong historical narrative on Nordic openness legitimizing the new commercial use. Though no major problems in the ethical infrastructure have been reported, the public's trust has been stretched to take in a new type of activity without their explicit mandate.

In foreign affairs, openness became a policy problem due to the change in the operative environment at the turn of the 2000s after a long, stagnant period of reforms. The end of the Cold War, globalization and Finland's EU membership created pressures for the Ministry for Foreign Affairs to legitimate itself in the new environment, where all the ministries now had international tasks. There was also significant external pressure for transparency through the use of indicators and measurable results, which led to an increase in media appearances by civil servants, information services and information campaigns directed towards the public. Openness is a new strategic choice, separating the Foreign Service symbolically from the secretive past of the Cold War era. The term of secrecy for foreign policy information has been cut and the amount of secret and confidential material has arguably diminished in the foreign ministry. Yet, as there are now EU documents circulating throughout the Finnish public administration, the amount of foreign political material has increased, making it difficult to assess whether the level of confidentiality within the whole public administration has diminished, or vice versa.

Openness has since become a strategy for pursuing goals both home and abroad, now discussed as Public Diplomacy, an Anglo-Saxon model. In shifting to a new mode of operating, a tradition of a consensual openness has been cherished in this context. In constructing an analogy of inclusive policy-making that has existed in labor market policies, openness is reframed as a non-public grey area. The new practice of circulating confidential information to strategic partners poses potential limits for public debate and also entails an element of self-censorship. The justification for this is the global economic competition and the new demands for transparency.

To sum up, the ideational change that has occurred concerning access to government information complies with the general transformations in the accountability system, which now highlights both performance and deliberation (see Chapter 1). The international discourse on transparency has drawn attention to the Nordic tradition of governance, making it the subject of deliberate reforms. Moreover, the new performance ideas discussed within the notion of transparency have also provided the key policy ideas that have been referred to in the recasting of the state information strategy. There are claims that the publicity of governance has historically had not only a controlling function in Finland but also an integrative function. Since the late 1990s, there have been ideational addendums to the institution, which are now posited as openness, public sector information and transparency implying redeployment of an old institution for new purposes. These conceptual shifts are expressions of an emerging economic function for the institution, now complementing the control and integration functions. As a result there are paradoxes and social contradictions involved, such as unintended consequences and trade-offs resulting from the policies to address access to government information from a perspective of performance.

The current institutional turn in economic competitiveness presents us with a paradox. As the policy actors become aware of an institutional trajectory of national economic advantage, such as that of institutional openness, it becomes a policy concern and subject of active development. Consequently, the institutional practices change and may even be deracinated. The Nordic principle of publicity is now complemented by ideas of performance and strategic communication, and public information is increasingly seen as a commodity. In financial steering, new economic ideas of transparency are coupled with the pursuit of effectiveness through public hearings and the production of performance information. Surprisingly, the reflexivity over a democratic trajectory leads to its reframing in economic terms.

Paradoxically, the new practices of transparency might lead to a closure in attaining public information. As the civil service is increasingly being held responsible for the results of its activities in economic terms, the public information resources it manages might become its product to sell. In Europe, access to public sector information had already become a policy concern in the mid-1990s (see Chapter 4). The problem of the high pricing of government information results from performance management and budget transparency. This potential for closure is apparent with resources such as statistics and geographical information, which have become expensive commodities sold by the state. But commodification can also involve personal information of citizens. In this area, performance management has provided incentives to sell these information resources for private sector use.

The commercial use of the personal information held by the state involves a further paradox. For historical reasons, the codifications on privacy and registry keeping may differ greatly from one country to another. In countries where the state has enjoyed a greater hold over the private information of its citizens, the marketization of public registry keeping may go further than in those countries where there has been a relative lack of trust in such registry keeping. The high level of trust in this state activity may pave the way to its privatization. Or, at least, trust in the state's registry keeping may allow for a far-reaching commercial use of public registry information.

The privatization of public information is a clear case of an unintended consequence of budget transparency, discussed now as an unintended consequence of the NPM by the policy actors themselves (Chapter 4). This shows the limits of rationales for introducing efficiency-enhancing practices of budget transparency to a domain where normative principles have prevailed. Government information relevant to public debate has become a costly resource. Those in need of it, for instance universities and NGOs that use cartographic data, have to pay for it, which is contrary to publicity in the traditional sense. Moreover, because agencies now consider personal data to be a market commodity, there is a clear tension between the activities of the civil service and privacy as a citizen right, which is indeed a painful trade-off.

There are also perspectival errors in understanding efficient governance, whether understood holistically (state administration) or atomically (agency). The aspirations of the information economy could be fulfilled with information as a public asset, regulated by laws, not market mechanisms. But reframing an information resource in market terms may cause it to become a costly resource, with a negative influence on the cohesion of the state administration and general economic development. As we have seen, the above negative development has taken place in Europe. Initially this was a counter-finality in terms of efficiency; commercializing activities can be highly beneficial for the agencies that engage in this, though the overall results of it, especially since several other agencies joined in, were negative. But as all actors in the field are now aware of the situation, this classifies as sub-optimality.

Transparency is often seen to increase trust in government and consensus through deliberation. However, the control of government builds on the idea of potential conflict in state–citizen relations. Paradoxically, the broad circulation of information among trusted partners may have a negative influence on publicity. This is an important observation regarding the practices of consensual governance and access to government information, and sheds some light on the low level of conflict in accessing the government information in some countries. For example, in states with consensual traditions of governance such as the Nordic countries, consensual and trust-based relations between various actors permit a wide circulation of confidential information. As central actors and even members of the media may be included in the distribution of government documents they may grow dependent on them, though they are not necessarily always able to use them. This may even entail self-censorship through a dependency on the information provided. The consensual practices of decision-making, which are evolving amid economic globalization, also possess a power relation between the civil service and those it chooses to inform.

Somewhat surprisingly, the drive for performance management and competitiveness can have counterproductive impacts on market transparency, as the information held by a civil service becomes a strategic asset shared mostly to domestic actors only (see Chapter 5). Openness becomes a non-public 'grey area', where the information circulates among the policy actors and, even to the media, without necessarily reaching the public. It is valued as a new bond within the political community. In market terms, the actors' reflexivity on the new demands for transparency is leading to the practice where domestic companies and actors of other sorts are treated exclusively. That the 'openness' of administration can amount to its opacity in democratic and market terms could be seen as an unintended consequence, a counter-finality in terms of the initial intention. It is worth noting that this is, again, the result of the civil service trying to cope with the new demands of performance and market transparency.

On a general level, by reframing access to government information – an element of process accountability – in economic terms, a shift in the accountability system is produced, now emphasizing performance over process. The concepts of transparency and openness circulating internationally allow re-descriptions of the previous ideas of publicity. Now understood as strategic communication, openness becomes part of the performance management paradigm. Though there are deliberate policies for enhancing the performance of governance through transparency and access to information, the potential trade-offs that are involved may remain tacit even to the actors involved, as there are contradictory terms in the different policies that are pursued in the name of openness and transparency. Hence, the potential negative effects can be seen as unintended consequences of such reforms.

While the above transformations are difficult to reduce to a single idea or policy initiative, the economic ideas of transparency are most remarkably at odds with the traditional ideas of publicity. In particular, the new ideas of performance management and budget transparency bring a new logic to the state information strategy. On a general level, there now is an economic function developing for access to state information. This does not necessarily mean abandoning the previous control and integration functions that institutional openness has had. On the contrary, the integration function and social trust is central in the emerging institutional forms of openness, whether in the new commercial use of registry data or the sharing of information with an extended circle of policy actors in tackling the challenges of economic competition.

The outcomes of this reflexivity over the new demands of transparent governance also touch upon structuration as a type of unintended consequence: even if actors refer to the internationally circulating ideas of transparency or the knowledge economy, they end up reproducing a culturally shaped variant of these. The reassessment of an institutional history thus entails an unintended consequence. This is an important mechanism in understanding the contextuality and path dependencies in ideational change. It also helps us to understand why reforms tend to take differing institutional forms in national contexts and therefore often bring about surprising results.

As this summary on the paradoxes, unintended consequences and trade-offs shows, there is no single rationality behind political acts done in the name of transparency and openness. Though they are discussed in logical terms here, it is worth noting that outcomes and institutional consequences are contingent, owing to path dependencies, and an ideational and cultural context. However, the aggregate effect of re-describing publicity of governance in economic terms can be negative, pointing to a trade-off of a sort: should the public administration stress performance through public acts of governance, it might shift its focus from democratic control.

At present, democratic institutions are valued by their economic qualities and the attempts at their reform also stress economic perspectives. As the market logic enters these institutions, the institutional evolution is tempered. The results of this are likely to be seen in long-term institutional developments. Unintended consequences are often perceived in negative terms. Nevertheless, one could also see them as bringing about the possibility to escape the captivating effects of policy ideas. They can be seen as expressions of political conflict, often a necessity for institutional change. In analyzing the interplay of discourses, ideational changes, and institutional transformations, institutional studies can contribute by bringing these conflicts to light.

Notes

1 Paradoxes and Unintended Consequences of Transparency

1. As a result of increasing international trade and citizen participation in state activities, a new awareness of politics is said to have been born in eighteenth-century Europe. Political opinions and even secret information based on official documents spread through Europe by means of new information networks (Würgler 2002, pp. 126–7). Improved means of transport also enabled ideas to diffuse as members of the academic elite travelled in Europe (see Manninen 1996, 2000). This allowed the ideas of the Enlightenment to spread, which influenced state thinking and debates on politics even in peripheral areas. Hagen Schulz-Forberg and Bo Stråth have identified communicative and discursive networks of academics, royals and tradesmen as a 'soft European public sphere' that has existed since the eighteenth century, and in some cases even in the sixteenth and seventeenth centuries Europe (Schulz-Forberg and Stråth 2010).

2. The public sphere as a social category has been widely seen as a site for maintaining and constructing these differences (cf. Habermas 1989; Arendt 1958; Anderson 1991). The contemporary accounts of the public sphere often treat it either as an idealized, normative structure constituting or hindering democratization, or as a discursive space where power is used (Marx Ferree et al. 2002). The institutionalization of the public sphere thus affects national understandings of public and private, as well as understandings of political accountability (Eisenstadt and Schluchter 2001, pp. 10–12, 15–16).

3. As a social structure, the public sphere is itself the subject of an institutionalization process in which structural, institutional and cultural factors collide (Eisenstadt and Schluchter 2001, pp. 17–18; Somers 1993).

4. Europe perhaps provides the best context in which to appreciate the shared lineages of modernization and nation-building (cf. Eisenstadt and Schluchter 2001; Eder 2006).

5. The accounts of failed attempts to break away from absolutist secrecy offer informal narratives on how Enlightenment ideas on free speech and freedom of the press battled the 'mystery of the state' – though in vain.

6. Bennett 1997; Freedominfo 2010

7. The term has no direct English equivalent. Acknowledged as a constitutional right, the principle is conceptually broader than mere public access to official documents, and is often seen as covering freedom of expression, public access to court rooms and public access to decision-making venues.

8. Jürgen Habermas's idealized and linear view of history is often contested (Dean 1994; Skinner 1999). The debate comes down to the position that the authors have on the Enlightenment as an historical development, including its normative principles and ethical heritage (compare Calhoun 1992, p. 28; Ashenden and Owen 1999; Dean 1994, 98; Skinner 1999, p. 65).

9. There are also other historical cases, often disregarded in the analysis of 'historical publics', in which religion and science provided both topics and forums for public debate (Zaret 1992; Forster 2002; von Friedeburg 2002).

10. In Denmark, freedom of the press was debated in the early 1770s, leading to a short-lived liberalization of printing (Knudsen 2003). It did not acquire the same institutional status or position as in Sweden, and did not lead to the breaching of administrative secrecy. In Norway, then part of Denmark, proposals for breaking absolutist secrecy had a similar fate. The issue of institutional openness was debated on several occasions from the mid 1800s onwards, but it was not until 1970 that both Denmark and Norway passed legislation on access to information.

11. Larsson's account of the Swedish experience points in the same direction: the openness of Swedish government builds trust, and vice versa; government can afford to be open because there is no mounting social pressure from the general public to get involved in its work (Larsson 1998).

12. The extensive collaboration of labor market organizations in the Nordic countries, and administrative peculiarities such as State Committees, often serve as examples of sites of consensual decision-making.

13. The conceptualization of accountability and transparency here seems vague and ambiguous, as does the understanding of their interrelation (see Mulgan 2000; Dubnick 2003; Sinclair 1995; Žižek 1997, p. 133). The problem of holding politics and administration accountable in the new environment of globalizing governance has become a pressing issue for academics and political actors alike. Accountability and transparency have rapidly become keywords in the current political vocabulary, appearing often as key concepts, if not synonyms, for modern representative democracy. Neither of these concepts was much used before the early 1990s.

14. The literature on governance describes the changes in politics and administration that have been taking place throughout the Western world from the late 1980s to the present: changes in conditions, patterns and structures of governance, along with changes in the nature, number and relations of actors involved (Pierre and Peters 2000, pp. 14–23). The term 'governance' has been criticized for its inconsistent use (Stoker 1998, pp. 17–18; Pierre 2000, p. 3; Smouts 1998, p. 81; Jessop 1998, p. 29), and it has had a dual use as both a phenomenon and an analytical framework (Pierre and Peters 2000, p. 24; Stoker 1998, p. 18). Accountability has become a topic of concern throughout the literature, and the question of accountability can be seen as one of the reasons that governance has come to be so hotly debated in recent years.

15. I have used previous interpretations of accountability as a starting point for my own, especially a classification by Richard Mulgan and a typology by Barbara Romzek and Melvin Dubnick (Mulgan 2000; Romzek and Dubnick 1987).

16. The recent shift in thinking on deliberative democracy has emphasized the role of institutional arrangements in the organization of democracy (Fung 2003). Whether the ideal site of deliberation is within the space of public administration (Habermas 1996), a forum added to administration (Young 2000) or existing outside public administration altogether (Cohen 1997), scholars of deliberative democracy see deliberation as being possible on one

condition only: that there is unrestricted information available to everyone engaged in the process.

17. The Nobel Laureate of 1970, Paul Samuelson claimed in his renowned elementary book *Economics* (first published in 1948) that the Soviet Union would outrun the United States in economic growth simply due to its central planning and coercive and autocratic institutions (Skousen 1997). With intellectual roots in Keynesian economic theory, Samuelson was not skeptical of ideas of central planning and governmental alleviation, but doubted whether laissez-faire economics would bring about the desired outcomes, such as full employment, in the long run. This line of reasoning went as far as seeing Soviet autocracy as an efficient form of government. In the total of fifteen volumes of *Economics* that followed, the insight on the Soviet system was downplayed over time and, finally, omitted altogether (Skousen 1997, pp. 148–9). In his retrospective analysis of the influence of Samuelson's book, Skousen considers that it steered the national economy of the United States. This might well also apply to the general understanding of efficiency that prevailed at the time.

18. At the core of New Public Management thinking stood the claim that the public–private dichotomy was no longer valid or necessary. Also, most of the literature on governance has downplayed the importance of traditional political-scientific dichotomies.

19. According to some critics, the pursuit of good governance can even undermine the preconditions of political action (Mouffe 1999, p. 752).

20. George Gallup famously called his use of survey information on political opinion the 'pulse of democracy'.

21. This is particularly true of the indices relevant to this study, namely the World Bank Institute's World Governance Index (WGI), the World Economic Forum's Global Competitiveness Index (GCI), Transparency International's Corruption Perception Index (PCI), Freedom House's Freedom of the Press and Freedom in the World indices, the OECD's Government at a Glance, and the UN's e-Government Readiness Index. These indices enjoy broad exposure, and were referred to in the interviews conducted for the empirical section of this book. Finland fares well in all of the above indices and rankings.

22. The concept of transparency is referred to in Transparency International's fight against corruption and in World Economic Forum's attempts to enhance economic competitiveness. Standard & Poor's, an international credit-rating organization, issues a newsletter named *Transparency*.

23. The cost of acquiring information on a country and its development has fallen significantly. Governance indices dismiss the notion of comparability assumed by traditional comparative politics. Instead, various different societies and forms of rule are assessed by the same criteria, regardless of their applicability, which users of the indices now often bypass.

24. Elster defines counter-finality as 'the unintended consequences that arise when each individual in a group acts upon an assumption about his relations to others that, when generalized, yields the contradiction in the consequent of fallacy the of composition, the antecedent of that fallacy being true' (Elster 1978, p. 106). The classic case of this is Sartre's example of woodcutting and erosion. If a peasant cuts down a tree to obtain land, he is better off; but if all other peasants do the same, erosion would ensue. Another

classic example is that of bank deposits: if everyone were simultaneously to deposit or withdraw their money, there would be no interest available in the first case and no money in the second. (Elster 1978, p. 110.)

25. Elster defines sub-optimality as 'the deliberate realization of a non-cooperative solution that is Pareto-inferior to some other payoff set obtainable by individual choices of strategy' (Elster 1978, p. 122).

26. Referring to Roy Bhaskar and Anthony Giddens's theory of structuration, Baert defines it as a case of unintended consequences: 'people are unaware of the occurrence of unintended consequences, and these come back into social reality as unacknowledged conditions or, even, again as unintended consequences of future actions. In particular, every form of self-conscious conduct is only possible through the more or less unconscious reproduction of routine practices.' (Baert 1991, p. 209).

27. The Habermasian notion of 'private' implied both the private sphere of individuals and the private sphere of market actors. The double conceptualization also applies here. The dichotomized view, albeit simplistic, aims to serve as a generalization pointing towards a conceptual shift in the understanding of 'accountability'.

28. Scharpf's idea of input legitimacy refers to the traditional idea of government by the people emphasizing accountability in the process of decision-making, whereas output legitimacy, focusing on government for the people, emphasizes positive and efficient policy outcomes as a legitimizing element (Scharpf 1999, p. 6; Papadopoulos 2003, pp. 482–3).

29. For instance, Scharpf has identified a trend towards policy choices being increasingly made by non-accountable bodies, especially in Western Europe – although concerns about the democracy deficit do not seem to represent an insurmountable obstacle to EU decision-making (Scharpf 1999, pp. 26–7). The reason for this is the compensating effect of 'output legitimacy' gained through satisfactory policy outcomes (Scharpf 1999, p. 12). However, this does not compensate for the lack of accountability through process (Scharpf 1999, pp. 26–7).

30. For instance, some classifications of accountability refer to legal and bureaucratic accountability as two different types. For civil servants, this division is not likely to be clear, which is the reason for merging the two (Erkkilä 2007).

31. According to Mulgan, the defining questions for accountability are: accountable to whom, for what, and how (Mulgan 2000).

32. In her assessment of the dangers to democracy in Finland, Paula Tiihonen has concluded that, though there are very few cases of corruption and many institutions (social and political) render the processes of government somewhat immune to such behavior, there are still other institutions that can be seen as problematic for democracy (Tiihonen 2003, p. 112; cf. Isaksson 1997). For example, Tiihonen mentions the tradition of consensuual decision making, such as the incomes policy agreements, and a fairly unanimous power elite can pose problems for public integrity. These problems largely arise from those mechanisms of inclusion and exclusion that evolve around the trust-based sharing of information.

33. Current attempts to measure administrative ethics and good governance may lead to their instrumentalization, particularly as they are now also

seen as being virtues for economic performance (Erkkilä and Piironen 2009). Similarly, Max Weber saw the calculative logic of bookkeeping as an inherent part of bureaucracy – an iron cage that left no room for ethics or politics (Weber 1978). In the 1930s Edmund Husserl had already published his thesis about the 'crisis of European sciences', criticizing the mathematization of natural phenomena (Husserl 1970). Husserl saw the quantification of social phenomena as having serious consequences for ethics as such (Husserl 1970). In which case, what is to be said of quantification of administrative ethics?

34. For example, the government's program makes explicit reference to its responsibility to the market. In normative steering, the current Better Regulation programmes stress the idea of regulatory competition, assessing the regulatory framework exclusively from the perspective of economic actors.

35. Many institutional structures in the transnational policy making still overlap, which also allows agenda shopping, moving a controversial issue to a decision making venue where it is most likely to pass, making accountability even more difficult (see Hosein 2004). Moreover, discourses are important, since references to democratic principles such as rights may lead to undesired outcomes if they are poorly codified (Borowiak 2004).

36. In this respect, institutionalization is an open-ended process (Judge 2003, pp. 497–8).

37. The idea of a 'trajectory' in administrative studies can be understood as 'an intentional pattern – a route that someone is trying to take' (Pollitt and Bouckaert 2004, pp. 65–6). Scholars of historical institutionalism have been most prominent in discussing historical patterns, often debated in terms of path-dependence (Pierson 2000a; Mahoney 2000). Here intentionality in institutional design is not seen as mandatory; on the contrary, social patterns occurring over time may be obscured and in contradiction with desired ends, while still determining institutional developments (Pierson 2000b).

38. Some scholars of sociological institutionalism have even argued for institutional isomorphism on a global scale, emerging through a convergence of institutional ideas and practices (Meyer et al. 1997; DiMaggio and Powell 1983).

39. This isomorphism is conceived as arising through coercion, competition, learning and emulation (Simmons et al. 2006; cf. DiMaggio and Powell 1983).

40. According to Haas, epistemic communities comprise: 1) a shared set of normative and principled beliefs, 2) shared causal beliefs in policy actions (also entailing a shared set of perceived problems), 3) shared notions of validity, and 4) a common policy enterprise (Haas 1992, 3). Though the concept of an epistemic community has been used before, particularly in scientific studies, it is now used increasingly in the context of policy coordination of the modern administrative state, marked by 'deference to the "knowledge elite"' (Haas 1992, pp. 3, 7).

41. Schmidt is referring here to the sociological institutionalist idea of the logic of appropriateness (March and Olsen 1989, p. 25): the normatively appealing (communicative) discourse frames the new cognitive arguments of the coordinative discourse in a way that makes it fit into the values and culture of the institutional context (Schmidt 2006a, p. 252).

42. Foucauldian reflexivity does pose a problem for an understanding of agency in processes of change, as there is necessarily none anticipated, though contemporary studies building on the Foucauldian notion of governmentality do not dismiss actors completely (Dean 1999; Rose 1999; Dean and Hindess 1998). Moreover, the notion of 'governing at a distance' does indeed assume that there are actors involved (Miller and Rose 1990).

43. This conception of the power relation in terms of governmentality is being used increasingly in the analysis of globalization and global governance (Shore 2006; Zanotti 2005; Larner and Walters 2004).

44. Ideational schemas underlying institutions are highly persistent (Rothstein and Steinmo 2002, p. 5; Pierson 2000a; Mahoney 2000), but they can change disruptively and cause significant institutional changes (Somers and Block 2005; Marcussen 2000, p. 17; Douglas 1987). In institutionalist accounts on path-dependence, actors are likely to escape this inertia only when structures of knowledge are delegitimized, deemed inappropriate, disconfirmed or destabilized, which is likely to occur at a time of crisis (compare Douglas 1987; March and Olsen 1989; Marcussen 2000, p. 17; Thelen 2004; Blyth 2002, p. 252; Peters et al. 2005; Schmidt 2008).

45. When the interview data are used to make factual claims, several sources of information are deployed (see Davies 2001). Findings had to be confirmed in other interviews or documents, or at least to be clearly consistent with them. In producing the 'facts' represented here, this procedure of triangulation was used in order to eliminate errors arising from failures of memory, missing data, misunderstandings on my part, and so on. The time series data presented in the book was received from the organizations in question, unless indicated otherwise.

2   Transparency and Ideational Changes: Nordic Openness as a Policy Discourse

1. According to Koselleck, conceptual change occurs during historical junctures (*Sattelzeit*) – or crises – when the gap between our experiences (*Erfahrungsraum*) and future expectations (*Erwartungshorizont*) grows too large (Koselleck 2004, p. 256; Richter 1995, p. 17).

2. As a term, 'offentlighetsprincip' has been used since 1931 (Nationalencyklopedins ordbok 2004).

3. Nationalencyklopedins ordbok 2004.

4. Nykysuomen sanakirja 1978.

5. Nykysuomen sanakirja 1978; Nykysuomen etymologinen sanakirja 2004.

6. The current *Oxford English Dictionary* does not speak of any clear political connotations for the terms 'transparency' (Latin: *transpārēnti-a*) or 'transparent', or their antonyms 'opacity' and 'opaque' (*Oxford English Dictionary* 2010). Optical and material connotations also dominate the French and German linguistic accounts of transparency (Duden 2001; TLFI 2010).

7. Nykysuomen sanakirja 1978 ; Nationalencyklopedins ordbok 2004.

8. The government program of Matti Vanhanen, published in 24 June 2003 after the resignation of Jäättenmäki government, is the same document as that of Jäätteenmäki's program. Anneli Jäättenmäki had to resign due to

her use of classified foreign political material in the pre-election debates. The material concerned Prime Minister Paavo Lipponen's discussions with George W. Bush regarding the war in Iraq.

9. Finnish Government, 1998 (HE 30/1998).
10. HE 30/1998 1 K Ed. Mikkola; HE 30/1998 1 K Ed. Brax (16.02.1999); HE 30/1998 1 K Ed. Jäätteenmäki (16.02.1999); Compare also: HE 30/1998 LK Ed. Karpio (23.04.1998).
11. HE 30/1998 1 K Ed. Kallio (16.2.1999).
12. HE 30/1998 LK Min. Järventaus (23.4.1998).
13. HE 30/1998 LK Ed. Wideroos (23.4.1998).
14. HE 30/1998 LK Ed. Karpio (23.4.1998).
15. HE 30/1998 1 K Ed. Kallio (16.2.1999); HE 30/1998 3 K Ed. Pulliainen (19.2.1999).
16. HE 30/1998 1 K Ed. Brax (16.2.1999).
17. HE 30/1998 1 K Ed. Kallio (16.2.1999).
18. HE 30/1998 1 K Ed. Kankaanniemi (16.2.1999).
19. HE 30/1998 LK Ed. Tulonen (23.4.1998).
20. HE 30/1998 LK Ed. Kekkonen (23.4.1998).
21. HE 30/1998 LK Ed. M. Pohjola (23.4.1998); HE 30/1998 LK Ed. Mikkola (23.4.1998).
22. HE 30/1998 LK Min. Järventaus (23.4.1998).
23. Söderman was largely responsible for establishing the institution of European Ombudsman (Magnette 2003; cf. Söderman 2005). But the rise of openness in the EU was a result of many factors, not least the loss of credibility of the European Commission through cases of corruption (Héritier 2003; Lodge 2003; Gammeltoft-Hansen 2005; Shore 2006; Cini 2007).
24. HE 30/1998 1 K Ed. Jäätteenmäki (16.2.1999); HE 30/1998 3 K Ed. Kankaanniemi (19.2.1999).
25. HE 30/1998 1 K Ed. Jäätteenmäki; HE 30/1998 1 K Ed. Kaarilahti (16.2.1999).
26. HE 30/1998 1 K Ed. Jansson (16.2.1999).
27. HE 30/1998 1 K Ed. Kankaanniemi (16.2.1999).
28. HE 30/1998 1 K Ed. Kankaanniemi (16.2.1999); HE 30/1998 LK Ed. M. Pohjola (23.4.1998).
29. HE 30/1998 1 K Ed. Brax (16.2.1999).
30. HE 30/1998 1 K Ed. Brax (16.2.1999).
31. HE 30/1998 LK Ed. Viljamaa (23.4.1998).
32. HE 30/1998 1 K Ed. Kankaanniemi (16.2.1999).
33. HE 30/1998 1 K Ed. Kankaanniemi (16.2.1999).
34. HE 30/1998 1 K Ed. Ryhänen (16.2.1999).
35. HE 30/1998 LK Ed. Huotari (23.4.1998).
36. HE 30/1998 LK Ed. Lahtela (23.4.1998).
37. HE 30/1998 LK Ed. Tiusanen (23.4.1998).
38. HE 30/1998 LK Ed. Tiusanen (23.4.1998).
39. HE 30/1998 LK Ed. M. Pohjola (23.4.1998).
40. Picture used with the kind permission of the Prime Minister's Office.
41. K.J. Ståhlberg acted as the first Finnish president (1919–25) and was also a long term member of the parliament.
42. State committees, an institutional peculiarity of Nordic participatory governance, brought together different experts and representatives of interest

groups. The committee reports often gave an insight on the preparation of laws and sometimes also legislative proposals.

43. Henkilötietolaki 22.4.1999/523, Luottotietolaki 11.5.2007/527
44. Laki viranomaisten toiminnan julkisuudesta 21.5.1999/621
45. Suomen perustuslaki 11.6.1999/731, 12 §
46. Act on the Openness of Government Activities (621/1999), Unofficial translation.
47. Viljanen (1996, p. 791) also claims that the notion of good governance, mentioned in the basic rights, is of Finnish origin, which, assessed against the rise of the international discourse of 'good governance' (Seppänen 2003; Drechsler 2004; cf. Tiihonen 2004; Zanotti 2005), seems doubtful.
48. Asetus valtioneuvoston viestinnästä (380/2002)
49. Act on the Openness of Government Activities (621/1999), Unofficial translation.
50. Towards the present, however, the tripartite agreements, a process involving the government, labour unions and employers' organizations, have been increasingly of a lessening significance and they have been labeled outright 'dysfunctional' particularly by the representatives of employers' organizations but also by certain key civil servants of the Ministry of Finance (see, for example, Helsingin Sanomat 2007a, Helsingin Sanomat 2007b).
51. For background see HE 72/2002 vp.
52. Hallintolaki 6.6.2003/434.
53. HE 72/2002 vp.
54. HE 72/2002 vp.
55. Apart from the developments in the sphere of European Union institutions and international human rights, the law draft presents summaries of development of similar legislation in Sweden, Norway, Denmark, Iceland, Germany, Switzerland, France, Netherlands, Spain, and Portugal.
56. HE 30/1998 Yksityiskohtaiset perustelut 1/3 vp , 8 §: Asiakirjan saattaminen yleisesti julkisuuteen
57. There were also international examples of the same development. In terms of timing, the drafting of the Finnish law in 1998/99 coincided with the economic crises in Asia, where the opacity of administration expedited the fleeing of foreign direct investment from the countries. The measure adopted to prevent this was a transparency reform that increased the business trust in these countries (Rodan 2004).
58. HE 30/1998 Yleisperustelut 1/2 vp.
59. Valtion maksuperustelaki 1992/150
60. In the first quarter of 2005 alone, 7,700 requests for information were filed to government departments and further 5,700 to other government bodies in the UK (James 2006, p. 19).
61. Picture used with the kind permission of the Ministry of Finance.

3 Transparency and Institutions of Public Accountability

1. Figures given by the Finnish Supreme Administrative Court.
2. Further, the majority respondents (57 percent) had not used the features of the new law when asking civil servants for information. The main reported problem was too broad interpretations of secrecy exemptions. The

respondents thought that the civil servants did not know the law too well. The study also concluded this to have been the likely case with journalists themselves at the time. (Mörä & Tarkiainen 2003.)

3. Of this 2004 figure, 42 percent of which were initiated by the citizens, 35 percent comprised of preventive control and guidance, and the final 23 percent comprised of various statements, hearings, administrative matters and international cooperation (Muttilainen 2006).

4. Liikenne ja viestintäministeriön työjärjestys, 627/2007, 41 § Julkisuus ja avoimuus; Valtioneuvoston kanslian työjärjestys, 394/2007, 35 §; Ulkoasiainministeriön työjärjestys, 550/2008, 7 §, 74 §

5. The civil servants named the following eight top values: legality, service orientation, expertise, impartiality, justice, openness, result orientation, and integrity. The legislators' rank-order was following: expertise, trustworthiness, impartiality, responsibility, equality, service orientation, openness, and efficiency.

6. The figures between 1976–1990 are based on compilation by the Library of Parliament (Eduskunnan kirjasto 1992). The 1991–2008 figures are derived from the Library of Parliament information system (Selma).

7. Source: Valtioneuvoston hankerekisteri HARE / Valtiovarainministeriö 2008a, liite 1 a. Note: Since 2008, Ministry of Labour and the Ministry of Trade and Industry were merged into the Ministry of Employment and the Economy.

8. The Finnish news agency STT asked the Ministry of Education for school evaluation information in 2002 (Kemppainen 2005). The Ministry dismissed the request arguing that the evaluations had been produced on behalf of the municipalities. When asked from the city of Vantaa, the request was also turned down. After the decisions of the Chancellor of Justice and a ruling by the Administrative Court, the evaluations were made public. However, the city of Vantaa filed a complaint to the Supreme Administrative Court. In a commentary written by a civil servant of the Ministry of Finance, this was regretted and the quality of the evaluations was seen to benefit from their publicity, and institutional openness was named as a 'comparative advantage' of the Finnish state (Holkeri 2005).

4   NPM, Budget Transparency and Census Information

1. For example, the Soros Foundation helped several public institutions to get photocopy equipment under the Hungarian communist regime in the 1980s. This did not lead to enhancing existing administrative processes but instead had a big impact on the dissemination of anti-government material. (Dányi 2006)

2. The timeline of EU policies follows ePSIplus Analyst Chris Corbin's presentation in ePSIplus National Meeting at Tampere, 2 October 2007.

3. The Finnish information society strategy, published in 1998, calls for cooperation between the public and private sector to exploit the economic potential of public information resources through commodification (SITRA 1998).

4. Table used with the kind permission of the Ministry of Finance.

5. Liikenne- ja viestintäministeriön asetus Tiehallinnon maksuista, 1132/2007.

6. Source: Väestörekisterikeskus, 1999.

7. There were significant changes during the period 1997–2000 in the use of subcontractors and counting the revenues attained through them. In

October 1999, there was a large transfer to a new information system, which caused slowing to the use of the system and also lower volumes and revenues particularly for private sector conveyance in 2000 and perhaps even afterwards.

8. Sisäasiainministeriön asetus rekisterihallinnon suoritteiden maksuista, 19.12.2007.

9. The Swedish state has a single SPAR register (Statens Person- och Adressregister) from where the address information of citizens can be obtained. As with Finland, a private company is responsible for the operation and selling of the data in SPAR (see Infodata 2010).

10. There has been a significant amount of joint cooperation among the Nordic countries involving the exchange of registry data over the years. The public officials have joint information systems that help to keep track of people moving from one Nordic country to another.

11. Henkilötietolaki 22.4.1999/523, Väestötietolaki 11.6.1993/507, Act on the Publicity of Government Activities 621/1999.

12. For instance, in some cases address information could not be given out for security reasons. A specific code of conduct was applied for these cases.

13. The economic issues had already dominated the agenda around the time the previous act on census information was being drafted (see Korhonen 1997).

14. Until the end of 2007 the Population Register Centre was still placed under the Ministry of Interior but was moved under the Ministry of Finance in early 2008, along with a wider restructuring, aiming to enhance the coordination of policies, particularly within the domain of local government.

15. Hätäkeskuslaki 2000/157, §8.

16. The ranking was based on so called e-Government readiness index. For a clearer picture on the composition of the index see its Technical Annex.

17. Throughout the reorganization of the former tasks of the Ministry of Interior under the Ministry of Finance, the latter was also given the means to tighten its control on coordination.

18. However, the Ministry of Finance should by no means be regarded as a single entity in the debate. On the contrary, there were also tensions inside the ministry as the department of budgeting was coordinating the budgetary process and a separate department on administrative reform is responsible for the information society issues and IT management.

19. Even though the reuse of public information set the agenda for most of the 1990s and was to make an encore in 2008 in the form of directive follow-up, the Lisbon strategy makes no mention of PSI. The topic seems to have momentarily fallen off the agenda, even if the initial policy problems remain unresolved.

20. For instance, anyone who has spent more time in the Finnish research community would know stories about high prices paid for statistical or geographical information, and the peculiarities in interpreting the law on accrual charges (see, for example, Tietoarkisto 2006).

21. Borowiak has studied new digital dilemmas of intellectual property rights, revealing the potential of unintended consequences for the discourse of rights in this context (Borowiak 2004).

5 New Domains of Openness and Transparency: Performing Foreign Affairs

1. The issue was publicly addressed by Chancellor of State Pertti Torstila, at the Finnish Institute of International Affairs seminar on EU Foreign Policy and the European External Action Service, 25 February 2008.
2. The final conclusion of the document was that in order to remain at its operative level, the ministry would be in need of €37 million worth of supplementary funding in 2002 (Ulkoasiainministeriö 2001a, p. 56). This particular financial function of the document was also openly referred to in the interviews.
3. L.A. Puntila, Professor of History, and a Social Democratic parliamentarian (1966–1970), made public appeals for attaining primary research material from the archives.
4. An example of this was the report on the Finnish–Soviet trade negotiations of Zavidovo that was leaked to the Swedish media, which published the content of the document, leading to internal investigations within the administration (cf. Holopainen, et al. 1973). This led finally to the setting up of a specific committee on secrecy that tried to establish new means for keeping documents from being leaked (Salassapitokomitea, Komiteanmietintö 1974, p. 70).
5. Sources: Ulkoasiainministeriö 1984; Ulkoasiainministeriö 1992; Ulkoasiainministeriö 2001b; Favorin 2003.
6. In fact, between the time frame 1 January 1952 – 5 June 1952, Finland probably had the most liberal term of secrecy for foreign political information in the world, set briefly to 25 years before being corrected to 50 years.
7. This is part of the still ongoing debate on the reorganization of the mandates and power relations of the Prime Minister and President in Finland. While the Finnish political system was previously characterized as semi-presidential, the early 2000s constitutional reform shifted the balance towards a more parliamentarian system. Taking the EU coordination to the Council of State brought them under the oversight of the Prime Minister.
8. In a public interview in 2005, the retiring Head of Information Management of the Foreign Ministry stressed the diminishing number of secret documents (see Helsingin Sanomat 2005).
9. This is also a general development that can be observed internationally, and there are increasing pressures to introduce transparency to international organizations (cf. Kahler 2004; Nanz and Steffek 2004).
10. For example, during the Finnish EU presidency in 2006, Erkki Tuomioja, Finnish Foreign Minister at the time, publicly criticized EU officials for 'false transparency'; that is leaking out documents in pursuit of their own interests (Tuomioja 2006).
11. On 5 June 1952, when the 50-year term of secrecy was issued to the Foreign Political Material, the Council of State, after a proposal from the ministry, gave exemptions for research permits. This lasted until the end of the 1980s.
12. The standard procedure had it that instead of documents civil servants gave information. In particular, when a document contained classified material, civil servants were instructed to give information about the document, but not the document itself. If the document was requested, the issue was most often passed to the Information Service, whose head made the necessary

decision. The decision-making process seldom involved legal assistance, though this was sought in some cases. Business confidentiality was referred to in particular as constituting difficult cases of this nature.

13. According to the ministry, there was no overall account available. Some information requests only reach the telephone exchange and some proceed to civil servants in charge of the issue, without the Information Service being aware of them. Also, in cases where information was not given and the person filing the request settled for the result, there was no reporting. The requests that reached the Information Service were collected in a file, but more to maintain a consistent line in the decisions than to keep track of the number of requests.

14. Figure used with the kind permission of the Ministry for Foreign Affairs.

15. One should note that the particular exemptions on the Foreign Political material were removed first in 8 February 2001.

16. Source: Ministry for Foreign Affairs. The figures are from the record of secret documents of the ministry.

17. Section 24(2), 'Act on the Publicity of Government Activities'. Unofficial translation.

18. I gained personal experience on the non-publicity of the positions of member states, when trying to receive information on the drafting of the privacy codification for the EU's third pillar (Justice and Home Affairs) for another study (see Erkkilä 2010b). A contact in the Ministry of Justice declined to say how different countries had acted in the long negotiations leading to a compromise solution in establishing privacy standards for the EU's third pillar in exchanging criminal data between the EU countries.

19. Source: Prime Minister's Office. The figures include documents without different language versions. There was often a Swedish translation of the same document, which is excluded from the numbers.

20. Source: Prime Minister's Office. The information was available starting from 2003.

21. The actual assessment on the status of a document was made at its request, which was also the procedure according to the law. It could be that they should not have been secret to begin with or that the information that was perceived as classified a month ago would be public knowledge today, making the document public in full when requested.

22. 4 §, Ulkoasiainministeriön työjärjestys, 550/2008.

23. Yet the biggest media case regarding foreign political information during the time frame investigated was in 2003 as Anneli Jääteenmäki, the opposition leader of the Centre Party had used secret documents in her campaigning, leading to her resignation after serving only 68 days as Prime Minister. The documents were leaked from the President's Office. The issue concerned a discussion between Finnish at the time Prime Minister Paavo Lipponen (Social Democratic Party) and George W. Bush concerning Finland's stance on the war in Iraq. The documents were leaked from the President's Office. A court case that followed found the person leaking the documents guilty but Anneli Jäätteenmäki was freed of charges. She had already resigned due to political pressure.

24. This particular insight referred to the adopted practice of Finland's permanent representation to the European Union, which had handed confidential

EU documents to Finnish journalists. These were not to write about but they were given in order to share the information behind the policies that were then pursued.

25. This trend was attaining global media attention at the time: 'Escape to New Zealand', BBC Podcast, Documentary Archive, Global Perspectives, 2.5.2008.

Bibliography

Alasuutari, Pertti (2006) 'Suunnittelutaloudesta kilpailutalouteen: miten muutos oli ideologisesti mahdollinen?' In Heiskala, Risto and Luhtakallio, Eeva (eds) *Uusi jako. Miten Suomesta tuli kilpailukyky-yhteiskunta?* Gaudeamus, Helsinki.

Anders Chydenius Foundation (2006) 'The World's First Freedom of Information Act. Anders Chydenius' Legacy Today.' Anders Chydenius Foundation, Kokkola, available at http://www.chydenius.net/pdf/worlds_first_foia.pdf.

Anderson, Benedict (1991) *Imagined Communities: Reflections on the Origin and Spread of Nationalism*. Verso, London.

Anderson, Perry (1993) *Lineages of the Absolutist State*. Verso, London.

Arendt, Hannah (1958) *The Human Condition*. The University of Chicago Press, Chicago.

Arjen tietoyhteiskunnan neuvottelukunta (2008) Arjen tietoyhteiskunta. Toimintaohjelma 2008–2011. Liite: Toimintaohjelman hankkeet ja toimenpiteet.

Arjen tietoyhteiskunnan neuvottelukunta (2009) Tietoyhteiskunta suomalaisten arjessa-saavutettuja edistysaskeleita ja tulevaisuuden haasteita. Arjen tietoyhteiskunnan neuvottelukunnan vuosiraportti 2008 valtioneuvostolle.

Ashenden, Samantha and Owen, David, (eds) (1999) *Foucault contra Habermas: Recasting the Dialogue between Genealogy and Critical Theory*. Sage, London.

Azubuike, Abraham (2008) 'Accessibility of Government Information as a Determinant of Inward Foreign Direct Investment in Africa'. In Lynden, Irina and Wu, Jane (eds) *Best Practices in Government Information: A Global Perspective*. K.G. Saur, München. pp.85–98.

Bacchi, Carol Lee (1999) *Women, Policy and Politics. The Construction of Policy Problems*. Sage, London.

Baert, Patrick (1991) 'Unintended Consequences: A Typology and Examples'. *International Sociology* 6(2), pp.201–210.

Beck Jørgensen, Torben and Larsen, Bøje (1987) 'Control – An Attempt at Forming a Theory'. *Scandinavian Political Studies* 10(4), pp.279–299.

Beck Jørgensen, Torben (1993) 'Modes of Governance and Administrative Change'. In Kooiman, Jan (ed.) *Modern Governance. New Government-Society Interactions*. Sage Publications, London.

Beck, Ulrich (1992) *Risk Society: Towards a New Modernity*. Sage, London.

Behn, Robert (2001) *Rethinking Democratic Accountability*. Brookings Institution Press, Washington D.C.

Béland, Daniel and Hacker, Jacob (2004) 'Ideas, Private Institutions and American Welfare State "Exceptionalism": the Case of Health and Old-Age Insurance, 1915–1965'. *International Journal of Social Welfare*, 13, pp.42–54.

Bennett, Colin (1997) 'Understanding the Ripple Effects: The Cross-National Adoption of Policy Instruments for Bureaucratic Accountability'. *Governance. An International Journal of Public Policy and Administration*, 10(3), pp.213–233.

Berman, Sheri (1997) 'Civil Society and Political Institutionalization'. *American Behavioral Scientist*, 40(5), pp.562–574.

Best, Jacqueline (2005) *The Limits of Transparency: Ambiguity and the History of International Finance.* Cornell University Press, Ithaca.

Blakemore, Michael and Craglia, Max (2006) 'Access to Public-Sector Information in Europe: Policy, Rights, and Obligations'. *Information Society,* 22(1), pp. 13–24.

Blomgren, Maria and Sahlin, Kerstin (2007) 'Quests for Transparency – Signs of a New Institutional Era?' In Christensen, Thomas and Lægreid, Per (eds) *Transcending New Public Management.* Ashgate, Aldershot.

Blomgren, Maria (2007) 'The Drive for Transparency: Organizational Field Transformations in Swedish Healthcare'. *Public Administration* 85(1), pp. 67–82.

Blume, Peter (2001) *Nordic Data Protection Law.* Kauppakaari, Helsinki.

Blyth, Mark (2002) *Great Transformations: Economic Ideas and Institutional Change in the Twentieth Century.* Cambridge University Press, Cambridge.

Boltanski, Luc and Chiapello, Ève (2005) *The New Spirit of Capitalism.* Verso, New York.

Borowiak, Craig (2004) 'Farmers' Rights: Intellectual Property Regimes and the Struggle over Seeds'. *Politics & Society,* 32(4), pp.511–543.

Bouckaert, Geert, Ormond, Derry and Peters, Guy (2000) *A Potential Governance Agenda for Finland.* Ministry of Finance, Helsinki.

Bovens, Mark and Loos, Eugène (2002) 'The Digital Constitutional State: Democracy and Law in the Information Society'. *Information Polity,* 7(4), pp.185–197.

Bovens, Mark (2005) 'Public Accountability'. In Ferlie, E., Lynne, L. and Pollitt, C. (eds) 'The Oxford Handbook of Public Management'. Oxford University Press.

Brax, Tuija (2007) Julkisuusperiaatteen haasteet. Puhe tietämisen vapauden päivän seminaarissa 30.11.2007, available at http://www.om.fi/Etusivu/ Ajankohtaista/Ministerinpuheita/Puhearkisto/Puheet2007Brax/11961593288 43,30 November 2007.

Breton, Albert (2007) 'Transparency and Efficiency'. In Breton, Albert, Galeotti, Gianluigi, Salmon, Pierre and Wintrobe, Ronald (eds) *The Economics of Transparency in Politics.* Ashgate, Aldershot. pp.55–70.

Brown, Wendy (2003) 'Neo-liberalism and the End of Liberal Democracy'. *Theory & Event,* 7(1).

Brunila, Anne (2005) 'Osaava, avautuva ja uudistuva Suomi'. *Kansantaloudellinen aikakauskirja,* 101(1), s. 31–37.

Calhoun, Craig, (ed.) (1992) *Habermas and the Public Sphere.* MIT Press, Cambridge.

Campbell, John (2004) *Institutional Change and Globalisation.* Princeton University Press, New Jersey.

Castells, Manuel and Himanen, Pekka (2002) *The Information Society and the Welfare State: The Finnish Model.* Oxford University Press, Oxford.

Castells, Manuel (1996) *The Rise of the Network Society.* Blackwell, Oxford.

Cejudo, Guillermo M. (2008) 'Explaining Change in the Mexican Public Sector: The Limits of New Public Management'. *International Review of Administrative Sciences,* 74(1), pp.111–127.

Chapman, Richard and Hunt, Michael, (eds) (2006) *Open Government in a Theoretical and Practical Context.* Ashgate, Aldershot.

Cheung, Anthony (2005) 'The Politics of Administrative Reforms in Asia: Paradigms and Legacies, Paths and Diversities'. *Governance: An International Journal of Policy, Administration, and Institutions*, 18(2), pp.257–282.

Christensen, Tom and Lægreid, Per (eds) (2001) *New Public Management: The Transformation of Ideas and Practice*. Ashgate, Aldershot.

Christensen, Tom and Lægreid, Per (eds) (2007) *Transcending New Public Management: The Transformation of Public Sector Reforms*. Ashgate, Aldershot.

Chydenius, Anders (1880a) 'Den nationala vinsten'. In *Politiska skrifter af Anders Chydenius*. G.W. Edlunds Förlag, Helsinki. [Original 1765]

Chydenius, Anders (1880b) 'Hvad kan vara orsaken, att sådan myckenhet svenskt folk årligen flyttar utur landet? Och genom hvad författningar det kan bäst förekommas?' In *Politiska skrifter af Anders Chydenius*. G.W. Edlunds Förlag, Helsinki. [Original 1765]

Chydenius, Anders (1880c) 'Källan till rikets vanmagt'. In *Politiska skrifter af Anders Chydenius*. G.W. Edlunds Förlag, Helsinki. [Original 1765]

Chydenius, Anders (1880d) 'Vederläggning af de skäl, hvarmed man söker bestrida Öster-och Vesterbottniska samt Vesternoorländska städerna fri seglation'. In *Politiska skrifter af Anders Chydenius*. G.W. Edlunds Förlag, Helsinki. [Original 1765]

Chydenius, Anders (1929a) 'Antti Chydeniuksen Göteporin tiede-ja kirjallisuusseuralle lähettämä omatekoinen elämäkerta'. In Chydenius, Antti (ed.) (1929) *Valitut kirjoitukset*. Werner Söderström, Porvoo. [Original 1780]

Chydenius, Anders [Antti] (1929b) *Valitut kirjoitukset*. Werner Söderström, Porvoo.

Cini, Michelle (2007) *From Integration to Integrity: Administrative Ethics and Reform in the European Commission*. Manchester University Press, Manchester.

Cogburn, Derrick (2005) 'Partners or Pawns? The Impact of Elite Decision-Making and Epistemic Communities in Global Information Policy on Developing Countries and Transnational Civil Society'. *Knowledge, Technology & Politics*, 18(2), pp.52–82.

Cohen, Joshua (1997) 'Deliberation and Democratic Legitimacy'. In Bohman, James and Rehg, William (eds) *Deliberative Democracy: Essays on Reason and Politics*. MIT Press, Cambridge.

Craglia, Max (1999) 'Geographic Information Policies in Europe: National and Regional Perspectives'. Report of the EUROGI-EC Data Policy Workshop. Amersfoort, 15.11.1999.

Curtis, Bruce (2001) *The Politics of Population: State Formation, Statistics, and the Census of Canada, 1840–1875*. University of Toronto Press, Toronto.

Dányi, Endre (2006) 'Xerox Project: Photocopy Machines as a Metaphor for an "Open Society"'. *The Information Society*, 22, pp.111–115.

Davies, Philip (2001) 'Spies as Informants: Triangulation and Interpretation of Elite Interview Data in the Study of the Intelligence and Security Service'. *Politics*, 21(1), pp.73–80.

Dean, Mitchell and Hindess, Barry, (eds) (1998) *Governing Australia: Studies in Contemporary Rationalities of Government*. Cambridge University Press, Cambridge.

Dean, Mitchell (1994) *Critical and Effective Histories: Foucault's Methods and Historical Sociology*. Routledge, London.

Dean, Mitchell (1999) *Governmentality: Power and Rule in Modern Society*. Sage, London.

Desrosières, Alain (1998) *The Politics of Large Numbers: A History of Statistical Reasoning*. Harvard University Press, Cambridge.

DiMaggio, Paul and Powell, Walter W. (1983) 'The Iron Cage Revisited: Institutional Isomorphism and Collective Rationality in Organizational Fields'. *American Sociological Review*, 48(2), pp.147–160.

Dolowitz, David and Marsh, David (2000) 'Learning From Abroad: The Role of Policy Transfer in Contemporary Policy-Making'. *Governance: An International Journal of Policy and Administration*, 13(1), pp.5–24.

Douglas, Mary (1987) *How Institutions Think?* In Routledge and Kegan, Paul. London.

Drechsler, Wolfgang (2004) 'Governance, Good Governance, and Government: The Case for Estonian Administrative Capacity'. *Trames*, 8(4), pp.388–396.

Drezner, Daniel and Farrell, Henry (2004) 'Web of Influence'. *Foreign Policy*, 145.

Drezner, Daniel (2004) 'The Global Governance of the Internet: Bringing the State Back In'. *Political Science Quarterly*, 119(3), pp.477–498.

Dryzek, John (2002) *Deliberative Democracy and Beyond: Liberals, Critics, Contestations*. Oxford University Press, Oxford.

Dubnick, Melvin (2003) 'Accountability and Ethics: Reconsidering the Relationships'. *International Journal of Organisation Theory and Behavior*, 6(3), pp.405–441.

Dubnick, Melvin (2005) 'Accountability and the Promise of Performance: In Search of the Mechanisms'. *Public Performance and Management Review*, 28(3), pp.376–417.

Duden (2001) 'Duden: Deutsches Universalwörterbuch' (4th Edition). Dudenverlag, Mannheim.

Dunn, John (2006) *Setting the People Free: The Story of Democracy*. Atlantic Books, London.

Dülmen, Richard van (1986) *Die Gesellschaft der Aufklärer: Zur bürgerlichen Emanzipation und aufklärerischen Kultur in Deutschland*. Fischer Taschenbuch Verlag, Frankfurt/M.

Durham Peters, John (2005) *Courting the Abyss: Free Speech and the Liberal Tradition*. Chicago University Press, Chicago.

Dwivedi, O.P. and Jabbra, Joseph (1988) 'Introduction: Public Service Responsibility and Accountability'. In Jabbra, Joseph and Dwivedi, O.P. (eds) *Public Service Accountability: A Comparative Perspective*. Kumarian Press, Hartford.

Economic Council of Finland (2010) 'Economic Council of Finland', front page, available at http://www.valtioneuvosto.fi/hallitus/talousneuvosto/en.jsp, date accessed 12 April 2010.

Economist, The (2010a) 'Data and Transparency. Of Governments and Geeks'. Newspaper article 6.2.2010.

Economist, The (2010b) 'Leviathan's Spyglass'. Newspaper article 17.7.2010.

Eder, Klaus (2006) 'The Public Sphere'. *Theory, Culture and Society*, 23(2–3), pp. 607–611.

Eduskunnan kirjasto (1992) 'Valtion komiteanmietinnöt 1976–1990'. Eduskunnan kirjasto, Helsinki.

Eduskunta (2005) 'EU-menettelyjen kehittäminen. EU-menettelyjen tarkastus-toimikunnan mietintö'. Eduskunnan kanslian julkaisu 2/2005.

Eijnatten, Joris van (2004) 'Between Practice and Principle: Dutch Ideas on Censorship and Press Freedom, 1579–1795'. *Redescriptions. Yearbook of Political Thought and Conceptual History*, 8, pp.85–113.

Eisenstadt, Shmuel N. and Schluchter, Wolfgang (2001) 'Introduction: Paths to Early Modernities – A Comparative View'. In Eisenstadt, Shmuel N., Schluchter, Wolfgang, Wittrock, Björn (eds) *Public Spheres & Collective Identities*. Transaction Publishers, New Brunswick.

Elster, Jon (1978) *Logic and Society: Contradictions and Possible Worlds*. Wiley, Chichester.

Embassy of Finland in Tokyo (2010) 'Project Finland', available at http://www.projectfinland.jp/, date accessed 12 April 2010.

Emirbayer, Mustafa and Sheller, Mimi (1999) 'Publics in History'. In *History and Theory*, 28, pp.145–197.

Erkkilä, Tero and Piironen, Ossi (2009) 'Politics and Numbers: The Iron Cage of Governance Indices'. In Cox, Raymond (ed.) *Ethics and Integrity in Public Administration: Concepts and Cases*. M.E. Sharpe, Armonk. pp.125–145.

Erkkilä, Tero (2007) 'Governance and Accountability – A Shift in Conceptualisation'. *Public Administration Quarterly*, 31(1), pp.1–38.

Erkkilä, Tero (2008) 'Communicating Political Institutions. The Ombudsman in Finland and in the European Union'. Paper presented at the ECPR (Standing Group on the European Union) Fourth Pan-European Conference on EU Politics, 25–27 September 2008. Riga, Latvia.

Erkkilä, Tero (2010a) 'Transparency and Nordic Openness: State Tradition and New Governance Ideas in Finland'. In Jansen, St.A., Schröter E., B.P., Stehr, N. (eds) *Transparenz. Multidisciplinäre Durchsichten durch Phänomene und Theorien des Undurchsichtigen. Zu-Schriften*. Jahrbuch der Zeppelin University Friedrichshafen, pp.348–372. VS-Verlag, Wiesbaden.

Erkkilä, Tero (2010b) 'Viranomaistiedonvaihdon kulttuuriset haasteet Euroopan unionin oikeus-ja sisäasioissa'. In Nuotio, Kimmo and Malkki, Leena (eds) *Vapauden, turvallisuuden ja oikeuden Eurooppa*. Forum Iuris, Oikeustieteellinen tiedekunta, Helsinki.

Espeland, Wendy Nelson and Stevens, Mitchell L. (2008) 'A Sociology of Quantification'. *European Journal of Sociology*, 49(3), pp.401–436.

EU Presidency (2006a) Finland's EU Presidency: Logo, available at http://www.eu2006.fi/THE_PRESIDENCY/EN_GB/LOGO/INDEX.HTM

EU Presidency (2006b) 'The objective for Finland's EU Presidency: a transparent and effective Union', available at http://www.eu2006.fi/NEWS_AND_DOCUMENTS/PRESS_RELEASES/VKO26_/EN_GB/162650

Eurooppatiedotus (2010) 'Eurooppatiedotus', available at http://www.eurooppatiedotus.fi, date accessed 12 April 2010.

European Commission (1998) 'Public Sector Information: A Key Resource for Europe'. Green Paper on Public Sector Information in the Information Society. COM(1998)585. European Commission, Brussels.

European Commission (2001) 'European Governance'. A White Paper. COM (2001)428 final. European Commission, Brussels.

European Commission (2005) 'Guide to the Archives of Member States' Foreign Ministries and European Union Institutions' (3rd Edition). Office for Official Publications of the European Communities, Luxembourg.

Eymeri, Jean-Michel (2001) 'The Electronic Identification of Citizens and Organisations in the European Union: State of Affairs'. A Report for 37th Meeting of the Directors-General of the Public Service of the Member States of the European Union. Federal Ministry of the Civil Service, Brussels.

Farr, James (1989) 'Understanding Conceptual Change Politically'. In Ball, Terrence, Farr, James and Hanson, Russell (eds) *Political Innovation and Conceptual Change*. Cambridge University Press, Cambridge.

Favorin, Martti (2003) 'Mennyttä aikaa etsimässä – UM:n salassapidon historiaa'. *UMIIRI* 2/2003, pp.22–23.

Financial Times (2011) 'Livable v lovable'. Newspaper article, 7.5.2011.

Finlex (2010) 'Finlex Valtion säädöstietopankki', available at http://www.finlex.fi/, date accessed 12 April 2010.

Finnish Competition Authority (2002) 'Finnish Meteorological Institute fined for abuse of dominant position', available at http://www.kilpailuvirasto.fi/cgi-bin/english.cgi?sivu=news/n-2002–01–23, date accessed 23 January 2002.

Finnish Government (1999) 'Comments on the Green Paper on Public Sector Information in the Information Society (COM 1998/585)', available at http://cordis.europa.eu/econtent/publicsector/comments/fingov.html

Finnish Government (2010a) 'Finnish Government Programmes 1917–2007', available at http://www.valtioneuvosto.fi/tietoa-valtioneuvostosta/hallitukset/hallitusohjelmat/fi.jsp, date accessed 12 April 2010.

Finnish Government (2010b) 'Contact information in EU affairs', available at http://www.valtioneuvosto.fi/eu/suomi-ja-eu/yhteystietoja/en.jsp, date accessed 12 April 2010.

Forlano, Laura (2004) 'The Emergence of Digital Government: International Perspectives'. In Pavlichev, Alexei and Garson, David (eds) *Digital Government: Principles and Best Practices*. Idea Group Publishing, Hershey.

Formin (2002) 'Alivaltiosihteeri Pertti Torstila: Ulkoasiainhallinto 2000-selvityksen jatko', available at http://www.formin.fi/public/?contentid=57516&contentlan=1&culture=fi-FI, date accessed 12 April 2010.

Formin (2006) 'Ulkoministeriön tulevaisuuskatsaus 2006', available at http://formin.finland.fi/public/default.aspx?contentid=77880, date accessed 17 August 2006.

Formin (2007) 'Suurlähettiläät saivat Katajanokalle tuhatkunta vierasta', available at http://www.formin.fi/public/default.aspx?contentid=100009&nodeid=15148&contentlan=1&culture=fi-FI, date accessed 12 April 2010.

Formin (2009) 'Toimivasta brändistä on apua ulkopolitiikalle', available at http://www.formin.fi/public/default.aspx?contentId=160296&nodeId=15145, date accessed 4 March 2009.

Formin (2010) 'Suomi ulkomaisissa tiedotusvälineissä', available at http://formin.finland.fi/public/default.aspx?nodeid=40007&contentlan=1&culture=fi-FI, date accessed 12 April 2010.

Forster, Marc (2002) 'Debating the Meaning of Pilgrimage: Maria Steinbach 1733.' In Melton, James Van Horn (ed.) *Cultures of Communication from Reformation to Enlightenment: Constructing Publics in Early Modern German Lands*. Ashgate, Aldershot.

Freedom House (2006) *Freedom in the World 2006*, available at http://www.freedomhouse.org/.

Freedominfo (2010) 'Freedominfo. Global Network of Freedom of Information Advocates', available at http://www.freedominfo.org, date accessed 12 April 2010.

FreeOurData (2011) 'Free Our Data: Make taxpayers' data available to them', available at http://www.freeourdata.org.uk/, date accessed 17 July 2011.

Friedeburg, Robert von (2002) 'The public of confessional identity: territorial church and church discipline in 18th-century Hesse'. In Melton, James Van Horn (ed.) *Cultures of Communication from Reformation to Enlightenment: Constructing Publics in Early Modern German Lands*. Ashgate, Aldershot.

Fukuyama, Francis (2004) *State-Building: Governance and World Order in the 21st Century*. Cornell University Press, Ithaca.

Fung, Archong (2003) Survey Article: 'Recipes for Public Spheres: Eight Institutional Design Choices and Their Consequences'. *The Journal of Political Philosophy*, 11(3), pp.338–367.

Fung, Archon, Graham, Mary and Weil, David (2008) *Full Disclosure: The Perils and Promise of Transparency*. Cambridge University Press, Cambridge.

Gammeltoft-Hansen, Hans (2005) 'Trends Leading to the Establishment of a European Ombudsman'. In *The European Ombudsman: Origins, Establishment, Evolution*. Office for Official Publications of the European Communities, Luxembourg.

Garrett, Geoffrey (1998) 'Global Markets and National Politics: Collision Course or Virtuous Circle?' *International Organisation*, 52(4), pp.787–824.

Garson, David (2004) 'The Promise of Digital Government'. In Pavlichev, Alexei and Garson, David (eds) *Digital Government: Principles and Best Practices*. Idea Group Publishing, Hershey.

Gestrich, Andreas (1994) *Absolutismus und Öffentlichkeit: Politische Kommunikation in Deutschland zu Beginn des 18. Jahrhunderts*. Vandenhoeck & Ruprecht, Göttingen.

Giddens, Anthony (1984) *The Constitution of Society: Outline of the Theory of Structuration*. Polity Press, Cambridge.

Giddens, Anthony (1985) *The Nation-State and Violence: Volume Two of a Critique of Historical Materialism*. Cambridge: Polity Press.

Glatzer, Miguel and Rueschemeyer, Dietrich (2005) 'Conclusion: Politics Matters'. In Glatzer, Miguel and Rueschemeyer, Dietrich (eds) *Globalization and the Future of the Welfare State*. University of Pittsburgh Press, Pittsburgh. pp.203–225.

Goodin, Robert (2003) 'Democratic Accountability: The Distinctiveness of the Third Sector'. *Archives Européennes de Sociologie*, 44(3), pp.359–396.

Gregory, Robert (2007) 'New Public Management and the Ghost of Max Weber: Exorcized or still haunting'. In Christensen, Tom and Laegreid, Per (eds), *Transcending New Public Management: The Transformation of Public Sector Reforms*. Ashgate, Aldershot.

Grønlie, Tore and Nagel, Anne-Hilde (1998) 'Administrative History in Norway'. *Jahrbuch für Europäische Verwaltungsgeschichte*, 10, pp.307–332.

Haas, Peter M. (1992) 'Introduction: Epistemic Communities and International Policy Coordination'. *International Organisation*, 46(1), pp.1–35.

Habermas, Jürgen (1989) *The Structural Transformation of the Public Sphere: An Inquiry into a Category of Bourgeois Society*. Polity Press, London.

Habermas, Jürgen (1996) *Between Facts and Norms: Contributions to a Discourse Theory of Law and Democracy*. Polity Press, Cambridge.

Habermas, Jürgen (1997) 'The Public Sphere'. In Goodin, Robert E. and Pettit, Philip (eds) *Contemporary Political Philosophy: An Anthology*. Blackwell, Oxford. pp.105–108.

Hall, Peter and Soskice, David (2001) 'An Introduction to Varieties of Capitalism'. In Hall, Peter and Soskice, David (eds) *Varieties of Capitalism: The Institutional Foundations of Comparative Advantage*. Oxford University Press. pp.1–70.

Halonen, Tarja (2005) 'Puhe Anders Chydeniuksen juhlavuoden pääjuhlassa Kokkolassa 1.3.2003'. In Anders Chydenius Säätiö (2005) *Yhteinen vapaus. Anders Chydeniuksen ajatukset nykyajassa*. Anders Chydenius Säätiö, Kokkola.

Hamilton, Gary and Feenstra, Robert (1998) 'The Organization of Economies'. In Brinton, Mary and Nee, Victor (eds) *The New Institutionalism in Sociology*. Stanford University Press, Stanford. pp.153–180.

Harisalo, Risto and Stenvall, Jari (2001) *Luottamus kansalaisyhteiskunnan peruskivenä: Kansalaisten luottamus ministeriöihin*. Edita, Helsinki.

Harlow, Carol (2002) *Accountability in the European Union*. Oxford University Press: Oxford.

Harlow, Carol (2006) 'Global Administrative Law: The Quest for Principles and Values'. *The European Journal of International Law*, 17(1), pp.187–214.

Harvey, David (2005) *A Brief History of Neoliberalism*. Oxford University Press, Oxford.

Harvey, David (2006) *Spaces of Global Capitalism: Towards a Theory of Uneven Geographical Development*. Verso, New York.

Hautamäki, Antti and Mäkipeska, Marja (1994) *Laatupolitiikkaa julkiselle sektorille? Peruspalvelujen laadunhallinnan tarve ja keinot*. Valtiovarainministeriö, Painatuskeskus, Helsinki 1994.

Hay, Colin (2001) 'The "Crisis" of Keynesianism and the Rise of Neoliberalism in Britain: An Ideational Institutionalist Approach'. In Campbell, John and Pedersen, Ove K. (eds) *The Rise of Neoliberalism and Institutional Analysis*. Princeton University Press, New Jersey. pp.193–218.

Heiskala, Risto and Luhtakallio, Eeva, (eds) (2006) *Uusi jako. Miten Suomesta tuli kilpailukyky-yhteiskunta?* Gaudeamus, Helsinki.

Heiskala, Risto (2006) 'Kansainvälisen toimintaympäristön muutos ja Suomen yhteiskunnallinen murros'. In Heiskala, Risto and Luhtakallio, Eeva (eds) *Uusi jako. Miten Suomesta tuli kilpailukyky-yhteiskunta?* Gaudeamus, Helsinki.

Heiskanen, Ilkka (1977) *Julkinen, kollektiivinen ja markkinaperusteinen: Suomalaisen yhteiskunnan hallintajärjestelmien ja julkisen päätöksenteon ja hallinnon kehitys ja kehittäminen 1960- ja 1970-luvuilla*. Helsingin yliopiston yleisen valtio-opin laitoksen tutkimuksia. Sarja C, DETA 31.

Helsingin Sanomat (1991) 'Itsesensuurin aika (HS kuukausiliite)'. Newspaper article, 24.8.1991.

Helsingin Sanomat (2005) 'Valtion salaisuuksien vartija'. Newspaper article, 29.5.2005.

Helsingin Sanomat (2006) 'Jäätäviä päätöksiä'. Newspaper article, 29.7.2006.

Helsingin Sanomat (2007a) 'Riski: Isänmaata voi rakentaa ilman tupojakin'. Newspaper article, 9.12.2007.

Helsingin Sanomat (2007b) 'Missä luuraa Lauri?' Newspaper article, 16.12.2007.

Helsingin Sanomat (2008a) 'Julkiset verkkopalvelut luotava käyttäjän eikä tarjoajan ehdoilla'. Newspaper article, 3.3.2008.

Helsingin Sanomat (2008b) 'Tietoyhteiskunnan takapajula: Suomi'. Newspaper article, 3.3.2008.

Helsingin Sanomat (2009) 'Talouspappi Chydenius pääsi valtiovarainministerin seinälle Ruotsissa'. Newspaper article, 1.9.2009.

Héritier, Adrienne (2003) 'Composite Democracy in Europe: The Role of Transparency and Access to Information'. *Journal of European Public Policy*, 10(5), pp.814–833.

Hermans, Outi and Hermans, Raine (2007) Paikkatietojen yhteiskäyttö ja jakeluperiaatteet. Hinnoitteluperiaatteiden analyysi ja kansantaloudellisten vaikutusten simulointi. Maa- ja metsätalousministeriö. Paikkatietoasiain neuvottelukunta 6.2.2007.

Hidén, Mikael (1970) *Eduskunnan oikeusasiamies*. Suomalainen lakimiesyhdistys, Helsinki.

Hidén, Mikael (2000) 'Finnish Parliamentary Ombudsman as a Guardian of Human Rights and Constitutional Rights: An Integrated Approach'. In Rautio, Ilkka (ed.), *Parliamentary Ombudsman of Finland 80 Years*. Parliamentary Ombudsman of Finland, Helsinki.

Hill, Christopher (2002) *The Changing Politics of Foreign Policy*. Palgrave, Basingstoke.

Hobsbawm, Eric (1987) 'Introduction: Inventing Traditions'. In Hobsbawm, Eric and Ranger, Terrence (eds) *The Invention of Traditions*. Cambridge University Press, Cambridge.

Holkeri, Katju (2005) 'Kouluarvioinnit julkisiksi – kommentti'. *Hallinnon tutkimus*, Arvioinnin teemanumero, p.135.

Holkeri, Katju (2007) 'Kuka kuulee ja mitä?, Onko periaatteilla merkitystä-tilaisuus Säätytalo', available at http://www.vm.fi/vm/fi/04_julkaisut_ja_asiakirjat/03_muut_asiakirjat/20070910Tilais/02_Kysely_KUKA_050907.pdf, 5 September 2007.

Holliday, Ian (2001) 'Steering the British State in the Information Age'. *Government and Opposition*, 36(3), pp.314–330.

Holopainen, Kauko, Tor, Högnäs, Heikki, Jokela (eds) (1973) *Tapaus Zavidovo*. Kirjayhtymä, Helsinki.

Hood, Christopher (1986) 'Concepts of Control over Public Bureaucracies: "Comptrol" and "Interpolable Balance" '. In Kaufmann, Franz-Xaver, Majone Giandomenico and Ostrom Vincent (eds) *Guidance, Control, and Evaluation in the Public Sector*. Walter de Gruyter, Berlin.

Hood, Christopher (1998) *The Art of the State: Culture, Rhetoric, and Public Management*. Oxford University Press, Oxford.

Hood, Christopher (2006) 'Transparency in Historical Perspective'. In Hood, Christopher and Heald, David (eds) *Transparency: The Key to Better Governance?* Oxford University Press, Oxford. pp.3–23.

Hood, Christopher (2010) 'Accountability and Transparency: Siamese Twins, Matching Parts, Awkward Couple?' *West European Politics*, 33(5), pp. 989–1009.

Hood, Christopher, Peters, Guy B., Wollmann, Hellmut (1996) 'Sixteen Ways to Consumerize Public Services: Pick'n Mix or Painful Trade-Offs?' *Public Money & Management*, October-December, pp.43–50.

Hood, Christopher and Schuppert, Gunnar Folke (1988) 'Evaluation and Review'. In Hood, Christopher and Schuppert, Gunnar Folke (eds) *Delivering*

Public Services in Western Europe: Sharing Western European Experience of Para-Government Organization. Sage Publications, London.

Hood, Christopher and Peters, Guy B. (2004) 'The Middle Aging of New Public Management: Into the Age of Paradox?' *Journal of Public Administration Research and Theory*, 14(3), pp.267–282.

Hood, Christopher and Heald, David, (eds) (2006) *Transparency: The Key to Better Governance?* Oxford University Press, Oxford.

Hood, Christopher and Margetts, Helen (2007) *The Tools of Government in the Digital Age*. Palgrave Macmillan, Basingstoke.

Hopwood, Anthony and Miller, Peter (1994) *Accounting as Social and Institutional Practice*. Cambridge University Press.

Hosein, Ian (2004) 'The Sources of Laws: Policy Dynamics in a Digital and Terrorized World'. *The Information Society*, 20, pp.187–199.

Hummel, Ralph P. (2006) 'The Triumph of Numbers: Knowledges and the Mismeasure of Management'. *Administration & Society*, 38(1), pp.58–78.

Husserl, Edmund (1970) *The Crisis of European Sciences and Transcendental Phenomenology: An Introduction to Phenomenological Philosophy*. Northwestern University Press, Evanston.

Hynninen, Asko, ja työryhmä (2001) *Demokratian kivijalka vai susi jo syntyessään? Suomalainen julkisuusperiaate ja julkisuuslaki käytännön syynissä*, available at http://www.kaapeli.fi/tutki/Julkisuusperiaate.pdf.

Hynninen, Asko (2000) *Periaatteessa julkista: julkisuusperiaatteen käytäntö EU-Suomen päätöksenteossa ja journalismissa*. Jyväskylä studies in communication / 10. Jyväskylän yliopisto, Jyväskylä.

Hyvärinen, Matti (2003) 'Valta'. In Hyvärinen, Matti, Kurunmäki, Jussi, Palonen, Kari, Pulkkinen, Tuija and Stenius, Henrik (eds) *Käsitteet liikkeessä. Suomen poliittisen kulttuurin käsitehistoria*. Vastapaino, Tampere.

Häner, Isabelle (1990) 'Öffentlichkeit und Verwaltung'. Schulthess Polygraphisher Verlag, Zürich.

Høgetveit, Einar (1981) *Hvor hemmelig? Offentlighetsprinsippet i Norge og USA, særlig med henblikk på militærpolitiske spørsmål*. Pax Forlag, Oslo.

Hölscher, Lucian (1978) 'Öffentlichkeit'. In O. Brunner, W. Conze and R. Koselleck (eds) *Geschichtliche Grundbegriffe* Vol. 4, pp. 413–67. Klett-Cotta, Stuttgart.

Infodata (2010) 'Infodata', available at http://www.infodata.se/, date accessed 12 April 2010.

Inha, Jyri (2003) *Elämä ja oikeus. K.J. Ståhlberg oikeusajattelijana*. Suomalainen lakimiesyhdistys, Helsinki.

Inha, Jyri (2005) *Haminasta Maastrichtiin – Modernin suomalaisen valtio-sääntöhistorian pääpiirteet*. Oikeustieteellinen tiedekunta, Helsinki.

Invest in France (2010) 'Invest in France', available at http://www.invest-in-france.org/, date accessed 12 April 2010.

Invest in Georgia (2010) 'Invest in Georgia', available at http://www.investin-georgia.org/, date accessed 12 April 2010.

Isaksson, Paavo (1997) *Korruptio ja julkinen valta*. Tampereen yliopisto. Yhteiskuntatieteiden tutkimuslaitos. Julkaisuja 15/1997, Tampere.

Ivanov, Kalin (2009) 'Fighting Corruption Globally and Locally'. In Cox, Raymond (ed.) *Ethics and Integrity in Public Administration: Concepts and Cases*. M.E.Sharpe, Armonk. pp.146–154.

Iversen, Torben (2001) 'The Dynamics of Welfare State Expansion: Trade Openness, De-industrialisation and Partisan Politics'. In Pierson, Paul (2001) *The New Politics of the Welfare State*. Oxford University Press, Oxford. pp. 45–79.

James, Simon (2006) 'The Potential Benefits of Freedom of Information'. In Chapman, Richard and Hunt, Michael (eds) *Open Government in Theoretical and Practical Context*. Ashgate, Aldershot.

Jansson, Jan-Magnus (1993) *Hajaannuksesta yhteistoimintaan. Suomalaisen parlamentarismin vaiheita*. Gaudeamus, Tampere.

Jenkins, Glenn B. and Kuo, Chan-Yan (2007) 'Information, Corruption, and Measures for the Promotion of Manufactured Exports'. In Breton, Albert, Galeotti, Gianluigi, Salmon, Pierre and Wintrobe, Ronald (eds) *The Economics of Transparency in Politics*. Ashgate, Aldershot. pp.151–172.

Jessop, Bop (1998) 'The Rise of Governance and the Risks of Failure: The Case of Economic Development'. *International Social Science Journal*, 155, pp.29–45.

Judge, David (2003) 'Legislative Institutionalisation: A Bent Analytical Arrow?' *Government and Opposition*, 38(4), pp.497–516.

JUHTA (1996a) 'Perusrekistereiden tietopalvelun kehittäminen, 8/1996'. Sisäasiainministeriö, Helsinki.

JUHTA (1996b) 'Kansallinen paikkatiedon infrastruktuuri, 2/1996'. Sisäasiainministeriö, Helsinki.

JUHTA (1996c) 'Paikkatietoydin – kansallisesti merkittävät tietovarannot, 9/1996'. Sisäasiainministeriö, Helsinki.

JUHTA (1997) 'Tietoyhteiskunnan perusrekisterit 3/1997'. Sisäasiainministeriö, Helsinki.

Jyränki, Antero (2006) 'Kansanedustuslaitos ja valtiosääntö 1906–2005'. In Mylly, Juhani, Pernaa, Ville, Niemi, Mari K. and Heino, Laura (eds) *Suomen eduskunta 100 vuotta. Osa 2: Eduskunnan muuttuva asema*. Edita, Helsinki.

Kahler, Miles (2004) 'Defining Accountability Up: The Global Economic Multilaterals'. *Government and Opposition*, 39(2), pp.132–158.

Käkönen, Jyrki. 1983. "Anders Chydenius ja 1700-luvun suomalainen valtio-opillinen ajattelu." In *Valtio ja yhteiskunta. Tutkielmia suomalaisen valtiollisen ajattelun ja valtio-opin historiasta.*, eds. Jaakko Nousiainen and Dag Anckar. Juva: Werner Söderström.

Kananen, Johannes and Kantola, Anu (2009) 'Kilpailukyky ja tuottavuus – Kuinka uudet käsitteet saavuttivat hallitsevan aseman hyvinvointivaltion muutoksessa'. In Kananen, Johannes and Saari, Juho (eds) *Ajatuksen voima – Ideat hyvinvointivaltion uudistamisessa*. Sophi/Minerva, Jyväskylä.

Kantola, Anu (2002) *Markkinakuri ja managerivalta: poliittinen hallinta Suomen 1990-luvun talouskriisissä*. Loki-kirjat, Helsinki.

Kantola, Anu (2006) 'Suomea trimmaamassa: suomalaisen kilpailuvaltion sanastot'. In Heiskala, Risto and Luhtakallio, Eeva (eds) *Uusi jako. Miten Suomesta tuli kilpailukyky-yhteiskunta?* Gaudeamus, Helsinki.

Karimaa, Erkki (ed.) (2001) *Perusrekisterit: yhteiskunnan perustietojärjestelmien käsitteet, tietojen hankinta ja tietopalvelut*. Kuntaliitto, Helsinki.

Kauppi, Niilo (1997) 'Kohti post-absoluuttista valtiota?: EU-tutkimus haasteena politiikan tutkimukselle'. *Politiikka*, 39(1), pp.60–63.

Kelly, Terrence (2004) 'Unlocking the Iron Cage: Public Administration in the Deliberative Theory of Jürgen Habermas'. *Administration & Society*, 36(1), pp. 38–61.

Kemppainen, Olli (2005) 'Kouluarvioinnit tulivat julkisiksi. Journalismin tehtävänä on kertoa yleisölle olennaisista asioista'. *Hallinnon tutkimus*, Arvioinnin teemanumero, pp.131–132.

Kertzer, David I. and Arel, Dominique (2002) *Census and Identity: The Politics of Race, Ethnicity, and Language in National Censuses*. Cambridge University Press, Cambridge.

Kettunen, Pauli (1997) 'The Society of Virtuous Circles'. In Kettunen, Pauli and Eskola, Hanna (eds) *Models, Modernity and the Myrdals*. Renvall Institute Publications 8, University of Helsinki.

Kettunen, Pauli (1999) 'The Nordic Model and the Making of the Competitive "Us" '. In Edwards, Paul and Elger, Tony (eds) *The Global Economy, National States and the Regulation of Labour*. Mansell Publishing, London.

Kettunen, Pauli (2003a) 'Yhteiskunta'. In Hyvärinen, Matti, Kurunmäki, Jussi, Palonen, Kari, Pulkkinen, Tuija and Stenius, Henrik (eds) *Käsitteet liikkeessä. Suomen poliittisen kulttuurin käsitehistoria*. Vastapaino, Tampere.

Kettunen, Pauli (2003b) 'Yhteiskunta ohjattavana ja ohjaajana – historiallinen näkökulma. Monikäyttöinen Chydenius'. Alustus Anders Chydenius – seminaarissa 13.10.2003, available at http://www.chydenius.net, 13 October 2003.

Kettunen, Pauli (2008) *Globalisaatio ja kansallinen me. Kansallisen katseen historiallinen kritiikki*. Vastapaino, Tampere.

Kettunen, Pekka and Kiviniemi, Markku (2006) 'Policy-Making in Finland: Consensus and Change'. In Colebatch, Hal (ed.) *The Work of Policy – an International Survey*. Lexington Books, New York. pp.147–160.

Kingdom, John (2000) 'Britain'. In Chandler, J.A. (ed.) *Comparative Public Administration*. Routledge, London.

Klagge, Jay (1997) 'Approaches to the Iron Cage: Reconstructing the Bars of Weber's Metaphor'. *Administration & Society*, 29(1), pp. 63–77.

Knorr Cetina, Karin (1999) *Epistemic Cultures: How the Sciences make Knowledge*. Harvard University Press, Cambridge (MA)

Knudsen, Tim (2003) *Offentlighed i det offentlige. Om historiens magt*. Aarhus Universitetsforlag.

Kokkonen, Arvo (2007) 'Sähköinen asiointi valtionhallinnossa. Maanmittaustieteiden Seura ry:n julkaisu n:o 44', available at http://mts.fgi.fi/paivat/2007/Arvo_Kokkonen.pdf.

Kolstad, Ivar and Wiig, Arne (2009) 'Is Transparency the Key to Reducing Corruption in Resource-Rich Countries?' *World Development*, 37(3), pp. 521–532.

Kono, Daniel Y. (2006) 'Optimal Obfuscation: Democracy and Trade Policy Transparency'. *American Political Science Review*, 100(3), pp.369–384.

Konstari, Timo (1977) *Asiakirjajulkisuudesta hallinnossa. Tutkimus yleisten asiakirjain julkisuudesta hallinnon kontrollivälineenä*. Suomalainen lakimiesyhdistys, Helsinki.

Konstari, Timo (1999) 'Perusoikeudet, lainkäyttö ja julkisuus'. *Lakimies*, 6–7, pp.943–951.

Konstari, Timo, Salovaara, Christa, Tala, Jyrki, Vettenranta, Leena, Wallin, Anna-Riitta (2003) *Julkisuuslakia koskevan oikeuskäytännön esittelyä ja erittelyä*. Oikeuspoliittisen tutkimuslaitoksen julkaisuja 205. Helsinki.

Korhonen, Rauno (1997) 'Väestötietojärjestelmä ja oikeus'. In Haavisto, Risto (ed.) *Oikeuskirja 2, Lapin yliopiston oikeustieteellisiä julkaisuja B 27*. Lapin yliopiston oikeustieteiden tiedekunta, Kitee.

Korhonen, Rauno (2003) 'Perusrekisterit ja tietosuoja'. Edita, Helsinki.

Korkein hallinto-oikeus (2007) *Vuosikertomus 2006*. Korkein hallinto-oikeus, Helsinki.

Kort & Matrikelstyrelsen (2006) *Ejendomsregistrering i de nordiske lande*. Kort & Matrikelstyrelsen, København.

Koselleck, Reinhart (2004) *Futures Past: On the Semantics of Historical Time*. Columbia University Press, New York. [Original 1979: Vergangene Zukunft: zur Semantik geschichtlicher Zeiten]

Koski, Heli, Rouvinen, Petri and Ylä-Anttila, Pekka (2002) *Tieto & talous. Mitä "uudesta taloudesta" jäi?* Edita, Helsinki.

Koskiaho, Briitta (1973) 'Hallitusohjelma ei ole puu. Analyysi hallitusohjelmien yhteiskuntapoliittisista arvoista, tavoitteista ja keinoista'. In Hakovirta, Harto and Koskiaho, Tapio (eds) *Suomen hallitukset ja hallitusohjelmat 1945–1973*. Gaudeamus, Helsinki.

Krasner, Stephen (1984) 'Approaches to the State: Alternative Conceptions and Historical Dynamics'. *Comparative Politics*, 16(2), pp.223–246.

Krasner, Stephen (1988) 'Sovereignty: An institutional Perspective'. *Comparative Political Studies*, 21(1), pp.66–94.

Kuronen, Timo (1998) Tietovarantojen hyödyntäminen ja demokratia (SITRA 174) Suomen itsenäisyyden juhlarahasto, Helsinki.

Kytömäki, Päivi (1999) Yliopistojen tietoaineistot ja niiden saatavuus ja hyödynnettävyys EU:n ja Suomen tietoyhteiskuntapolitiikan valossa. Oulun yliopisto, available at http://herkules.oulu.fi/isbn9514255178/.

Käkönen, Jyrki (1983) 'Anders Chydenius ja 1700-luvun suomalainen valtio-opillinen ajattelu'. In Nousiainen, Jaakko and Anckar, Dag (eds) *Valtio ja yhteiskunta. Tutkielmia suomalaisen valtiollisen ajattelun ja valtio-opin historiasta*. Werner Söderström Oy, Juva.

Lamble, Stephen (2002) 'Freedom of Information, a Finnish Clergyman's Gift to Democracy'. *Freedom of Information Review*, 97, February 2002, pp.2–8.

Lambsdorff, Johann (2007) 'Invisible Feet and Grabbing Hands: The Political Economy of Corruption and Welfare'. In Breton, Albert, Galeotti, Gianluigi, Salmon, Pierre and Wintrobe, Ronald (eds) *The Economics of Transparency in Politics*. Ashgate, Aldershot. pp.123–150.

Lane, Jan-Erik (1993) 'The Public Sector: Concepts, Models and Approaches'. Sage Publications, London.

Lane, Jan-Erik (1997) 'Introduction – Public Sector Reform: Only Deregulation, Privatization and Marketization?' In Lane, Jan-Erik (ed.) *Public Sector Reform: Rationale, Trends and Problems*. Sage Publications, London.

Lane, Jan-Erik (2000) *New Public Management*. Routledge, London.

Larner, Wendy and Walters, William (2004) 'Globalization as Governmentality'. *Alternatives*, 29(5), pp.495–514.

Larsson, Thornbjörn (1998) 'How Open Can a Government Be? The Swedish Experience'. In Deckmyn, Veerle and Thomason, Ian (eds) *Openness and Transparency in the European Union*. European Institute of Public Administration, Maastricht.

Lash, Scott (2000) 'Risk Culture'. In Beck, Ulrich (ed.) *The Risk Society and Beyond: Critical Issues for Social Theory*. Sage Publications, London.

Lash, Scott (2002) *Critique of Information*. Sage Publications, London.

Lee, Chang Kil and Strang, David (2006) 'The International Diffusion of Public-Sector Downsizing: Network Emulation and Theory-Driven Learning'. *International Organization*, 60(4), pp.883–909.

Libich, Jan (2006) 'Should Monetary Policy be Transparent?' *Policy*, 22(1), pp.28–33.

Lodge, Juliet (2003) 'Transparency and EU Governance: Balancing Openness with Security'. *Journal of Contemporary European Studies*, 11(1), pp.95–117.

Lopez-Claros, Augusto, (ed.) (2006) *The Global Competitiveness Report 2006–2007*. A Report by the World Economic Forum. Palgrave, Houndmills.

Lord, Kristin (2006) *The Perils and Promise of Global Transparency: Why the Information revolution may not lead to security, democracy or peace*. State University of New York Press, Albany.

Luther, Georg (1993) 'Suomen tilastotoimen historia vuoteen 1970'. WSOY, Porvoo.

Lynden, Irina and Wu, Jane (eds) (2008) *Best Practices in Government Information: A Global Perspective*. K.G.Saur, München.

Lähteenkorva, Pekka and Pekkarinen, Jussi (2005) 'Asiakirjojen avoimuudessa Suomi on Euroopan kärkimaita'. Newspaper article in Helsingin Sanomat, 4.11.2005.

Maa- ja metsätalousministeriö (2008) 'INSPIRE-työryhmän loppuraportti. Työryhmämuistio 2008:2'. Maa- ja metsätalousministeriö, Helsinki.

Maesschalck, Jeroen (2004) 'The Impact of New Public Management Reforms on Public Servants' Ethics: Towards a Theory'. *Public Administration*, 82(2), pp.465–489.

Magnette, Paul (2003) 'Between Parliamentary Control and the Rule of Law: The Political Role of the Ombudsman in the European Union'. *Journal of European Public Policy*, 10(5), pp.677–694.

Mahon, Rianne and McBride, Stephen (2009) 'Standardizing and Disseminating Knowledge: The Role of the OECD in Global Governance'. *European Political Science Review*, 1(1), pp.83–101.

Mahoney, James (2000) 'Path Dependence in Historical Sociology'. *Theory and Society*, 29, pp.507–548.

Mahoney, James (2003) 'Strategies of Causal Assessment in Comparative Historical Analysis'. In Mahoney, James and Rueschemeyer, Dietrich (eds) *Comparative Historical Analysis in the Social Sciences*. Cambridge University Press, Cambridge. pp.337–372.

Majone, Giandomenico (1997) 'From the Positive to the Regulatory State: Causes and Consequences of Changes in the Mode of Governance'. *Journal of Public Policy*, 17, pp.139–167.

Manninen, Juha (1996) *Feuer am Pol. Zum Aufbau der Vernunft im europäischen Norden*. Peter Lang, Frankfurt am Main.

Manninen, Juha (2000) *Valistus ja kansallinen identiteetti. Aatehistoriallinen tutkimus 1700-luvun Pohjolasta*. Suomalaisen Kirjallisuuden Seura, Helsinki.

Manninen, Juha (2006) 'Anders Chydenius and the Origins of World's First Freedom of Information Act'. In Anders Chydenius Foundation (ed.) *The World's First Freedom of Information Act: Anders Chydenius' Legacy Today*. Anders Chydenius Foundation, Kokkola.

Mansala, Arto and Suomi, Juhani (2003) *Suomalainen diplomaatti*. Muotokuvia muistista ja arkistojen kätköistä. Suomalaisen Kirjallisuuden Seura, Helsinki.

Maravic, Patrick von (2007) *Verwaltungsmodernisierung und dezentrale Korruption: Lernen aus unbeabsichtigten Konsequenzen*. Haupt, Berne.

March, James and Olsen Johan (1989) *Rediscovering Institutions: The Organizational Basis for Politics*. The Free Press, New York.

Marcussen, Martin and Ronit, Karsten (2003) *Internationaliseringen af den offentlige forvaltning i Danmark. Forandring og kontinuitet*. Aarhus Universitetsforlag, 2003.

Marcussen, Martin (2000) *Ideas and Elites: The Social Construction of Economic and Monetary Union*. Aalborg University Press, Aalborg.

Marcussen, Martin (2002) *OECD og idéspillet – game over?* Hans Reitzels Forlag, Kobenhavn.

Marcussen, Martin (2007) 'Central Bank Reform across the World: Only by Night are all Cats Grey'. In Christensen, Tom and Laegreid, Per (eds) *Transcending New Public Management: The Transformation of Public Sector Reforms*. Ashgate, Aldershot.

Martens, Wolfgang (1971) *Die Botschaft der Tugend: Die Aufklärung im Spiegel der deutschen Moralischen Wochenschriften*. Metzler, Stuttgart.

Marx Ferree, Myra, Gamson, William, Gerhards, Jürgen and Rucht, Dieter (2002) 'Four Models of the Public Sphere in Modern Democracies'. *Theory and Society*, 31, pp.289–324.

Meklin, Pentti and Näsi, Salme (1994) 'Budjettiohjauksen uudistus ja laskentatoimen muuttuva rooli julkisessa hallinnossa'. *Hallinnon tutkimus*, 4/1994, pp.231–243.

Meyer, John, Boli, John, Thomas, George, Ramirez, Francisco (1997) 'World Society and the Nation State'. *American Journal of Sociology*, 103(1), pp.144–81.

Miller, Peter and Rose, Nikolas (1990) 'Political Rationalities and Technologies of Government'. In Hänninen, Sakari and Palonen, Kari (eds) *Texts, Contexts, Concepts. Studies on Politics and Power in Language*. The Finnish Political Science Association, Helsinki.

Ministry of Agriculture and Forestry (2004) 'National Geographic Information Strategy'. Publication 10a/2004. Ministry of Agriculture and Forestry of Finland, Helsinki.

Ministry of Finance (2006) 'Handbook on Performance Management'. Series: Governance and Accountability 2/2006. Ministry of Finance, Helsinki.

Mittelman, James (2004) 'Whither Globalization? The Vortex of Knowledge and Ideology'. Routledge, London.

Moilanen, Timo (1999) *Hallinto muuttuu, muuttuuko virkamiesetiikka? Valtionhallinnon virkamiesetiikka julkisen keskustelun, hallinnon kehittämisen ja kansainvälisen vertailun näkökulmasta*. Valtiovarainministeriö, hallinnon kehittämisosasto, Helsinki.

Moisio, Sami (2006) 'Kansallisesta Suomesta kilpailukyky-yhteiskuntaan: maantieteen ja tieteellisen tutkimuksen muuttuva toimintaympäristö'. *Terra*, 118(3–4), pp.218–228.

Moisio, Sami (2008) 'Towards Attractive and Cost-Efficient State Space: Political Geography of the Production of State Transformation in Finland'. *World Political Science Review*, 4(3), Art. 2.

Mouffe, Chantal (1999) 'Deliberative Democracy or Agonistic Pluralism'. *Social Research*, 66(3), pp.745–758.

Mulgan, Richard (2000) '"Accountability": An Ever-expanding Concept?' *Public Administration*, 78(3), pp.555–573.

Mulgan, Richard (2003) 'One Cheer for Hierarchy – Accountability in Disjointed Governance'. *Political Science*, 55(2), pp.6–18.

Muttilainen, Vesa (2006) *Suomalaiset ja henkilötietojen suoja. Kyselytutkimusten ja viranomaistilastojen tietoja 1990-luvulta ja 2000-luvun alusta.* Oikeuspoliittisen tutkimuslaitoksen julkaisuja 218. Oikeuspoliittinen tutkimuslaitos, Helsinki.

Myllymäki, Arvo and Vakkuri, Jarmo, (eds) (2001) *Tulos, normi, tilivelvollisuus. Näkökulmia tilintarkastukseen ja arviointiin.* Tampere University Press, Tampere.

Mäenpää, Olli (2008a) *Julkisuusperiaate.* WSOY, Helsinki.

Mäenpää, Olli (2008b) *Oikeus hyvään hallintoon.* Helsingin yliopiston oikeustieteellinen tiedekunta, Helsinki.

Mörä, Tuomo and Tarkiainen, Johanna (2003) 'Toimittajien kokemukset uudesta julkisuuslaista'. Lausuntoja ja selvityksiä, 2003:36. Oikeusministeriö, Helsinki.

Nanz, Patrizia and Steffek, Jens (2004) 'Global Governance, Participation and the Public Sphere'. *Government and Opposition,* 39(2), pp.314–335.

Nationalencyklopedins ordbok (2004) Språkdata, Göteborg.

Neustadt, Richard and May, Ernest (eds) (1986) *Thinking in Time: The Uses of History for Decision Makers.* The Free Press, New York.

Nevalainen, Risto (1999) *Suomi tietoyhteiskunnaksi – eespäin tiedon poluilla ja valtateillä. Tietoyhteiskuntatoiminnan lyhyt historia.* Sitra, Helsinki.

Newman, Abraham L. and Bach, David (2004) 'Self-Regulatory Trajectories in the Shadow of Public Power: Resolving Digital Dilemmas in Europe and the United States'. *Governance: An International Journal of Policy, Administration, and Institutions,* 17(3), pp.387–413.

Nieminen, Hannu (2006) *Kansa seisoi loitompana: kansallisen julkisuuden rakentuminen Suomessa 1809–1917.* Vastapaino, Tampere.

Nonaka, Ikujiro and Takeuchi, Hirotaka (1995) *The Knowledge-Creating Company: How Japanese Companies Create the Dynamics of Innovation.* Oxford University Press, New York.

North, Douglas C. (1998) 'Economic Performance through Time'. In Brinton, Mary and Nee, Victor (eds) *The New Institutionalism in Sociology.* Stanford University Press, Stanford. pp.247–257.

North, Douglas C. (2005) *Understanding the Process of Economic Change.* Princeton University Press, Princeton.

Nousiainen, Jaakko (2006) 'Suomalainen parlamentarismi'. In Mylly, Juhani, Pernaa, Ville, Niemi, Mari K. and Heino, Laura (eds) *Suomen eduskunta 100 vuotta. Osa 2: Eduskunnan muuttuva asema.* Edita, Helsinki.

Nykysuomen etymologinen sanakirja (2004) WS Bookwell Oy, Juva.

Nykysuomen sanakirja (1978) Werner Söderström Oy, Porvoo.

OECD (1996) Public Management Occasional Papers. 'Ethics in the Public Service: Current issues and Practices'. OECD, Paris.

OECD (1997) 'In Seach of Results: Performance Management Practices'. OECD, Paris.

OECD (1999) 'How to Strengthen Government-Citizen Connections'. Meeting of Senior Officials from Centres of Government on How to Strengthen Government-Citizen Connections. Naples, 11–12 October 1999. PUMA/MPM(99)2.

OECD (2000) 'Trust in Government: Ethics Measures in OECD Countries'. OECD, Paris.

OECD (2001a) 'Citizens as Partners: Information, Consultation and Public Participation in Policy-making'. OECD, Paris.

OECD (2001b) 'Citizens as Partners' OECD Handbook on 'Information, Consultation and Public Participation in Policy-Making'. OECD, Paris.

OECD (2002a) 'Public Sector Transparency and Accountability: Making It Happen'. OECD, Paris.

OECD (2002b) 'Budgeting in Finland'. PUMA/SBO(2002)8/FINAL. OECD, Paris.

OECD (2003a) 'Open Government: Fostering Dialogue with Civil Society'. OECD, Paris.

OECD (2003b) 'International Investment Perspectives 2003'. OECD, Paris.

OECD (2005a) 'Evaluating Public Participation in Policy-Making'. OECD, Paris.

OECD (2005b) 'Public Sector Modernisation: Open Government'. Policy Brief. OECD, Paris.

Oikeusministeriö (2006) Suomen demokratiaindikaattorit. Oikeusministeriön julkaisu 1/2006. Oikeusministeriö, Helsinki.

Olsen, Johan P. (2009) 'Change and Continuity: An Institutional Approach to Institutions of Democratic Government'. *European Political Science Review*, 1(1), pp.3–32.

Opetusministeriö (2007) Onko kulttuurilla vientiä? ON! Esitys Suomen kulttuuriviennin kehiittämisohjelmaksi 2007–2011. Opetusministeriön julkaisuja 2007:9. Opetusministeriö, Helsinki.

OSCE (2010) 'Remove small arms from conflict areas', available at http://www.removearms.com/, date accessed 12 April 2010.

Otakantaa (2010) 'Valtionhallinnon keskustelufoorumi', available at http://www.otakantaa.fi/, date accessed 12 April 2010.

Ottaviano, Gianmarco I.P. and Pinelli Dino (2004) 'The challenge of globalization for Finland and its regions: The new economic geography perspective'. Valtioneuvoston kanslian julkaisusarja 24/2004. Valtioneuvoston kanslia, Helsinki.

Oulasvirta, Leena (1993) *Julkisen toiminnan eettisiä kysymyksiä*. Valtionhallinnon kehittämiskeskus, Helsinki.

Owen, Barry (2000) 'France'. In Chandler, J.A. (ed.) *Comparative Public Administration*. Routledge, London.

Oxford English Dictionary (2010) 'Oxford English Dictionary', available at http://dictionary.oed.com/, date accessed 12 April 2010.

Paastela, Jukka (1995) *Valhe ja politiikka: tutkimus hyveestä ja paheesta yhteiskunnallisessa kanssakäymisessä*. Gaudeamus, Helsinki.

Pagano, Ugo (2004) 'Economics of Institutions and the Institutions of Economics'. In Lewis, Paul (2004) (ed.) *Transforming Economics: Perspectives on the Critical Realist Project*. Routledge, London.

Painter, Martin and Peters, Guy B. (eds) (2010) *Tradition and Public Administration*. Palgrave Macmillan, Basingstoke.

Pakarinen, Mirja, Tammisalpa, Eija, Tenhunen, Susanna (2002) 'Hyvä tiedonhallintatapa viranomaistoiminnassa'. Dipoli raportit 2002:6. Teknillinen korkeakoulu, Espoo.

Pakkasvirta, Jussi (2008) *Pulp & Fiction: Tarinoita globalisaatiosta ja sellutehtaasta*. Gaudeamus Helsinki University Press, Helsinki.

Palonen, Kari (2003) 'Four Times of Politics: Policy, Polity, Politicking, and Politicization'. *Alternatives*, 28(2), pp.171–186.

Papadopoulos, Yannis (2003) 'Cooperative Forms of Governance: Problems of Democratic Accountability in Complex Environments'. *European Journal of Political Research*, 42, pp.473–501.

Patoluoto, Ilkka (1986) 'Hyödyllinen luomakunta. Hyötyajattelun maailmankuvalliset perusteet 1700-luvun Ruotsin valtakunnassa'. In Manninen, Juha and Patoluoto, Ilkka (eds) *Hyöty, sivistys, kansakunta. Suomalaista aatehistoriaa.* Kustannusosakeyhtiö Pohjoinen, Oulu.

Patomäki, Heikki (2004) 'Salaisen diplomatian aika on ohi'. *Ulkopolitiikka*, 40(1), pp.76–80.

Pekonen, Kyösti (1995a) 'Käskyjä kansalle, mannaa markkinoille'. Newspaper article published in Helsingin Sanomat 14.4.1995.

Pekonen, Kyösti (1995b) *Kohti uutta hallintoajattelua julkisessa hallinnossa?* Hallinnon kehittämiskeskus, Helsinki.

Pekonen, Kyösti (2003) 'Hallitseminen'. In Hyvärinen, Matti, Kurunmäki, Jussi, Palonen, Kari, Pulkkinen, Tuija and Stenius, Henrik (eds) *Käsitteet liikkeessä. Suomen poliittisen kulttuurin käsitehistoria.* Vastapaino, Tampere.

Pelkonen, Antti (2008) 'The Finnish Competition State and Entrepreneurial Policies in the Helsinki Region'. Research Report 254. Department of Sociology, University of Helsinki.

Peters, Guy B. (1989) *The Politics of Bureaucracy* (3rd Edition). Longman, New York.

Peters, Guy B. (1999) *Institutional Theory in Political Science: The 'New Institutionalism'.* Pinter, London.

Peters, Guy B. (2008) 'Performance Management in the Nordic Countries: One Pattern or Many?' A Report to the Swedish Ministry of Finance.

Peters, Guy B., Pierre, Jon and King, Desmond S. (2005) 'The Politics of Path Dependency: Political Conflict in Historical Institutionalism'. *The Journal of Politics*, Vol. 67, No. 4, pp.1275–1300.

Pierre, Jon (ed.) (2000) *Debating Governance: Authority, Steering, and Democracy.* Oxford University Press, New York.

Pierre, Jon and Peters, Guy B. (2000) *Governance, Politics and the State.* St. Martin's Press, New York.

Pierson, Paul (2000a) 'Increasing Returns, Path Dependence, and the Study of Politics'. *The American Political Science Review*, 94(2), pp.251–267.

Pierson, Paul (2000b) 'The Limits of Design: Explaining Institutional Origins and Change'. *Governance: An International Journal of Policy and Administration*, 13(4), pp.475–499.

Pietrowski, Suzanne, Zhang, Yahong, Lin, Weiwei and Yu, Wenxuan (2009) 'Key Issues for Implementation of Chinese Open Government Information Regulations'. *Public Administration Review*, 69(s1), pp.s129-s135.

Pollitt, Christopher, Hanney, Stephen, Packwood, Tim, Rothwell, Sandra and Roberts, Simon (1997) *Trajectories and Options: An International Perspective on the Implementation of Finnish Public Management Reforms.* Ministry of Finance, Helsinki.

Pollitt, Christopher and Bouckaert, Geert (2004) *Public Management Reform: A Comparative Analysis* (2nd Edition). Oxford University Press, Oxford.

Pollitt, Christopher, Talbot, Colin, Caulfield, Janice, Smullen, Amanda (eds) (2004) *Agencies: How Governments Do Things through Semi-Autonomous Organizations.* Palgrave Macmillan, Basingstoke.

Porter, Michael E. (1990) *The Competitive Advantage of Nations*. Macmillan Press, London.

Porter, Theodore M. (1996) *Trust in Numbers: The Pursuit of Objectivity in Science and Public Life*. Princeton University Press, Princeton.

Power, Michael (1999) *The Audit Society: Rituals of Verification*. Oxford University Press, Oxford.

Prime Minister's Office (2003) 'Recommendation on Central Government Communication'. Prime Minister's Office Publications 2003/4, Helsinki.

Prime Minister's Office (2007) 'Programme Management within the Finnish Government'. Prime Minister's Office Publications 12/2007.

Przeworski, A. (2004) 'Institutions matter?' *Government and Opposition*, 39(4), pp.527–540.

Pöysti, Tuomas (1999) *Tehokkuus, informaatio ja eurooppalainen oikeusalue*. Helsingin yliopisto, oikeustieteellinen tiedekunta, Helsinki.

Radaelli, Claudio (2000) 'Policy Transfer in the European Union: Institutional Isomorphism as a Source of Legitimacy'. *Governance: An International Journal of Policy and Administration*, 13(1), pp.25–43.

Rainio-Niemi, Johanna (2008) 'Small State Cultures of Consensus: State Traditions and Consensus-Seeking in the Neo-Corporatist and Neutral Policies in Post-1945 Austria and Finland'. Doctoral Dissertation. University of Helsinki: Department of Social Science History, Political History.

Rajavaara, Marketta (2007) *Vaikuttavuusyhteiskunta. Sosiaalisten olojen arvostelusta vaikutusten todentamiseen*. Sosiaali- ja terveysturvan tutkimuksia 84. Kelan tutkimusosasto, Helsinki.

Raunio, Tapio and Tiilikainen, Teija (2003) *Finland in the European Union*. Frank Cass Publishers, London.

Raunio, Tapio and Wiberg, Matti (ed.) (2000) *EU ja Suomi. Unionijäsenyyden vaikutukset suomalaiseen yhteiskuntaan*. Edita, Helsinki.

Relly, Jeannine and Sabharwal, Meghna (2009) 'Perceptions of Transparency of Government Policymaking: A Cross-National Study'. In *Government Information Quarterly*, 26, pp.148–157.

Roberts, Alasdair (2006) *Blacked Out: Government Secrecy in the Information Age*. Cambridge press, New York.

Robertson, K.G. (1982) *Public Secrets: A Study in the Development of Government Secrecy*. St. Martin's Press, New York.

Rodan, Garry (2004) *Transparency and Authoritarian Rule in Southeast Asia: Singapore and Malaysia*. RoutledgeCruzon, New York.

Rodrik, Dani (1998) 'Why Do More Open Economies Have Bigger Governments?' *The Journal of Political Economy*, 106(5), pp.997–1032.

Romzek, Barbara and Dubnick, Melvin (1987) 'Accountability in the Public Sector: Lessons from the Challenger Tragedy'. *Public Administration Review*, 47, pp.227–238.

Romzek, Barbara (2000) 'Dynamics of Public Sector Accountability in an Era of Reform'. *International Review of Administrative Sciences*, 66, pp.21–44.

Rose, Nikolas (1999) *Powers of Freedom: Reframing Political Thought*. Cambridge University Press.

Rose, Nikolas (2000) 'Governing Liberty'. In Ericson, Richard and Stehr, Nico (eds) *Governing Modern Societies*. University of Toronto Press, Toronto. pp.141–176.

Rose-Ackerman, Susan (2005) 'From Elections to Democracy: Building Accountable Government in Hungary and Poland'. Cambridge University Press, New York.

Rothschild, Michael and Stiglitz, Joseph (1976) 'Equilibrium in Competitive Insurance Markets: An Essay on the Economics of Imperfect Information'. *The Quarterly Journal of Economics*, 90(4), pp.629–649.

Rothstein, Bo (2000) 'Trust, Social Dilemmas and Collective Memories'. *Journal of Theoretical Politics*, 12(4), pp.477–501.

Rothstein, Bo (2005) *Social Traps and the Problem of Trust*. Cambridge University Press, Cambridge.

Rothstein, Bo and Steinmo, Sven (2002) 'Restructuring Politics: Institutional Analysis and the Challenges of Modern Welfare States'. In Rothstein, Bo and Steinmo, Sven (eds) *Restructuring the Welfare State: Political Institutions and Policy Change*. Palgrave Macmillan, New York.

Rouvinen, Petri (2002) 'Kilpailukykyä etsimässä'. *Kansantaloudellinen aikakauskirja*, 98(1), pp.90–93.

Rowat, Donald C. (1973) *The Ombudsman Plan: Essays on the Worldwide Spread of an Idea*. McClelland and Stewart, Toronto.

Rowat, Donald C. (ed.) (1979) *Administrative Secrecy in Developed Countries*. Columbia University Press, New York

Rueschemeyer, Dietrich (2003) 'Can One or a Few Cases Yield Gains?' In Mahoney, James and Rueschemeyer, Dietrich (eds) *Comparative Historical Analysis in the Social Sciences*. Cambridge University Press, Cambridge. pp.305–336.

Sahlin-Andersson, Kerstin and Engwall, Lars (2002) *The Expansion of the Management Knowledge. Carriers, Flows and Sources*. Stanford University Press.

Salassapitokomitea (1974) 'Komiteanmietintö', 1974, p.70.

Salminen, Ari (2006) 'Accountability, Values and the Ethical Principles of Public Service: The Views of Finnish Legislators'. *International Review of Administrative Sciences*, 72(2), pp.171–185.

Salovaara, Christa and Tala, Jyrki (2003) 'Uuden julkisuuslainsäädännön toimivuus valtionhallinnossa'. Oikeuspoliittisen tutkimuslaitoksen julkaisuja 199. Helsinki.

Samaratunge, Ramanie, Alam, Quamrul and Teicher, Julian (2008) 'The New Public Management Reforms in Asia: A Comparison of South and Southeast Asian Countries'. *International Review of Administrative Sciences*, 74(1), pp. 25–46.

Sanders, Todd and West, Harry (2003) 'Power Revealed and Concealed in the New World Order'. In West, Harry and Sanders, Todd (eds) *Transparency and Conspiracy: Ethnographies of Suspicion in the New World Order*. Duke University Press, Durham.

Sartre, Jean-Paul (2004) *Critique of Dialectical Reason: Volume 1*. Verso, New York.

Savolainen, Raimo (1996) *Keskusvirastolinnakkeista virastoarmeijaksi: Senaatin ja valtioneuvoston alainen keskushallinto 1809–1995*. Edita, Helsinki.

Scharpf, Fritz (1999) *Governing in Europe. Effective and Democratic?* Oxford University Press.

Schmidt, Vivien (2000) 'Values and Discourse in Adjustment'. In Scharpf, Fritz and Schmidt, Vivien (eds) *Welfare and Work in the Open Economy: Volume I: From Vulnerability to Competitiveness*. Oxford University Press, Oxford. Pp.229–309.

Schmidt, Vivien (2002) *The Futures of European Capitalism*. Oxford University Press, Oxford.

Schmidt, Vivien (2006a) *Democracy in Europe: The EU and National Polities*. Oxford University Press, Oxford.
Schmidt, Vivien (2006b) 'Institutionalism'. In Hay, Colin, Lister, Michael and Marsh, David (eds) *The State: Theories and Issues*. Palgrave Macmillan, Basingstoke.
Schmidt, Vivien (2008) 'Discursive Institutionalism: The Explanatory Power of Ideas and Discourse'. *Annual Review of Political Science*, 11, pp.303–326.
Schmidt, Vivien (2010) 'Taking Ideas and Discourse Seriously: Explaining Change through Discursive Institutionalism as the Fourth "New Institutionalism"'. *European Political Science Review*, 2(1), pp.1–25.
Schmitter, Philippe C. (2005) 'The Ambiguous Virtues of Accountability'. In Diamond, Larry and Morlino, Leonardo (eds) *Assessing the Quality of Democracy*. The Johns Hopkins University Press, Baltimore.
Schulz-Forberg, Hagen and Stråth, Bo (2010) 'Soft and Strong European Public Spheres'. In Frank Robert, Kaelble, Hartmut, Lévy, M. and Passerini, Luisa (eds) *Building a European Public Sphere: From the 1950s to the Present*. PIE-Peter Lang, Brussels.
Seligman, Adam B. (1992) 'Trust and the Meaning of Civil Society'. *International Journal of Politics, Culture and Society*, 6(1), pp.5–21.
Seppänen, Samuli (2003) 'Good Governance in International Law'. The Erik Castrén Institute Research Reports 13/2003. Helsinki.
Setälä, Maija (2006) 'Demokratiakäsite ja demokratian normatiiviset perusteet'. In Oikeusministeriö (ed.) *Suomen demokratiaindikaattorit*. Oikeusministeriön julkaisu 1/2006. Oikeusministeriö, Helsinki.
Sheehan, James (2006) 'The Problem of Sovereignty in European History'. *American Historical Review*, 111(1), pp.1–15.
Shore, Cris (2006) 'Government Without Statehood? Anthropological Perspectives on Governance and Sovereignty in the European Union'. *European Law Journal*, 12(6), pp.709–724.
Simmons, Beth, Dobbin, Frank and Garrett, Geoffrey (2006) 'Introduction: The International Diffusion of Liberalism'. *International Organization*, 60, pp.781–810.
Sinclair, Amanda (1995) 'The Chameleon of Accountability: Forms and Discourses'. *Accounting, Organizations and Society*, 20(2), pp.219–237.
Sirbu, Marvin (1995) 'Creating an Open Market for Information'. *Journal of Academic Librarianship*, 21(6).
Sisäasiainministeriö (2006) 'Väestötietolain kokonaisuudistus'. Työryhmän mietintö 16 / 2006. Sisäasiainministeriö, Helsinki.
SITRA (1998) Elämänlaatu, Osaaminen ja Kilpailukyky. Tietoyhteiskunnan strategisen kehittämisen lähtökohdat ja päämäärät (Sitra 206). Suomen itsenäisyyden juhlarahasto, Helsinki.
Skinner, Quentin (1969) 'Meaning and Understanding in the History of Ideas'. *History and Theory*, 8, pp.3–53.
Skinner, Quentin (1989) 'Language and Political Change'. In Ball, Terrence, Farr, James and Hanson, Russell (eds) *Political Innovation and Conceptual Change*. Cambridge University Press, Cambridge.
Skinner, Quentin (1999) 'Rhetoric and Conceptual Change'. *Finnish Year Book of Political Thought*, 3.
Skinner, Quentin (2002a) *Visions of Politics: Volume 1: Regarding Method*. Cambridge University Press.

Skinner, Quentin (2003) *Kolmas vapauden käsite*. 23°45, Eurooppalaisen filoso-
fian seura, Tampere. [A Third Concept of Liberty]
Skogstad, Grace (2003) 'Who Governs? Who Should Govern? Political Authority
and Legitimacy in Canada in the Twenty-First Century'. *Canadian Journal of
Political Science*, 36(5), pp.955–973.
Skousen, Mark (1997) 'The Perseverance of Paul Samuelson's Economics'. *The
Journal of Economic Perspectives*, 11(2), pp.137–152.
Slaughter, Anne-Marie (2004) 'Disaggregated Sovereignty: Towards the Public
Accountability of Global Government Networks'. *Government and Opposition*,
39(2), pp.159–190.
Smouts, Marie-Claude (1998) 'The Proper Use of Governance in International
Relations'. *International Social Science Journal*, 155, pp.81–89.
Söderman, Jacob (2005) 'The Early Years of the European Ombudsman'. In *The
European Ombudsman – Origins, Establishment, Evolution*. Office for Official
Publications of the European Communities, Luxembourg.
Söderman, Jacob (2006a) 'Salailusta on tullut maan tapa'. Helsingin Sanomat.
19.11.2006, newspaper article.
Söderman, Jacob (2006b) Speech on Transparency, IIAS conference in Monterrey,
Mexico, 16–20 July 2006, http://www.chydenius.net/eng/articles/artikkeli.
asp?id=924.
Soikkanen, Timo (2003) *Presidentin ministeriö: Ulkoasiainhallinnon ja ulkopoliti-
ikan hoito Kekkosen kaudella. 1, Kansainvälistymisen ja muutosvaatimusten pain-
eessa 1956–69*. Ullkoasiainministeriö, Helsinki.
Soikkanen, Timo (2008) *Presidentin ministeriö: ulkoasiainhallinto ja ulkopoliti-
ikan hoito Kekkosen kaudella. 2, Uudistumisen, ristiriitojen ja menestyksen vuodet
1970–81*. Otava, Helsingissä.
Somers, Margaret (1993) 'Citizenship and the Place of the Public Sphere: Law,
Community, and Political Culture in the Transition to Democracy'. *American
Sociological Review*, 58, pp.587–620.
Somers, Margaret (1995) 'What's Political or Cultural about Political Culture
and the Public Sphere? Toward an Historical Sociology of Concept Formation'.
Sociological Theory, 13(2), pp.113–144.
Somers, Margaret (2005) 'Let Them Eat Social Capital: Socializing the Market
versus Marketizing the Social'. *Thesis Eleven*, 81, pp.5–19.
Somers, Margaret and Block, Fred (2005) 'From Poverty to Perversity: Ideas,
Markets, and Institutions over 200 Years of Welfare Debate'. *American
Sociological Review*, 70(2), pp.260–287.
Spence, R.E. (2000) 'Italy'. In Chandler, J.A. (ed.) *Comparative Public Administration*.
Routledge, London.
Sriramesh, Krishnamurthy and Rivera-Sánchez, Milagros (2006) 'E-Government
in a Corporatist, Communitarian Society: The Case of Singapore'. *New Media
& Society*, Vol 8(5), pp.707–730.
Stasavage, David (2006) 'Does Transparency Make a Difference? The Example of
the European Council of Ministers'. In Hood, Christopher and Heald, David
(eds) *Transparency: The Key to Better Governance?* Oxford University Press,
Oxford. pp.165–179.
Steinmo, Sven (2008) 'Historical Institutionalism'. In Donatella Della Porta and
Michael Keating (eds) *Approaches in the Social Sciences*. Cambridge University
Press, Cambridge. pp.113–138.

Stenvall, Jari (1995) *Herrasmiestaidosta asiantuntijatietoon. Virkamiehistön asiantutemuksen kehitys valtion keskushallinnossa.* Hallintohistoriakomitea, Helsinki.

Stiglitz, Joseph E. (1998) 'Distinguished Lecture on Economics in Government: The Private Use of Public Interests: Incentives and Institutions'. *The Journal of Economic Perspectives*, 12(2), pp.3–22.

Stiglitz, Joseph E. (2002) 'Information and the Change in the Paradigm in Economics'. *The American Economic Review*, 92(3), pp.460–501.

Stiglitz, Joseph E. (2008) Is there a Post-Washington Consensus Consensus? In Stiglitz, Joseph E. and Serra, Narcis (eds) *The Washington Consensus Reconsidered: Towards a New Global Governance.* Oxford University Press, Oxford. pp. 41–56.

Stoker, Gerry (1998) 'Governance as Theory: Five Propositions'. *International Journal of Public Administration*, 155, pp.17–28.

Strathern, Marilyn (2000) 'The Tyranny of Transparency'. *British Educational Research Journal*, 26(3), pp.309–321.

Streeck, Wolfgang and Thelen, Kathleen (2005) 'Introduction: Institutional Change in Advanced Political Economies'. In Streeck, Wolfgang and Thelen, Kathleen (eds) *Beyond Continuity: Institutional Change in Advanced Political Economies.* Oxford University Press, Oxford.

Sum, Ngai-Ling (2009) 'The Production of Hegemonic Policy Discourses: "Competitiveness" as a Knowledge Brand and Its (Re-)Contextualizations'. *Critical Policy Studies*, 3(2), pp.184–203.

Summa, Hilkka (1993) 'Julkinen toiminta ja taloudellinen vastuu'. In Oulasvirta, Leena (ed.) *Julkisen toiminnan eettisiä kysymyksiä.* Valtionhallinnon kehittämiskeskus, Helsinki.

Supreme Administrative Court (2007) 'Annual report 2006'. Supreme Administrative Court, Helsinki.

Susiluoto, Ilmari (2002) *Diplomatian taiturit.* Ajatus Kirjat, Helsinki.

Takala, Jukka-Pekka and Konstari, Timo (eds) (1982) *Mikä Suomessa salaista: Salaisen ja julkisen rajat.* WSOY, Juva.

Tant, A.P. (1993) *British Government: The Triumph of Elitism: A study of the British Political Tradition and Its Major Challenges.* Dartmouth, Aldershot.

Tarkastusvaliokunta (2007a) 'Hallituksen esitys valtion talousarvioksi vuodelle 2008'. Tarkastusvaliokunnan lausunto 1/2007 vp. Eduskunta, Helsinki.

Tarkastusvaliokunta (2007b) 'Valtiontalouden tarkastusviraston kertomus eduskunnalletoiminnastaanvarainhoitovuodelta2006'.Tarkastusvaliokunnan mietintö 2/2007 vp. Eduskunta, Helsinki.

Temmes, Markku (1998) 'Finland and New Public Management'. *International Review of Administrative Sciences*, 64(3), pp.441–56.

Thelen, Kathleen (1999) 'Historical Institutionalism in Comparative Politics'. *Annual Review of Political Science*, 2, pp.369–404.

Thelen, Kathleen (2004) *How Institutions Evolve. The Political Economy of Skills in Germany, Britain, the United States, and Japan.* Cambridge University Press, Cambridge.

Thurlow, Richard (1994) *The Secret State: British Internal Security in the Twentieth Century.* Blackwell, Oxford.

Tietoarkisto (2006) 'Rekisterit paljastavat moninaisen maailman'. Newspaper article published in Tietoarkisto 2/2006.

Tietojärjestelmäkomitea (1974) 'Tietojärjestelmäkomitean 1 osamietintö. Komitean työn lähtökohdat ja tavoitteet'. *Komiteanmietintö*, 1974, p.110. Helsinki, 1974.

Tiihonen, Paula (2003) 'Good Governance and Corruption in Finland'. In Tiihonen, Seppo (ed.) *The History of Corruption in Central Government*. IOS Press, Amsterdam. pp.99–118.

Tiihonen, Paula (2006) 'Democracy is Institutional Gardening: A Hundred Years is a Short Time'. In Mannermaa, Mika, Dator, Jim and Tiihonen, Paula (eds) *Democracy and Futures*. Parliament of Finland, Helsinki. pp.191–204.

Tiihonen, Seppo (1994) *Herruus. Ruotsi ja Venäjä*. Hallintohistoriakomitea, Helsinki.

Tiihonen, Seppo (1999) 'From Uniform Administration to Governance and Management of Diversity: Reforming State Functions and Public Administration in Finland'. OECD, Paris.

Tiihonen, Seppo (2000) 'Miten nostaa valtioneuvoston hallintakapasiteettia tietoyhteiskunnassa?' *Hallinnon tutkimus*, 4/2000, pp.347–367.

Tiihonen, Seppo (2003) 'Kovin epätasaista: Valtioneuvoston asiat internetissä'. *Hallinnon tutkimus*, 1/2003, pp.86–89.

Tiihonen, Seppo (2004) 'Maailmanpankin hyvä hallinta'. *Hallinnon tutkimus*, 23(1), pp.15–29.

Tiihonen, Seppo (2006) 'Poliittisen hallinnan ja hallintopolitiikan muutoksia 1980- ja 1990-luvulla'. In Heiskala, Risto and Luhtakallio, Eeva (eds) *Uusi jako, Miten Suomesta tuli kilpailukyky-yhteiskunta?* Gaudeamus, Helsinki. pp.82–102.

Tiihonen, Seppo and Tiihonen, Paula (2004) 'Kohti globaalivastuuta, Maailmanhallinta – politiikkaa, taloutta ja demokratiaa'. *VATT-julkaisuja*, 39. Valtion taloudellinen tutkimuskeskus, Helsinki.

Tilly, Charles (2004) 'Trust and rule'. *Theory and Society*, 33, pp.1–30.

Timmins, Graham (2000) 'Germany'. In Chandler, J.A. (ed.) *Comparative Public Administration*. Routledge, London.

TLFI (2010) 'Trésor de la Langue Française Informatisé', available at http://www.atilf.fr/tlfi.htm, date accessed 12 April 2010.

Tocqueville, Alexis de (1991) *Democracy in America*. Alfred A. Knopf, New York.

Torstila, Pertti (2001) 'Suomen kansainvälinen kilpailukyky'. Kilpailukyky-seminaari Haaga Instituutti, available at http://www.formin.fi/public/?contentid=56071&contentlan=1&culture=fi-FI, 14 November 2001.

Transparency International (2006) 'Corruption Perceptions Index 2006', available at http://www.transparency.org/.

Tsoukas, Haridimos (1997) 'The Tyranny of Light : The Temptations and the Paradoxes of the Information Society'. *Futures*, 29(9), pp.827–843.

Tuomioja, Erkki (2006) 'Den falska transparensen'. Hufvudstadsbladet 7.8.2006, newspaper article.

Tuori, Kaarlo (1976) 'Johdanto'. In Tuori, Kaarlo (ed.) *Suomen komitealaitos*. Valtiovarainministeriön järjestelyosasto, Helsinki.

Tuori, Kaarlo (1983) Valtionhallinnon sivuelinorganisaatiosta 2. Julkisoikeudellinen tutkimus komiteatyyppisten elinten asemasta Suomen valtio-organisaatiossa 2. nide. Positiivisoikeudelliset tarkastelut. Suomalainen lakimiesyhdistys, Helsinki.

Ulkoasiainministeriö (1984) Ulkoasiainhallinnon asiakirjojen salassapitoaika ja asiakirjojen käyttö pidennetyn salassapitokauden aikana. Muistio 29.8.1984.

Ulkoasiainministeriö (1992) Ulkopoliittisten asiakirjojen salassapitoajan lyhentäminen. Hallinnollinen osasto. Muistio 92, 9.10.1992.

Ulkoasiainvaliokunta (2001) Ulkoasiainvaliokunnan lausunto 8/2001 vp. UaVL 8/2001 vp – UTP 10/2001 vp, M 1/2001 vp.

Ulkoasiainministeriö (2001a) Ulkoasiainhallinnon haasteet 2000-luvun alussa. Ulkoasiainministeri Erkki Tuomiojan eduskunnan ulkoasiainvaliokunnalle antama selvitys 12.6.2001 Suomen ulkoasiainhallinnon tehtävistä ja voimavaroista. Ulkoasiainministeriö, Helsinki.

Ulkoasiainministeriö (2001b) Ulkoasiainhallinnon asiakirjojen salassapitoajan lyhentäminen. Muistio 2.2.2001.

Ulkoasiainministeriö (2001c) Ulkopoliittisten asiakirjojen salassapitoaika lyheni 25 vuoteen. Tiedote Nro 30, 8. 2.2001.

Ulkoasiainministeriö (2001d) Yleisiä ohjeita EU-asiakirjojen julkisuudesta. Ohje, HEL0603–7, 19.12.2002.

Ulkoasiainministeriö (2002) Ohje UH:n virkamiesten julkisista esiintymisistä. 3.6.2002, Intranet asiakirja.

Ulkoasiainministeriö (2003) Rajanvetoa salaisen ja julkisen välillä. Intranetjulkaisu, UM, 11.9.2003.

Ulkoasiainministeriö (2005) Suomen etu – Globaali vastuu. Ulkoministeriön strategia. Ulkoasiainministeriö, Helsinki.

Ulkoasiainministeriö (2006) Ulkoasiainministeriön tulevaisuuskatsaus 2006. Ulkoasiainministeriö, Helsinki, http://formin.finland.fi/public/default. aspx?contentid=77880.

Ulkoasiainministeriö (2007a) Edustustojen tulossopimusehdotusten, ministeriön osastojen vuosisuunnitelmien sekä toiminta- ja taloussuunnitelmien laadintaohjeet 2008–2012. HEL6303–19/Liite 4. Ulkoasiainministeriö, Helsinki.

Ulkoasiainministeriö (2007b) Tulossopimusmalli. Ulkoasiainministeriö ja Suomen suurlähetystön/Edustuston välinen tulossopimus vuodeksi 2008. HEL6306–19 Liite 5. Ulkoasiainministeriö, Helsinki.

Ulkoasiainministeriö (2007c) Tuloskortti vuodelle 2008. HAL-09.

Ulkoasiainministeriö (2007d) Edustustojen tulossopimusehdotukset 2008 sekä ministeriö osastojen vuosisuunnitelmat 2008 ja toiminta- ja taloussuunnitelmat 2009–2012. HEL6306–19.

Ulkoasiainministeriö (2009) Suomi ulkomaisissa tiedotusvälineissä 2008. Ulkoministeriön viestintä- ja kulttuuriosaston julkaisu. 10. vuosikerta. Ulkoasiainministeriö, Helsinki.

United Nations (2008) 'UN e-Government Survey: From e-Government to Connected Governance'. United Nations, New York.

Vakkuri, Jarmo (2001) 'Organisaation tuloksellisuusinformaatio tarkastus- ja arviointitoiminnassa: informaation tuotannon ja käytön näkökulma'. In Myllymäki, Arvo and Vakkuri, Jarmo (eds) *Tulos, normi, tilivelvollisuus: Näkökulmia tilintarkastukseen ja arviointiin*. Tampere University Press, Tampere.

Valtioneuvoston kanslia (2000a) 'Markkinointia vai avoimuutta. Selvitys markkinointiviestinnästä valtionhallinnon tiedotuksessa'. Valtioneuvoston kanslian raportteja 2000/10. Valtioneuvoston kanslia, Helsinki.

Valtioneuvoston kanslia (2000b) 'Alueellinen kehitys ja aluepolitiikka Suomessa'. Valtioneuvoston kanslian julkaisusarja 2000/6, Helsinki.

Valtioneuvoston kanslia (2001a) 'Informoi, neuvoo, keskustelee ja osallistuu. Valtionhallinnon viestintä 2000-luvulla'. Valtioneuvoston kanslian julkaisusarja, 2001/5. Valtioneuvoston kanslia, Helsinki.

Valtioneuvoston kanslia (2001b) 'EU:n laajeneminen ja Suomi'. Valtioneuvoston kanslian julkaisusarja 2001/1, Helsinki.

Valtioneuvoston kanslia (2001c) 'Työmarkkinoilta syrjäytyminen, tulonjako ja köyhyys'. Valtioneuvoston kanslian julkaisusarja 2001/13, Helsinki.

Valtioneuvoston kanslia (2002a) 'Valtionhallinnon viestintäsuositus'. Valtioneuvoston kanslian julkaisusarja 2002/6. Valtioneuvoston kanslia, Helsinki.

Valtioneuvoston kanslia (2002b) 'Euroopan rakenteelliset jäykkyydet'. Valtioneuvoston kanslian julkaisusarja 2002/4, Helsinki.

Valtioneuvoston kanslia (2003) 'Joukkoviestimien kokemuksia valtionhallinnon viestinnästä'. Valtioneuvoston kanslian raportteja 4/2003. Valtioneuvoston kanslia, Helsinki.

Valtioneuvoston kanslia (2004) 'Osaava, avautuva ja uudistuva Suomi. Suomi maailmantaloudessa –selvityksen loppuraportti'. Valtioneuvoston kanslian julkaisusarja 19/2004. Valtioneuvoston kanslia, Helsinki.

Valtioneuvoston kanslia (2005a) 'Julkinen hyvinvointivastuu sosiaali- ja terveydenhuollossa'. Valtioneuvoston kanslian julkaisusarja 5/2005, Helsinki.

Valtioneuvoston kanslia (2005b) 'Tuottavuus ja työllisyys. Mitä opittavaa muista Pohjoismaista?' Valtioneuvoston kanslian raportteja 3/2005, Helsinki.

Valtioneuvoston kanslia (2005c) 'VISA – valtionhallinnon viestinnän seuranta- ja arviointijärjestelmä'. Valtionhallinnon viestintä 2007 -hanke, Osa I. Valtioneuvoston kanslia, Helsinki.

Valtioneuvoston kanslia (2005d) 'VISA – valtionhallinnon viestinnän seuranta- ja arviointijärjestelmä'. Valtionhallinnon viestintä 2007 -hanke, Osa II: Tutkimusraportit. Valtioneuvoston kanslia, Helsinki.

Valtioneuvoston kanslia (2005e) 'Tiedonkulku ja viestintä Aasian hyökyaaltokatastrofissa'. Valtioneuvoston kanslian julkaisusarja 7/2005. Valtioneuvoston kanslia, Helsinki.

Valtioneuvoston kanslia (2006a) 'Politiikkaohjelmat hallitustyössä. Ohjelmajohtamisen uudistettu malli'. Valtioneuvoston kanslian julkaisusarja 13/2006.

Valtioneuvoston kanslia (2006b) 'Paremman sääntelyn toimintaohjelma'. Osa 1. Valtioneuvoston kanslian julkaisusarja 8/2006. Valtioneuvoston kanslia, Helsinki.

Valtioneuvoston kanslia (2006c) 'Katsauksia Suomen lainsäädäntökehitykseen 1985–2005. Paremman sääntelyn toimintaohjelma'. Osa 2. Valtioneuvoston kanslian julkaisusarja 9/2006. Valtioneuvoston kanslia, Helsinki.

Valtioneuvoston kanslia (2006d) 'Hallinnonalakohtaiset selvitykset lainsäädännön kehityksestä 1985–2005. Paremman sääntelyn toimintaohjelma'. Osa 3. Valtioneuvoston kanslian julkaisusarja 10/2006. Valtioneuvoston kanslia, Helsinki.

Valtioneuvoston kanslia (2007a) 'Ikääntymisen taloudelliset vaikutukset ja niihin varautuminen'. Valtioneuvoston kanslian julkaisusarja 10/2007.

Valtioneuvoston kanslia (2007b) 'Rekrytointiongelmat, työvoiman tarjonta ja liikkuvuus'. Valtioneuvoston kanslian julkaisusarja 5/2007.

Valtioneuvoston kanslia (2007c) 'Pääministeri Matti Vanhasen hallituksen ohjelman seuranta'. Valtioneuvoston kanslian julkaisusarja 6/2007.

Valtioneuvoston kanslia (2007d) 'Itämeren alue Suomen taloudellisena toimintaympäristönä'. Valtioneuvoston kanslian julkaisusarja 20/2007.

Valtioneuvoston kanslia (2008) 'Joukkoviestimien kokemuksia valtionhal-
linnon viestinnästä'. Valtioneuvoston kanslian julkaisusarja 12/2008.
Valtioneuvoston kanslia, Helsinki.
Valtiontalouden tarkastusvirasto (1997) Tarkastuskertomus 1/1997.
Nettobudjetointi. Virastojen uuden rahoitusmuodon arviointia. Edita,
Helsinki.
Valtiontalouden tarkastusvirasto (2006) Tilintarkastajan väliraportti-luonnos
Ulkoasiainministeriön toimenpiteistä vuoden 2005 tilintarkastuskertomuksen
ilmoitusvelvollisuuden johdosta. 05.09.2006. Valtiovaraintarkastusvirasto,
Helsinki.
Valtiontalouden tarkastusvirasto (2007) Avoimuus ja hallinnon hyvä eettinen
taso parantavat vaikuttavuutta ja tehokkuutta, available athttp://www.vtv.fi/
ajankohtaista/tiedotearkisto/2007/avoimuus_ja_hallinnon_hyva_eettinen_
taso_parantavat_vaikuttavuutta_ja_tehokkuutta.html, 4 July 2007
Valtiontalouden tarkastusvirasto (2008) Tunnistuspalveluiden kehittäminen
ja käyttö julkisessa hallinnossa. Valtiontalouden tarkastusviraston toimin-
nantarkastuskertomukset 161/2008. Edita, Helsinki.
Valtiovarainministeriö (1995) 'Suomi tietoyhteiskunnaksi – kansalliset linjauk-
set strategiassa'. Valtiovarainministeriö, Helsinki.
Valtiovarainministeriö (1997) Valtiovarainministeriön työryhmämuistioita
10/1997. Valtion tietosuoritteiden maksuperusteet, Oy Edita Ab, Helsinki.
Valtiovarainministeriö (1998) Laadukkaat palvelut, hyvä hallinto ja vastuul-
linen kansalaisyhteiskunta. Hallintopolitiikan suuntalinjat. Valtioneuvoston
periaatepäätös. Valtiovarainministeriö, hallinnon kehittämisosasto, Helsinki.
Valtiovarainministeriö (1999) 'Euroopan komission vihreä kirja julkisen sek-
torin tiedosta'. Tiedote 22.02.1999, VM 9/071/99.
Valtiovarainministeriö (2000) Keskushallinnon uudistaminen, osahanke 3.1:
Kuule kansalaista. Kansalaisten ja kansalaisjärjestöjen osallistumismahdol-
lisuudet yhteiskuntapoliittisessa valmistelussa. Asettamispäätös VM0539,
12.9.2000. Valtiovarainministeriö, Helsinki.
Valtiovarainministeriö (2001) Kuule kansalaista –hankkeen loppuraportti.
Valtiovarainministeriö, Hallinnon kehittämisosasto, Helsinki 2001.
Valtiovarainministeriö (2002) 'Suomen kilpailukyky ja sen kehittämistarve'.
Edita Oyj, Helsinki.
Valtiovarainministeriö (2003a) Parempaan tilivelvollisuuteen. Valtion tilin-
päätösuudistuksen periaatteet. Valtiovarainministeriön työryhmämuistio 2 /
2003. Edita, Helsinki.
Valtiovarainministeriö (2003b) Hallinnon sisäisten tietoluovutusten hinnoit-
telu. Hallinnon tietoluovutusten hinnoitteluhankkeen raportti 30.5.2003
(Työryhmämuistio 16/2003). Edita, Helsinki.
Valtiovarainministeriö (2004) Arvot arkeen. Pilottivirastojen kokemukset ja
työryhmän johtopäätökset. Työryhmämuistio 6/2004, Valtiovarainministeriö,
Helsinki.
Valtiovarainministeriö (2005a) Kuule kansalaista – valmistele viisaasti! Käsikirja
virkamiehille ja viranhaltioille. Edita, Helsinki.
Valtiovarainministeriö (2005b) 'Hallinnon yhteiset periaatteet kansalaisten
kuulemiseen'. Valtiovarainministeriö, Helsinki.
Valtiovarainministeriö (2005c) Arvot arjessa – virkamiehen etiikka.
Valtionhallinnon käsikirja. Edita, Helsinki.

Valtiovarainministeriö(2005d)Tulosohjauksenkäsikirja.Valtiovarainministeriön julkaisuja 2/2005, Helsinki.

Valtiovarainministeriö (2005e) Indikaattorit ohjauksen ja seurannan välineinä. Valtiovarainministeriön Indikaattori-työryhmän raportti.

Valtiovarainministeriö (2006a) Ministeriöiden kustannuslaskennan kehittäminen. Valtiovarainministeriö, Hallinnon kehittämisosaston työryhmämuistio 1/2006. Edita, Helsinki.

Valtiovarainministeriö (2006b) Laajapohjaisen valmistelun kehittäminen. Laajapohjaisen valmistelutyön käytön edistämistä selvittäneen työryhmän raportti. Valtiovarainministeriö, Helsinki.

Valtiovarainministeriö (2007a) Perustietovarantojen yhteiskäytön nykytila ja kehittäminen. Perustietovarannot-projektin raportti, available at http://www.vm.fi/vm/fi/04_julkaisut_ja_asiakirjat/03_muut_ asiakirjat/20070628Kokona/07_Liite_05_Perustieovarantojen_yhteenveto.pdf.

Valtiovarainministeriö (2007b) Hallinnon sisäisten tietoluovutusten hinnoittelun selkeyttäminen, available at http://www.vm.fi/vm/ fi/04_julkaisut_ja_asiakirjat/03_muut_asiakirjat/20070628Kokona/09_ Liite_07_Perustietovarantojen__hinnoittelu.pdf.

Valtiovarainministeriö (2008a) Valtioneuvoston hanketyön tietojärjestelmätuen kehittäminen – Valtioneuvoston hankerekisterin (HARE) uudistaminen -hanke. Esiselvitysraportti 31.3.2009. VM086:01/2008.

Valtiovarainministeriö (2008b) Alue ja rekisterihallinnon tulosneuvottelut. Tulosneuvottelu: Väestörekisterikeskus. Muistio 30.1.2008.

Valtiovarainvaliokunta (2001) Valtiovarainlautakunnan lausunto 27/2001 vp. VaVL 27/2001 vp – UTP 10/2001 vp, M 1/2001 vp.

Van Kersbergen, Kees and Van Waarden, Frans (2004) 'Governance as a Bridge between Disciplines: Cross-Disciplinary Inspiration Regarding Shifts in Governance and Problems of Governability, Accountability and Legitimacy'. *European Journal of Political Research*, 43, pp.143–171.

Vihavainen, Timo (1991) *Kansakunta rähmällään. Suomettumisen lyhyt historia.* Otava, Helsinki.

Viljanen, Veli-Pekka (1996) 'Perusoikeusuudistus ja kansainväliset ihmisoikeussopimukset'. *Lakimies*, 94, pp.788–815.

Virrankoski, Pentti (1986) *Anders Chydenius. Demokraattinen poliitikko valistuksen vuosisadalta.* Werner Söderström, Juva.

Väestörekisterikeskus (2004a) Väestötietojärjestelmän julkishallinnon tietopalvelun käytännesäännöt (868/79/04). Väestörekisterikeskus, Helsinki.

Väestörekisterikeskus (2004b) Väestötietojärjestelmän yksityisen sektorin tietopalvelun käytännesäännöt (360/79/04). Väestörekisterikeskus, Helsinki.

Väyrynen, Raimo (1999) *Suomi avoimessa maailmassa. Globalisaatio ja sen vaikutukset.* Taloustieto, Helsinki.

Wallin, Anna-Riitta and Konstari, Timo (2000) *Julkisuus- ja salassapitolainsäädäntö : laki viranomaisten toiminnan julkisuudesta ja siihen liittyvät lait.* Suomalaiset oikeusjulkaisut, Helsinki.

Weber, Edward (1999) 'The Question of Accountability in Historical Perspective: From Jackson to Contemporary Grassroots Ecosystem Management'. *Administration & Society*, 31(4), pp.451–494.

Weber, Max (1978) *Economy and Society (Vol. 1 and 2).* University of California Press, Berkeley.

West, Darrell (2005) *Digital Government. Technology and Public Sector Performance.* Princeton University Press, Princeton.

West, Harry and Sanders, Todd (eds) (2003) *Transparency and Conspiracy: Ethnographies of Suspicion in the New World Order.* Duke University Press, Durham.

White, Hayden (1987) *The Content of the Form: Narrative Discourse and Historical Representation.* The Johns Hopkins University Press, Baltimore.

White, Hayden (2005) 'The Public Relevance of Historical Studies: A Reply To Dirk Moses'. *History and Theory,* 44 (October 2005), pp.333–338.

White, Jonathan (2009) 'Thematisation and Collective Positioning in Everyday Political Talk'. *British Journal of Political Science,* 39(4), pp.699–709.

Wieland, Joachim (2000) 'Freedom of Information'. In Engel, Christoph and Keller, Kenneth (eds) *Governance of Global Networks in the Light of Differing Local Values.* Nomos-Verlag, Baden-Baden.

Wietog, Jutta (2001) *Volkszählungen unter dem Nationalsozialismus. Eine Dokumentation zur Bevölkerungsstatistik im Dritten Reich.* Duncker & Humblot, Berlin.

Williamson, Oliver E. (1981) 'The Economics of Organization: The Transaction Cost Approach'. *The American Journal of Sociology,* 87(3), pp.548–577.

Wilson, James Q. (1989) *Bureaucracy. What Government Agencies Do and Why They Do It.* Basic Books, New York.

Wintrobe, Ronald (2007) 'Jihad vs. McWorld: A Rational Choice Approach'. In Breton, Albert, Galeotti, Gianluigi, Salmon, Pierre and Wintrobe, Ronald (eds) *The Economics of Transparency in Politics.* Ashgate, Aldershot. pp.97–120.

World Economic Forum (2006) The Global Competitiveness Report 2005–06: Video Interviews, Augusto Lopez-Claros, Chief Economist and Director, Global Competitiveness Programme, available at http://www.weforum.org/en/initiatives/gcp/GCR20052006VideoInterviews/index.htm.

Würgler, Andreas (2002) 'Conspiracy and Denunciation: A Local Affair and its European Publics (Bern, 1749)'. In Melton, James Van Horn (ed.) *Cultures of Communication from Reformation to Enlightenment: Constructing Publics in Early Modern German Lands.* Ashgate, Aldershot.

Yiannis, Gabriel (2005) 'Glass Cages and Glass Palaces: Images of Organization in Image-Conscious Times'. *Organization,* 12(1), pp.9–27.

Ympäristöministeriö (2007) 'Ohje Ympäristöhallinnon tietoaineistojen julkisuudesta, luovuttamisesta ja hinnoittelusta'. Ympäristöministeriö, 9.11.2007.

Young, Iris Marion (2000) *Inclusion and Democracy.* Oxford University Press, Oxford.

Zanotti, Laura (2005) 'Governmentalizing the post-Cold War international regime: The UN debate on democratization and good governance'. *Alternatives,* 30(4), pp.461–487.

Zaret, David (1992) 'Religion, Science, and Printing in the Public Spheres in Seventeenth-Century England'. In Calhoun, Craig (ed.) *Habermas and the Public Sphere.* MIT Press, Cambridge, Massachusetts.

Žižek, Slavoj (1997) *The Plague of Fantasies.* Verso, London.

Zysman, John (2004) 'Finland in a Digital Era: How Do Wealthy Nations Stay Wealthy?' Valtioneuvoston kanslian julkaisusarja 25/2004. Valtioneuvoston kanslia, Helsinki.

Index